Carmen M. Enss, Luigi Monzo (eds.)
Townscapes in Transition

Urban Studies

Carmen M. Enss (PhD), born in 1975, is a researcher at the Centre for Heritage Conservation Studies and Technologies at the University of Bamberg. Her research links urban planning with heritage conservation.
Luigi Monzo (PhD), born in 1977, works as an architect in Germany and teaches architectural history and design at the University of Innsbruck. His research addresses the intersections between architectural culture, design process and political conditions in regimes of totalitarian aspiration, especially in fascist Italy.

Carmen M. Enss, Luigi Monzo (eds.)
Townscapes in Transition
**Transformation and Reorganization of Italian Cities
and Their Architecture in the Interwar Period**

[transcript]

The conferences from which this anthology emerged took place as part of the DFG project »Planned Heritage«. Research for the introductory essay »Editing cities in Interwar Italy« was carried out as part of the DFG project EN 1135/1-1 »Planned Heritage«. The printing was co-financed by DFG funds and by the **Centre for Heritage Conservation Studies and Technologies (KDWT)**, Otto-Friedrich Universität Bamberg.

Bibliographic information published by the Deutsche Nationalbibliothek
The Deutsche Nationalbibliothek lists this publication in the Deutsche Nationalbibliografie; detailed bibliographic data are available in the Internet at http://dnb.d-nb.de

© 2019 transcript Verlag, Bielefeld

All rights reserved. No part of this book may be reprinted or reproduced or utilized in any form or by any electronic, mechanical, or other means, now known or hereafter invented, including photocopying and recording, or in any information storage or retrieval system, without permission in writing from the publisher.

Cover layout: Maria Arndt, Bielefeld, Concept: editors
Cover illustration: Adalberto Libera: Renovated little house in via San Basilio 53 Rome, so-called Piccola Casa da Pigione – Casa Nicoletti (1931-32); Photograph taken from the Journal »Architettura« 1933, p. 638.
Proofread by Sacha Anthony Berardo, Eleonora Bernardi, Johanna Blokker, Scott Budzynski, Ross Cioffi, Karl Eckert, Stacey-Ann Harrington, Carrie Giunta, Irina Oryshkevich, Eva Pedersen, Aban Tahmasebi
Translated by Gisella Calabrese, Enrico Cioni, David Antony Kelly, Susan Jane Kingshott, Letizia Maita, Doris Moreau, Richard Sadleir, LINKLAB – Laboratorio di Comunicazione Multilingue
Typeset by Carmen M. Enss, Farah Marie Berger

Print-ISBN 978-3-8376-4660-3
PDF-ISBN 978-3-8394-4660-7
https://doi.org/10.14361/9783839446607

Contents

INTRODUCTION

Editing Cities in Interwar Italy | 9
Carmen M. Enss, Luigi Monzo

TRADITION, ARCHITECTURE, HOMOGENIZATION

Piacentini and Unitary Architectural Directions for Italian Cities
Paolo Nicoloso | 47

The Concept of Tradition in the Theoretical and Aesthetic Debate from the 1920s to the Second Post-War Period
Cettina Lenza | 61

URBAN TRANSFORMATIONS

Transformations in Architectural and Urban Culture in the Sant'Ambrogio Area of Milan between the World Wars
Cecilia De Carli | 85

Transformation and the Vertical City: Milan's Early Skyscrapers
Scott Budzynski | 99

The Transformation of Rome and the Masterplan to Reconstruct Moscow: Historical Heritage between Modernity, Memory and Ideology
Anna G. Vyazemtseva | 113

Preserving the Old to Build the Modern: Visions of an Alternative Brescia in the Project by Pietro Aschieri
Alberto Coppo | 127

The Townscape of Bari: A Laboratory of Italian Urbanism during the Early Twentieth Century
Christine Beese | 141

Bergamo as a Case Study
Sandro Scarrocchia | 155

RESTORATION AND INVENTION

Planning the Past I: Giulio Ulisse Arata; Urban Renewal in Emilia Romagna
Elena Pozzi, Marco Pretelli, Leila Signorelli | 171

Planning the Past II: Rimini and Forlì in the 1920s; The Replanning of Two Squares in Romagna
Giulia Favaretto, Chiara Mariotti | 185

Architectural and Urban Transformations in Romagna during the Fascist Era between Tradition and Modernity: The Cases of Predappio, Forlì and Imola
Micaela Antonucci, Sofia Nannini | 203

Autarchy and Tradition in the Architecture during Italy's Fascist Period: Newly Founded Cities
Angela Pecorario Martucci | 221

CITY EXTENSIONS

Urban Expansion in Venice, 1918–1939: Continuity of the Urban Form in the Internal Periphery of the Residential Area of Santa Marta
Alexander Fichte | 233

Innocenzo Sabbatini and the Construction of Modern Rome
Lorenzo Ciccarelli | 247

Acknowledgements | 261

'Terms and Conditions' of Interwar Architecture and Urbanism in Italy: A Tentative Glossary
Carmen M. Enss, Luigi Monzo | 263

Authors | 271

Introduction

Editing Cities in Interwar Italy

Carmen M. Enss and Luigi Monzo

During the interwar period, a myriad of construction projects (cf. Nicoloso 2012: 9-11), major restoration measures and excavation campaigns were carried out in dozens of cities in Italy and its colonies. The nationwide construction effort was carried out as part of the cultural policy strategy of the Fascist party aimed at reshaping the urban and rural landscape.[1] In the decades of the *Ventennio,* political interest in connecting with a supposedly glorious past encountered an already well-established academic field of monument preservation and restoration theory. Artists and architects admired Italy's architectural heritage and longed for renewed national leadership (Nicoloso 1999: 41; Zucconi 1997: 20). The Fascist regime stimulated, as Claudia Lazzaro and Roger J. Crum observed, scholarship in Roman art and architecture, vernacular architecture and Italian gardens, and "[…] fostered the excavation and restoration of surviving examples" (Lazzaro/Crum 2005: 31). The intense awareness of national architectural heritage and an intention of connecting to historic building traditions informed modern architecture and urban development strategies and policies. They inspired plans for the redevelopment of historic urban quarters, where "existing structures were accentuated and perfected through a series of selective interventions" (Lasansky 2004a: 330). Despite a propagandistic commitment to the preservation of national monuments and historic urban spaces (cf. for Rome Insolera 2001), numerous historical, but often impoverished, areas were redeveloped – and thus ultimately demolished. The changes in townscapes and landscapes implemented in these decades have become part of Italy's history and determine its image until today. If we visit cities

---

1   For a propagandistic overview on large-scale restoration projects the first fascist decade after the First World War cf. Giovannoni 1932: 409-410, 419-20. For the context of modern Italian architecture between the nineteenth and early twentieth centuries in general see, exemplary for a large variety of titles, both volumes of Kirk 2005.

like Bari, Bergamo, Bologna, Brescia, Forlì, Milan, Rimini, Rome, Trieste, Turin, Venice and others analyzed in this book, we often do not notice where historic urban fabric dating from before the First World War are situated and at precisely which point new urban areas, which architects and planners created during the interwar period, begin. Interwar architecture and conservation thus shaped Italy's past and created Italy's future. The effects of the building policy at that time still influence our idea of the country's typical townscapes.

Research in the fields of architectural history, urban planning, historical urban studies or monument preservation looked at whole cities, city districts, or regions as being "edited" or curated in their architectural and social development. As Diana M. Lasansky (2004a: 347) observed, "the visitor's experience of a city was carefully choreographed as a series of encounters with historic landmarks". Concurrently, the concept of "other modernity" going back to Marcello Piacentini's notion of "una modernità diversa" (Pisani 1996: 172) is being rediscovered. Sandro Benedetti described Piacentini's vision of converging modalities of renewal: Piacentini aimed both a "rediscovery (return) of tradition in the form of a creatively recovered guiding idea" and an "adapted further development", so that a self-contained process of creation could bring forth fresh architectures that were valid expressions of new ways of life (Benedetti 2004: 11).[2] Connecting architecture to history was not an abstract idea but was fed by practical experience in Italian towns and cities.

This book looks at variations of passing down and appropriating architectural concepts and historical structures that led to combinations and architectural compositions of historic and modern buildings and urban quarters. By examining works of Marcello Piacentini, Giovanni Muzio, Pietro Aschieri, Giulio Ulisse Arata, Innocenzo Sabbatini, and others, this book focuses on individual model projects of leading architects who influenced city transformations and transition processes all over Italy.

Numerous publications describe a staging of monuments through urban planning in Rome and Benito Mussolini's efforts to create an idealized image of Italy for his rule and government (cf. Insolera 2001, Cederna 2006, Kirk 2006, Gentile 2008 [2007], Nicoloso 2012). The studies collected in this book extend the focus to cities and regions all over the country and confirm how thoroughly architects and engineers shaped the historical urban and rural landscapes in order to give birth to a modern state. Exemplified with the region of Romagna (see the chapter by Micaela Antonucci and Sofia Nannini in this book), this territorial editing can

---

2 "ritrovamento (ritorno) della tradizione, come recupero creativo di una guida"; "sviluppo evolutivo".

even be seen as a means of inner colonialization of Italian regions, inspired by a myth of centralized Roman empire.

This book makes an intervention in a transdisciplinary debate within architectural history and theory about architectural culture and cultural policy in Italy's interwar period. It contributes to this debate through the analysis of buildings, towns and quarters as well as theoretical texts. In the broader perspective, the project is part of a general debate on handing down the built heritage of historical cities as a process and a political practice that continues to this day (cf. Hökerberg 2018).

Research state on urban editing between the First and Second World War

Since World War II, research has focused primarily on a complex of design techniques subsumed under a rationalist style in Italian architecture (cf. Mras 1961; Ghirardo 1980; for a critical review on architectural history that often ignored political backgrounds see Spiegel 2015: 53-54). These studies recognized that rationalist architecture was derived notably from historical architecture or historical architectural theory. Daniela Spiegel suggested recently that this successful connection of tradition and modernity in fact "caused the widespread success of the Italian Razionalismo" (Spiegel 2015: 52-54). Henry Millon pointed to a political role that architectural history played in the late Ventennio as early as 1965 (Millon 1965). Italo Insolera published the book *Roma moderna,* a critical history of demolitions performed during the Ventennio (1976 [1962]). In 1978, Paolo Sica (1978) showed the quantitative importance of urban transformation projects in Italy's interwar city planning history by assessing contemporary publications. However, Diane Yvonne Ghirardo still had to complain in 1980: "Most historians have ignored the ardent Fascism of the best architects, while others simply avoid the issue altogether and study the buildings as stylistic phenomena." (1980: 109). While we know that a politicized urbanism focused on a staging and presentation of historical monuments and archeological remains, we still do not know much about the political role of monument preservation. This lack of attention may be due to the fact that, from today's perspective, the outcomes of monument preservation are less evident than those of new construction designs. As Lazzaro and Crum (2005: 31) observed: "inscriptions and fasces were later removed from [listed] buildings […] the crucial intervention of Fascism in these areas of study has been similarly erased." Christoph Thoenes (1995) responded to Millon's article and observed a restoration practice in the 1930s for renaissance palaces that followed the political intentions of a renewed renaissance. Klaus Tragbar (cf.

2009; 2010) analyzed not only restorations done in towns in Northern Italy, but, more importantly, the political intentions and implications for the restoration culture.

In recent years scholars have been rediscovering the abovementioned concept of "other modernity". They defined it as a way of designing in modern forms but referring to history or a particular regional context (cf. Docci/Turco 2010; Marcucci 2012; Neri 2011). While certain cases like breakthroughs in historical urban areas or specific historical zones, which were restored as a whole in combination with a thinning process, the Italian term was *diradamento*, have been studied in detail before, recent research observes urban transformation processes as a whole. Franz J. Bauer described Rome's urban development in the 19th and 20th century as a "Construction of a myth" (Bauer 2009). The essay collection *L'urbanistica a Roma durante il ventennio fascista* (Beese/Dobler 2018) shows how actors from different academic fields combined urban design with a staging of archeological or historical monuments. This phenomenon has been portrayed for Fascist Rome before by Kallis (2014), Nicoloso (2008, 2012), Bodenschatz (2011), Vidotto (2015), Kostof (1973) and Insolera (1976 [1962]). Diane Lasansky (2004a) was presumably the first to speak of an "urban editing, historic preservation, and political rhetoric" for analyzing restoration works in San Gimignano. In her book *The Renaissance perfected* she looked at the "selective preservation" of Arezzo (2004b: 107), which she described as aimed to design an idealized medieval townscape. Not only historic quarters, but new towns rely on design concepts that invoked historical images. After the First World War, the incipient Fascism was based on a strong national-conservative culture. In that intellectual climate, namely, e.g., at the Scuola Superiore di Architettura in Rome, founded in 1919/20 (cf. Colonna 1994), architecture was assigned the role of lifting an existing architectural culture and thus also a national architectural landscape into modern times. In recent years, scholars reflected various shadows of modernity and re-established "other modernity" (*altra modernità*) as a term. What remained untouched was to categorize different approaches to handing down a historic architectural culture to modernity. Cettina Lenza's chapter in this book responds to a theoretical background of that desideratum, whereas the other chapters analyze architecture and urban planning projects as practical examples for different strategies for reenacting architectural traditions.

The research focus for this book

This book aims to contextualize both new architecture and restoration efforts in architecture within urban and landscape transformation. We chose this overarching perspective in order to unfold a panorama of Italian townscapes in transition. Historical, architectural research often excluded monument conservation, which was commonly accompanied by efforts for staging surrounding areas, a practice of editing and integrating historical districts into the modern city. This book, *Townscapes in Transition*, looks at architecture and urban design as ways of transforming existing townscapes and landscapes to modernity and discusses theories of tradition in architecture and urban planning. The publication examines a wide range of construction and transformation processes from restoration campaigns for historic quarters up to new design concepts derived from historical models. We identify them as phenomena in a shared intellectual climate of a new renaissance of Italian architecture. The aspect of heritage was not only expressed in handing down monuments, physical structures, and the overall urban fabric but also through an architectural culture which was perceived as a tradition that could be inherited and yet modernized and transformed, – a concept that we would describe today as intangible heritage.

Departing from that heritage perspective, we can observe urban editing as a professional and political culture that included architecture, urban planning, and design, monument restoration, superordinate building programs like that of banks, fascist organizations or even the Catholic Church (for the Church cf. Monzo 2017). As we will show later, all these elements were incorporated into the field of *urbanistica* by the end of the 1920s. Because of their visible references to historical architecture, we suggest interpreting foundation cities as new editions of historic Italian or Mediterranean towns or cities.

In the first part of this introductory text, we give an overview of how an immense need for housing and urban expansion in Italy was joined to a political intention to connect to glorious ages in history. We describe how architecture and the restoration of monuments were assigned the task of simultaneously representing that past and connecting it to the present by drawing on myths and creating a backdrop to carry myths into the present. We give an overview of how architecture and commissioning were reorganized after the First World War and finally offer a panorama of significant urban development measures of that time.

In the second part, we introduce the understanding of urban planning at that time. We explain how investment in new public buildings, monument preservation, redevelopment of central urban areas and city extension were all conceived as an overall urban and regional development strategy. The different chapters of this book speak to different aspects and different scales of townscapes in transition and are shortly introduced here and contextualized within the overall strategies of *urbanistica*.

I: POLITICAL AND ARCHITECTURAL BACKDROPS OF THE INTERWAR PERIOD IN ITALY

Fascist self-fulfillment: Will for order and mobilization

After the First World War, Italy, like many other countries, is on an epochal threshold (cf. Münkler 2013: 797). Although the multi-layered processes of change that have been built up over decades are far more complex than can be captured in a central event, it is nevertheless the traumatic experience of the World War that produces a new kind of collective feeling that urges participation and change (cf. Leonhard 2018: 23-25). The well-nigh mystified "trench community" (Kershaw 2016: 105) is only the most extreme expression of a mass society that is now distinctly emerging and increasingly shaping cultural and political developments. A society of the masses that reveals itself to many contemporaries as a "deeply ambivalent result of demographic development, economic dynamism and social mobilization"[3] (Leonhard 2014: 25) and that expresses itself in new ways of living, of working, but also of organizing itself. Changes that do not fail to leave the built environment unscathed. On the contrary, they turn out to be driving forces of a substantial and visible change of the living environments.

The growing inflow of persons seeking work into urban centres and the considerable birth rates since 1900, which continued in Italy even throughout the war years, articulate themselves in a dynamic urban growth and increasing urbanization in the Interwar period. In parallel, however, a counter-movement to rapid urbanization is developing aiming at opening up new or previously neglected areas (regionalism). In this context, urbanization is reflected in the densification of existing urban structures and in urban expansions, while ruralization is expressed in regional, mostly agrarian settlement policy measures. Both strategies gain increasingly in importance in the Interwar period and form the basis on which the constructional changes of the Interwar period take place.

Simultaneously, the destructive force of the World War has disenchanted the bourgeois belief in progress of the 19th century (cf. Leonhard 2014: 24-26). In the search for individual and collective self-assurance, it is now a matter of repositioning oneself in a profoundly transformed reality of life (cf. Leonhard 2014: 25). The new dynamic society that emerged in the long 19th century thus becomes the field of action of modern political mass movements that offer orientation with programmatic and intuitive offers. And it is this reorientation accelerated by the

---

3   „zutiefst ambivalentes Ergebnis der demografischen Entwicklung, der wirtschaftlichen Dynamik und sozialen Mobilisierung".

First World War that characterizes the Interwar period as a transitional period between the world of the 19th and 20th centuries.

In a short post-war period, in which power in Italy is literally on the street due to a weakened liberal bourgeois government, the fascist mass movement under the leadership of the former interventionist Benito Mussolini (1883-1945) succeeds in seizing power in 1922 by a mixture of exuberant use of force and "pacification politics"[4] (Woller 2016: 73). Already at an early stage it became apparent that the fascist regime sees itself as a new power of order that pursues the goal of "motivating" and "mobilizing" the masses for a "strictly hierarchically ordered modern people's state without classes" that is also expansive in foreign and domestic policy (Woller 2016: 80).[5] This combination of the will to order and mobilization becomes the paradigm of fascist self-fulfillment: on the one hand, the fascist movement wants to be the perfecter of a lost, but culturally and historically founded greatness, on the other hand, it wants to embody a young, vital – and at times also brilliant – force leading Italy into a glorious future (cf. Payne 2006: 573-591). As a result, the promise of a deeper identification with one's own culture goes hand in hand with the demand for orientation and formation of a "new kind of civilization" (Washburn Child 1999 [1928]: 146).[6]

Towards a fascist building policy

The fascist regime, which was gradually installed in 1922 following Mussolini's takeover of the affairs of state, sees itself as a revolutionary force. Accordingly, the 1920s were marked by the reorganization of the state structure in the sense of a corporate and authoritarian order.[7] Through skillful consensus politics, the

---

4 „Pazifizierungs-Politik". There is a plethora of studies and publications on fascism that can hardly be overlooked. Stanley G. Payne's A History of Fascism (Payne 1995) and Emilio Gentile's Fascismo (Gentile 2007 [2005]) may still serve as an appropriate introduction. On Italian fascism, however, in addition to the extensive basic research of Renzo De Felice, the multi-layered research of Emilio Gentile is particularly worthy of note. On the history of society and culture in fascist Italy, the works of Richard J. B. Bosworth, Christopher Duggan, Patrizia Dogliani, Jens Petersen, Wolfgang Schieder and Alessandra Tarquini are particularly important.

5 „motivieren"; „mobilisieren"; „streng hierarchisch geordnete[n] modernen Volksstaat ohne Klassen".

6 "nuova via di civiltà".

7 For a brief explanation of fascist *corporatism* we refer to De Bernardi/Guarracino 2003: 233f.

transition to an increasingly totalitarian practice of rule is initiated. In this process, well described by Emilio Gentile as a phase of "totalitarian acceleration"[8] (Gentile 2007 [2005]: 27f), Italian fascism relies less on a self-contained, immovable logical order of ideas (ideology) than on an ideology of use without precise doctrine oriented towards the practical exploitation of emotional and mythical moments, such as liturgy-like organized mass dynamics, worship of the fallen, the myth of Rome, the cult of the leader, etc. (cf. Mack Smith 2004 [1981]: 224-232, Gentile 2001). "Myths and Rites of Fascism"[9] (Silva 1975 [1973]: 155; cf. Gentile 2005 [2001]) are stylized into connecting elements of a new mass society. In their visible counterparts, a propaganda that promises departure and novelty mixes with historical recourses creating continuity and a state supporting monumentality. Accordingly, fascist architectural politics aims at the dynamic embodiment of the Italian spirit and at the same time at the accomplishment of an Italian greatness perceived in myths. Building construction becomes the expression of a cultural ability that is experienced as superior. And yet the seeming contradiction between the fascist-sponsored recourse to tradition and the past and the simultaneous claim to be a modern nation dissolves in the ideological utility value of the newly shaped built environment.[10] The ultimate goal is an idea of identity legitimized by permanence and continuity, communicated by recognition and familiarity, and at the same time projected promisingly into eternity: "What we have created is destined to exist for centuries."[11]

Fascism uses architecture as a means of communicating with and influencing the masses; architecture is supposed to create consensus, secure acclamation and coin people in the sense of fascism by conveying its myths. In this way, architecture becomes part of a 'pedagogical' process in which identity creation and fascization merge in the education to a new 'fascist human being' (*uomo nuovo*). This ambition is particularly impressively reflected in the architecture of the holiday settlements commissioned by the *Opera Nazionale Balilla* (ONB), a fascist youth organization (cf. Capomolla/Mulazzani/Vittorini 2008). It is also found in the party buildings, the so-called Case del Fascio (cf. Portoghesi/Mangione/Soffitta 2006), as well as in the new town foundations of the Pontine Plain (cf.

---

8   "accelerazione totalitaria".
9   „Mythen und Riten des Faschismus".
10 On the more general theme of the search for an art and architecture which can be connotated to national motives we refer to the 2011 conference 'Kunst auf der Suche nach der Nation' (Art in Search of the Nation): cf. Dombrowski 2013.
11 "Quello che abbiamo fatto è destinato a rimanere nei secoli." Benito Mussolini, quoted from Estermann-Juchler 1982, p. 31.

Spiegel 2010), in the construction of which the *Opera Nazionale Combattenti* (ONC), the fascist veterans' association, plays a major role (for the specific use of building materials and autarchy see the chapter by Angela Pecorario Martucci in this book). Against this socio-political background, the fascist regime is building a system of institutionalized influence and control. In the field of building construction, this system is essentially based on control over the training of professionals involved in the construction sector, the legal definition and corporate organization of the same profession, as well as control over the press, especially the specialized press, and the commissioning of building projects. Particularly the latter is decisive for the development of an architectural language that can be related to the self-representation of the regime.

Reforming the architects education

In accordance with the demands of a great and modern nation already established in nationalism, the political and cultural initiatives, even before Mussolini took power, were aimed at making architects ambassadors of a new national identity by reorganizing the profession and centralizing architectural education. A not inconsiderable role in the reorganization of architectural training plays Freemasonry, which, until its prohibition in 1926, exerts a considerable influence on the Istituto di Belle Arti in Rome as a result of personal interweavements. At the time, the sculptor Ettore Ferrari (1845-1931), the Grand Master of the most influential lodge in Italy, chairs the Istituto di Belle Arti (cf. Nicoloso 2004 [1999]: 28-33). Unlike the Milan Polytechnic, founded in 1865, the Istituto di Belle Arti stands for an artistic teaching approach. The two institutions' exemplary different emphases in the training of architects are reflected in the legislative initiative of the architect and Member of Parliament Cesare Nava (1861-1933), which strengthens the technical point of view, and the legislative initiative of the State Secretary Giovanni Rosadi (1862-1925), which is oriented towards the traditional art academies, from which in turn the term 'academists', later used in contemporary discourse to describe the academically trained traditionalists of older generations, as a term of combat originates. In addition, Nava proposes the establishment of architecture academies or faculties in the country's largest cities, while Rosadi initially sees education centralized in Rome. In addition to strengthening Rosadi's proposal, Rosadi is also close to the environment of the Roman architect, engineer and leading architectural historian Gustavo Giovannoni (1873-1947). Together with the architect and Member of Parliament Manfredo Manfredi (1859-1927), Giovannoni leads a group of influential Roman professionals involved in the construction sector, who, in the then most important Italian association of architects and artists, the *Associazione Artistica fra i Cultori di Architettura* (1890-1927), dedicated themselves to the national renaissance of Italian architecture.[12] The group also includes later protagonists such as the architects Marcello Piacentini (1881-1960), who, thanks to Ferrari's intervention, is able to participate in the prestigious 1924 competition for the Memorial of the Fallen in Genoa, and Arnaldo Foschini (1884-1968), as well as the later president of the National Fascist Architects' Corporation Alberto Calza Bini (1881-1957), who, thanks to Ferrari's connections, is able to obtain a post in the Ministry of Education in 1919. As a result of the war, neither of the two legislative initiatives passes the parliament, but it becomes clear that, because of the gradually increasing influence of the Roman environment, Rome would play a central role in the training of architects.

Initially, Giovannoni is the formative figure in the debate about a scientifically founded architectural training. As spokesman, he succeeds in establishing the first Italian architecture college with the founding of the Scuola Superiore di Architettura in Rome (1919/20) (cf. Nicoloso 2004 [1999]: 23-49, Beese 2016: 110-113). The program of the new school adopts its training concept which is denominated *architetto integrale* (cf. Giovannoni 1916, Zucconi 1997a). It combines a profound knowledge of architectural history with an open attitude towards modern society and modern building materials and techniques. The knowledge of architectural history is applied to the discipline of *restauro*, restoration, conservation and preservation of cultural building heritage. In doing so, Giovannoni conveys a theoretical approach that emphasizes the determinant importance of the built context for new building types as well. Based on his understanding of a city being an agglomeration of building heritage, he demands extensive protection status for historical urban areas and sensitive building in the vicinity of monuments (*ambientismo*). Together with the preservation of historical monuments and decorative arts, the range of subjects furthermore includes the classical canon, typical of the turn of the century Europe, which plays into the still strong references to materiality and forms of existing architecture characterizing most of the Italian architectural designs of the Interwar period.

The reform of the professional education is accompanied by the journal *Architettura e Arti Decorative*, published since 1921 by the Associazione Artistica fra i Cultori di Architettura and directed by Giovannoni and Piacentini (cf. Beese 2016: 114-117). In this regard, the integral technical and artistic training aims at the development of an own, unmistakable Italian style (cf. Giovannoni 1921).

---

12 For the Associazione Artistica fra i Cultori di Architettura cf. Albrecht 2017: 29-39, see also glossary at the end of this book.

Thus, Giovannoni writes:

Please do not confuse stylistic inclinations with didactic orientation, these are two fundamentally different things. [...] in my opinion, transient fashions do not belong to what is to be taught; instead, the search for a constructive rationalism must take precedence. But on the other hand this must not lead us tearing down the bridges to the past and disrupting the line of continuity that constitutes the most praiseworthy tradition with which Italy in parts still dominates the world.[13] (Giovannoni 1929 [1925]: 51).

The increasing importance of the controlled design of the built environment, especially in view of the growing urbanization in Italy, also leads to the newly created subject Edilizia cittadina (Urban construction) at the Scuola Superiore di Architettura di Roma, taught by Piacentini, which subsequently gives rise to Urbanistica (Urban planning) as an independent discipline. Piacentini, however, already makes an early plea (cf. Piacentini 1922: 60-72) for an urban development adapted to the requirements of "the economization and rationalization of the construction industry as well as the 'de-individualization' of society"[14] (Beese 2016: 117). As a representative of an "Italian way to new tendencies"[15] (Nicoloso 2004: 60), Piacentini, who has meanwhile been promoted as the undisputed broker of Italian architecture for Mussolini, assumes from 1927 on the sole management of the country's most important architectural magazine Architettura e Arti Decorative.[16]

Reorganization of the profession

The development initiated by educational reform and journalism is flanked by a reorganization of the profession. On 24 June 1923, in Italy, the professional titles *architect* and *engineer* are legally protected for the first time in Europe, and in 1925 the transition from studies to professional life is linked to a state examination, which is still required today, for the ability to exercise the profession (cf. Tragbar 2012: 200-202). This coincides with the quasi-authoritarian corporate reorganization of the working class and the reorganization of the professions

---

13 "Non confondiamo due argomenti diversissimi, quali quelle delle tendenze stilistiche e dell'indirizzo didattico. [...] il mio pensiero: bando alle mode effimere [...] e ricerca di un razionalismo costruttivo, senza che questa ricerca ci faccia rompere i ponti con il passato ed interrompa il filo di una mirabile tradizione continua per la quale ancora in parte l'Italia domina il mondo."

14 „der Ökonomisierung und der Rationalisierung des Baugewerbes sowie der ‚Entindividualisierung' der Gesellschaft".

15 "via italiana alle nuove tendenze".

16 On the outstanding role of Piacentini see above all Nicoloso 2018.

(*corporatism*) that has been carried out since 1927 within the framework of the fascist restructuring of the state. During this process, a fascist professional representation of architects is founded under the name of *Sindacato Nazionale Architetti Fascisti* (National Fascist Architects' Corporation, see glossary) and taken under the leadership of Alberto Calza Bini.[17] Through its direct relationship with the Ministry of Corporation, which emerged from the Ministry of Economics in 1929, it serves above all to influencing building construction activities and thus indirectly to influence the creators of built environment (cf. Rifkind 2012a). With a view to the solidarity of Piacentini and Calza Bini in the architectural corporation the architect Giuseppe Pensabene (1898-1968) speaks even of an "artistic self-dictatorship"[18] (Pensabene 1933). The importance of the institution increases along with the extent to which Mussolini, after the consolidation of his rule (effectively staged in the *Lateran Treaties* with the Catholic Church, see glossary), increasingly focuses on architecture and building policy.

During the Second Congress of the Architects' Corporation on 17 July 1931, it became clear that from now on a strong influence on the built representation of the regime and infrastructural development of the country is to be aimed at through competitions and the awarding of contracts by taking a stand for a "[p]ropaganda without rest", so that "in every favorable circumstance the public administrations will announce competitions for works of some importance, giving the Architects' Corporation mandate for the preparation of the relative calls and recognizing to the same corporation the necessary function of control over the seriousness of the operations of competition both by the individual competitors, as well as by the juries and the same public authority."[19] (Architettura e arti Decorative 1931: 634) As early as 1932, the Architects' Corporation is able to set a moderately modern

---

17 The Sindacato Nazionale Fascista Ingegneri (National Fascist Engineers' Corporation) is also founded. The typical Italian confusion of that time between the professional titles of *architect* and *engineer* can be resolved by looking at the educational curricula: previously, building professionals were organised according to their education in the *Federazione Architetti Italiani* (for graduates of art schools) and in the Società degli Ingegneri e degli Architetti Italiani (for graduates of engineering schools and polytechnics) (cf. Albrecht 2017: 29 Footnote 60).

18 "autodittatura artistica".

19 "Propaganda senza riposo perché in ogni circostanza favorevole le pubbliche amministrazioni bandiscano concorsi per le opere di qualche importanza, dando ai sindacati mandato per la preparazione dei bandi relativi e riconoscendo ai sindacati medesimi la necessaria funzione di controllo sulla serietà delle operazioni di concorso tanto da parte dei singoli concorrenti, quanto da parte delle giurie e degli stessi Enti banditori."

stylistic standard by the organization and holding of a series of competitions for new churches in the earthquake-damaged area of the diocese of Messina, which is commissioned by the Bishop of Messina (cf. Monzo 2017, 699–769). This is followed by the so-called *stagione dei concorsi* (literally: season of competitions) (cf. Ciucci 2002 [1989]: 129-151, Casciato 2004: 208-233). Large-scale national competitions for public representative buildings and urban redevelopment through urban development plans (called *Piano Regolatore Generale* or simply *Piano Regolatore*, PRG or PR) are intended to shape the face of fascist Italy. In doing so, the strengthening of competition is aimed at increasing the influence of the Architects' Corporation vis-à-vis the local building and planning authorities through the composition of the juries and the selection of participants (cf. Calza Bini 1933). Among the tasks to be performed, the competitions for several post office buildings, the fascist party headquarters (Palazzo del Littorio) and the new university campus (Città universitaria) in Rome as well as for the new Santa Maria Novella railway station in Florence along with accompanying discussions on the orientation of Italian architecture stand out. However, a wide number of competitions and initiatives throughout the country testifies to a highly productive policy. Contemporaneous this policy is accompanied and channeled by Piacentini's ubiquitous presence.[20]

The magazine *Architettura* (1932-44), formerly *Architettura e Arti Decorative*, meanwhile transformed into the mouthpiece of the Architectural Corporation, becomes, under the leadership of Piacentini, a showcase for the building activity stimulated by the regime and, at the same time, a pace setter for the officially favored, moderately modern architectural language. Giovannoni, being considered too conservative, is marginalized; the Associazione Artistica fra i Cultori di Architettura is brought into line with the fascist architectural corporation. Piacentini 'dedusts' the editorial staff of the magazine by surrounding himself with young and familiar collaborators such as Plinio Marconi, Gaetano Minnucci and Giulio Pediconi, and significantly appoints with Giuseppe Pagano, Adalberto Libera, Giovanni Michelucci and Luigi Piccinato protagonists of the Italian avant-garde as correspondents (cf. Nicoloso 2018: 134).

---

20 Cf. in particular Paolo Nicoloso's chapter Piacentini and unitary architectural directions for Italian cities in this volume.

Creative homogenization and state architecture

The initial "pluralism of styles"[21] (Pfammatter 1996 [1990]), Daniela Spiegel even speaks of "extraordinary architectural variety" (Spiegel 2015: 43), is gradually becoming a relatively homogeneous national architectural trend, in which the various leading forces of Italian architecture participate. Still at the beginning of the 1930s, the fascist understanding of architecture oscillates between traditional and radically modern forms of expression, before these, accompanied by heated theoretical discussions (cf. Patetta 1972), are channeled through a real competition of currents into a unification of architectural language subserving the self-representation of the regime. This process is exemplarily reflected by the dissolution of the *Movimento Italiano per l'Architettura Razionale* (MIAR, see glossary), the Italian movement for rational architecture, which collected the representatives of a "radical rationalism"[22] (Benedetti 2010: 77), at the instigation of the Architectural Corporation, and the absorption of some of its leading members (Adalberto Libera, Sebastiano Larco, Carlo Enrico Rava) in the newly formed *Raggruppamento Architetti Moderni Italiani* (RAMI) controlled by Piacentini. It is through skillful mediation and by according changing favours that Mussolini's "architectural governors', Marcello Piacentini and Alberto Calza Bini, manage to bundle the various currents into a dynamic complex of creative homogenization.

Temporary sympathies of the regime, nurtured by the revolutionary left of the Fascist party (PNF) towards the *Razionalismo* represented by young radical architects, lead to an open confrontation, which finally merges into an "architectural trasformismo"[23] (Monzo 2017: 103). In this process, the permissive architectural policy of the early period is gradually being turned into the claim of a 'genuinely fascist' architecture – an architecture that consequently recalls fascist myths of national greatness. Such an architecture, while representing the claim of a modern revolution, must therefore speak a language understandable to the masses and easily accessible to collective memory; fully in the sense of an architecture that "speaks [...] to the memory of the nation"[24] (Nicoloso 2008: XVII). This, in turn, has the consequence that the importance that monuments have been attributed to the foundation and fortification of national identity since Italian unification is also accorded to the new monumental buildings of the fascist state. In this regard, the *Consiglio Superiore delle Belle Arti ed Antichità*, responsible for the uniform

---

21 „Pluralismus der Stile".
22 "razionalismo radicale".
23 „architektonischen trasformismo".
24 "che [...] parli alla memoria della nazione".

treatment of important monuments since the 19th century, also takes on responsibility for the city as a monument site with the new Town Planning Act and thus also for the integration of historical buildings and ensembles into modern urban planning (cf. Colavitti 2018: 100, Fontana 1999). In this way, the interlocking of building heritage with modern architecture and new structures referring to this heritage is ensured.

Figure 1: Angiolo Mazzoni, Termini Station, Rome, 1941, mockup of the frontal portico realized in Acque Albule near Tivoli

From: Ciucci, Giorgio (2004), p. 477

As Paolo Nicoloso has pointed out in his study *Mussollini architetto* (cf. 2008: 219-252) the development since the beginning of the 1930s towards a decided state architecture (the so-called *Stile Littorio* or *Licotrial Style*, cf. Palozzi 1936) is part of the integration of building production into the totalitarian acceleration processes of the regime. Characteristic of this period of transition to a unification of architectural trends in a "national modernity"[25] (Benedetti 2010: 67) – Piacentini also speaks here of "unitary physiognomy"[26] (Piacentini 1939: 6) – are the remarkably strong changes to which advanced projects in the construction and planning process are subjected, such as the Palazzo di Giustizia in Milan, the Ministero delle Corporazioni in Rome, the Palazzo delle Poste in Naples or even the church Sacro Cuore di Cristo Re in Rome. Another example, which has so far received little attention in this key function, is the result of the competition series for the diocese of Messina organized by the architects' corporation. In 1932, even before the decisions in the aforementioned major national architectural competitions in Rome and Florence, the chairman of the jury, Piacentini, and the organizer, Calza Bini, forced a clear shift towards a formal language that mediated between the Italian building heritage, which is important for national self-assurance, and the objectification of forms (Fig. 1). It is characteristic that the generally desire for representative size and monumentality which is authoritative in the Interwar period across countries (cf. Borsi 1986), is combined with the basic principles of the avant-garde to form a symbiosis of familiar design elements and reduced formulation: "in the most modern and functional forms of expression, the classical and the monumental must be the inspiration of architectural creation"[27] (Mariani 1987: 67). Accordingly, in 1931 Piacentini, in his attempt to identify a specifically Italian modernity, can refer to examples from the Netherlands, France and Scandinavia, where, in his opinion, a contemporary national architectural language had been developed that was not limited to arbitrarily interchangeable functionalist forms (cf. Piacentini 1931).

Piacentini thus underscores his plea for, in his words, "other modernity"[28] (Pisani 1996: 172), an Italian modernity. A modernity that – in contrast to the elitist colored understanding of modernity described by Sandro Benedetti as selective (because tending towards dissociation) – stands up for an inclusive concept taking the architectural and cultural diversity of the first half of the 20th century into account (cf. Benedetti 1998: 58).[29]

---

25 "modernità nazionale".
26 "fisionomia unitaria".
27 "il sentimento classico e monumentale, nel puro senso di atteggiamento dello spirito, [...] dovrà essere, pur nelle più moderne e funzionali forme, il fondamento dell'ispirazione architettonica", Mariani 1987: 67; see also Etlin 1991: 418-426 and 486-492.
28 "una modernità diversa".
29 Since the 1970s, the dualistic view of Interwar architecture from the perspective of a dogmatically perceived Classical Modern Architecture has given way to a more multilayered approach in the course of postmodern theory formation. Since then, this

Fascist building programs

The development of an architectural and urban design language that evokes associations with national myths as well as an ambitious building policy are essential elements of the fascist deployment of power. As Mussolini states: "For me, architecture is the highest of all the arts [...] because it encompasses everything"[30] (Mussolini/Ludwig 1932: 211). Keeping the goal of a visible change in the living environment in mind, fascist architectural policy leads to probably the largest building program in modern and contemporary history (cf. Nicoloso 2012: 9-11). This contains prestigious urban redevelopments and infrastructure measures in the urban centers of Turin, Milan, Rome and Naples as well as construction activity in smaller, rather regionally significant cities – treated in this volume – such as Bari, Brescia, Venice or the cities of the region where Mussolini was born and which was glorified to be the cradle of fascism: the Romagna. Additionally, there are many smaller and larger urban district and new town foundations. In detail, as suggested above, the measures mainly concern the design of the city centers through the construction of new government and administration buildings as well as buildings for public service, schools, post office buildings, railway stations, court buildings and branches of the fascist party. But also including sports facilities, holiday settlements for the fascist youth and leisure organizations as well as other state and semi-state welfare organizations and even state-subsidized church buildings in the new towns founded by the regime (cf. Gresleri/Gresleri/Culotta 2007). By the new buildings and the accompanying artistic-intellectual discourse propagandistically orchestrated in exhibitions, publications and excursions, the

---

approach has also understood architectural languages and design concepts with deeper roots in cultural history as part of modernity. However, it is only more recently that these have been detached from the perspective of postmodern overcoming strategies (Überwindungsstrategien) and have been recognized as equal as well as mutually conditioned and fertilizing expressions of one and the same time. Thus, the manifold expressions of modernity in the Interwar period have become a firmly established component of the consideration of architectural history. A circumstance that not least also contributes to opening up an ideologically undisguised view of architecture and urban planning in totalitarian regimes. Most recently, the diversity of modernity was the subject of a conference entitled The Multiple Modernity at the Archiv für Baukunst at the University of Innsbruck on the initiative of Klaus Tragbar (31 January - 2 February 2019).

30 „Die höchste unter allen Künsten [...] ist für mich die Architektur, denn sie fasst alles zusammen."

fascist regime gives itself an unmistakable physiognomy and creates for the fascist model of society its own built reality. Architecture becomes a means of self-representation, self-assurance and self-glorification, but also of permanent mass mobilization nourishing, thanks to its suggestive power, the myth of fascism promising splendor, greatness and welfare. Thus, for example, in the formal language of architecture, the myth of ancient imperial Rome (romanità) can be linked effectively and comprehensibly to the fascist revolution and transported to the present day in order to serve as a basis for the homogenization of fascism, people, state and its leader (*Duce*, for the term see glossary) (cf. Sarfatti 1926).

The concept or idea of *romanità* is not an invention of the fascists. Rather, it is an expression of a past that was already perceived in ancient Roman society as a living reference point (cf. Sommer 2016: XVIII). As a measure of cultural location and orientation, it is probably as old as Rome itself. But it gets a new dynamic in the context of fascist self-portrayal. The concept was probably first described in fascist interpretation by Margherita Sarfatti in her Mussolini biography *Dux* (1926). There *romanità* stands for the relatively diffuse cultural ideology of fascism, according to which one rejects the copy of the old, emphasizes one's own innovative power, but nevertheless strives for a visible relation to the cultural substrate of Italy because of the greatness of the nation. Together with the analogously interpreted *italianità* (e.g. through reminiscences of the Renaissance or the iconic Dante Alighieri), it forms the categories for a traditional fascist understanding of art.

In the built object, the fascist claim to power is given a physical presence; through the beauty of the forms, the value of the materials used, and the frequently programmatic reference to glorious epochs of Italian cultural history (*italianità*), architecture is also able to reach those parts of society and draw them under the spell of fascism that would otherwise be distant from political fascism. Paolo Nicoloso has aptly summarized this influential power of architecture as a structural shaping of power of the fascist regime: "The architectural monument has the ability to transmit meanings that can reach a whole community, which is then recognized in it."[31] (Nicoloso 2008: XVI.) As it were, it is the regime's aspiration to represent the historical continuity and legitimacy it claims through a "fascism of stone"[32] (Gentile 2008 [2007]). By employing, influencing and impressing the masses, the state architecture and building policy as an essential component of a broader cultural policy promises the consolidation of fascist power. At the same

---

31 "Il monumento architettonico ha la capacità di trasmettere significati in grado di raggiungere tutta una comunità, la quale in esso poi si viene a riconoscere."
32 "Fascismo di pietra."

time, however, the construction programs also serve economic interests, since in addition to the construction industry, the real estate market in particular is benefiting from increased construction activity and the willingness to open up inner-city areas by radical demolition (*sventramenti*) and to declare them building land.

II: MONUMENTS, HISTORIC URBAN FABRIC AND PROPAGANDA

Producing heritage

As shown in the first part, architects drew formal and stylistic connecting lines to a mystic Roman or Italian past by using specific design principles or stylistic elements for new buildings. What is more, also physical and structural urban connections were laid between historical locations and new parts of the city. New urban structures aimed to resemble historic streets or small squares (*piazze*) both inside and outside existing towns or cities. On the basis of the studies published in this book, we consider strong similarities between *romanità* or *italianità* in architecture and ways of restoration and urban planning. The design of the new urban area in Bologna between Via Marchesana and Via Piave, for example, followed the architectural and restoration practice for medieval architecture conducted by Alfonso Rubbiani (1848-1913) in Bologna in the years before (see the chapter by Elena Pozzi, Marco Pretelli and Leila Signorelli in this book). In other places like Milan, current design strategies for skyscrapers expressed *italianità* by underlining design connections via visual connecting lines to historical buildings representing authentic historical Italian-ness (see the chapter by Scot Budzynski). The insertion of new urban *fora* was sometimes directly connected to excavations and new presentations of ancient Roman ruins in the city like in Trieste (see the chapter by Paolo Nicoloso). However, even without direct historical connections to ancient buildings, a simulation of *romanità* was used to draw connections to a supposed grandiose past, as shown by Antonucci's and Nannini'chapter for the region of Romagna. How both ideas – a connection and exhibition of historical locations through urban planning and a creative reshaping of historic buildings towards an idealized past – correlated, is demonstrated by two examples from Forlì (chapters by Giulia Favaretto, Chiara Mariotti and Antonucci/Nannini). We can describe the whole phenomena of shaping and editing urban areas as the production of heritage (cf. Enss/Vinken 2016).

Apart from editing historic areas to idealized versions of ancient Italian towns, we even find forms of an invention of history. Pozzi, Pretelli, Signorelli, Favaretto, and Mariotti called this phenomenon in the titles of their chapters: "Planning the Past". Such inventions were primarily used in highly politicized areas like Romagna but were also described before for other cases (cf. Tragbar 2009). A 'medieval' reshaping of urban landscapes can be traced back to the nineteenth century when medieval often stood generally for the opposite of modernity (cf. Zucconi 1997b: 22).

The following text aims to structure the field of producing urban heritage into the sub-areas of a) preservation and restorations of monuments, b) urban planning and urban design based on minor modifications of existing cities and c) urban redevelopment and transformation.

Preservation of monuments

While a consistent modern architectural language that spoke, "to the memory of the Nation," (Nicoloso 2008: XVII, cit. above) surfaced only during the late years of the Fascist government, a canon of historic national buildings, National Monuments, had been identified and inventoried already beginning with the National unification in the nineteenth century (cf. Lamberini 2003). The abovementioned Consiglio Superiore delle Belle Arti ed Antichità, composed of leading specialists, architects, and art historians, e.g., restoration theorist Camillo Boito (1836-1914), had advised the relevant ministries in the way of restoring historical monuments consistently throughout the country (cf. Pane 2018). While monument preservation had affected mostly single buildings, the direct surrounding of monuments was protected from redevelopment in 1909 by law (cf. Lamberini 2003). This extension of the sphere of influence of monuments led to a disciplined cohesion of monument preservation and architecture in an urban context. The practice of planning urban development and redevelopment around safeguarded sites lead to an artistic and intellectual interaction between urbanism and architectural history that resulted in the idea of *ambientismo*.

Under the guidance of Gustavo Giovannoni, who joined the Consiglio in 1919, the concept of historic monuments opened up to whole historic quarters, city districts and even historical cultural landscapes. This affected city planning processes, since whole historic areas, vistas, and perspectives had to be taken into consideration for safeguarding in the redevelopment planning process. Conservation offices became part of planning processes. The Consiglio charged Giovannoni with providing expert opinions as commissioner for urban heritage conservation. He continuously aimed to reconcile urban planning and monumental preservation and can be considered in this role the first national heritage planner – being in charge during the whole Ventennio.

As part of an architectural culture that was under corporative fascist surveillance, restorations and archeological excavations were additionally put under a strict time regime in order to represent their results at national events, e.g., anniversaries of the *March on Rome* as exemplified recently for Rome by Sylvia Diebner (2018: 17-19).

As stated above, the fascist regime created its own built reality for the fascist model of society. That newly constructed environment included not only new buildings but existing constructions and urban fabric. Shaping and editing monuments and historic districts were very effective in creating suggestive vistas and scenes for mass spectacles and film. Architectural and urban strategies profited from a generally accepted pool of national memory as a backdrop for new buildings representing the regime. In Giovannoni's observation from a first international meeting of monument preservationists under the auspices of the League of Nations in Athens, Italy offered, compared with other nations attending the congress, with its over 40,000 listed buildings, a "unique number, importance and continuity of architectural manifestations from the past"[33] and an in his view progressive legislation that put national interests in conservation in front of those of private owners (Giovannoni 1932: 410).

In the interwar period, urban planning extended to regional and territorial planning, the concept of safeguarding urban areas, urban green and beautiful landscapes were developed likewise by architects and politicians around Giovannoni, resulting in the conservation law that included landscape protection in 1939 (Zucconi 2014: 85). The chapter by Antonucci and Nannini in this book shows explicitly how new public buildings, for example, Case del Fascio, were used to create a combination and a mutual accentuation or 'enhancement' of new monumental buildings and historical monuments. The campus of Milan's Catholic University (chapter in this book by Cecilia de Carli) can be considered a masterpiece in terms of such a combination and mythical reinterpretation of the existing historical area. New architecture, restoration, and preservation of monuments, garden planning, art, and sculpture were combined to complete artwork, a *Gesamtkunstwerk*. This example clearly shows how restoration works were used to draw connections to a glorious history in order to, as an exhibition catalog on *Urbanistica italiana in regime fascista* (1937) put it, "give back to the Nation all the artistic heritage that centuries passed down to it" ([Civico] 1937a: 32).[34] That practice included both references in modern buildings to the past and to a surrounding historical

---

33 "[…] dal numero, dall'importanza, dalla continuità unica al mondo delle manifestazioni architettoniche del passato."

34 "[…] per ridare alla Nazione tutto il patrimonio d'arte che i secoli le hanno trasmesso."

ambience plus an effort to restore historical buildings and structures to epitomize an ideal past.

Famous examples for a staging of ancient monuments in Rome were the breakthroughs of the Via della o (cf. Kirk 2006) and the Via dell'Impero, today's Via dei Fori Imperiali (cf. Baxa 2017), but similar measures were taken all over the country on smaller scales. Techniques of re-shaping the surroundings to help most significant historic monuments fulfil a representative role within the historic city and moderate between urban history and modernity were not new, as discussions around the staging of the capitol hill showed since the 19th century (cf. Vannelli 1992).

Yet, in fascist Italy, this staging was not only applied to historic works of art like monumental buildings (as shown for the Brescia case by Coppo), but also to memorial places connected to famous personalities of that time or friends and family of Benito Mussolini (see the chapters by Favaretto/Mariotti and Antonucci/Nannini).

Fascist policies led to an increased budget for the preservation of historical monuments. In some cases, political interests in restoration, induced to edit historic structures and the urban fabric to resemble a past that had never existed. Elena Pozzi, Marco Pretelli and Leila Signorelli speak even of 'fake[s]' (*falso*), which they observe in restoration examples in the Emilia region.

Urbanistica: Urban design for existing cities

Due to Giovannoni's role as an influential teacher at the *Scuola Romana* (the term refers to the loose aggregation of a Roman architectural class, see glossary) and to Piacentini's support for *ambientismo*, the urban design around historic monuments became part of *urbanistica*. The same was the case for new public buildings taking on monumental quality. Giovannoni emphasized this claim in his book *Vecchie città ed edilizia nuova* (1931). That volume, which was aimed to open a new series at the newly founded Istituto Nazionale di Urbanistica (INU), reflected the thinking of the whole Scuola Romana and was introduced by Calza Bini in a preface (Giovannoni 1931: V-VII) as a fundamental basis for the new discipline of *urbanistica*. The understanding of *urbanistica* as a mother discipline for architecture, urban redevelopment, restoration and archeology within urban contexts continues to be in use in that sense (cf. Beese/Dobler 2018: *L'Urbanistica a Roma durante il ventennio fascista*).

Giovannoni created in his master plans for new settlements of Aniene, Garbatella or Ostia, all near Rome, urban structures modeled on historical urban configurations of Rome. Piacentini, a supporter of Sitte's ideas, promoted together with Giovannoni the aim of drawing connection lines in design to historic quarters, but he focused more on references to existing neighboring buildings.

The chapters by Lorenzo Ciccarelli and Alexander Fichte show clearly for Rome and Venice that remarkable references were made for city extensions, both in regards to the general built history and the historic neighborhood (*ambiente*) of the new quarters. For example, in the Roman garden city district Garbatella, references are made to newly discovered Roman ruins of Ostia Antica and generally to historic architecture of the 'mother town'. The same was the case in Venice, where new streets were laid out to resemble historical Venetian canals. The above-mentioned district in Bologna, a redevelopment area in the old town, can likewise be read in that context – more than in a thinning context, which has been suggested before (Bodenschatz 2011: 309-310).

"Urbanistica italiana in regime fascista"

We mentioned above that ideas of creating a new specifically Italian architecture out of history existed before fascism and how the architectural profession was set gradually under state control. The same was the case for urban planning, *urbanistica*, organized in INU in 1930. At that time, fascism had grown into a stable political force and used cultural politics for propaganda purposes.

Urbanism in interwar Italy followed a general trend in urban planning that aimed to integrate individual plans into broader regional or territorial contexts (cf. Rifkind 2012a: 57). Experienced town planners as Giovannoni or Piacentini, who had followed the ideas of the garden city movement, took an active part in the International Federation for Housing and Planning (IFHTP) conference 1929 in Rome. The functionary Alberto Calza Bini was a co-organizer of that conference. He was interested in gaining sovereignty over the interpretation of urban planning in Fascist Italy and became the first president of the INU in 1930 (Wagner 2018: 158). However, self-declared rationalists from the intellectual environment of the journal *Quadrante* took advantage and gained prestige from their international contacts. All the diverse groups instrumentalized IFHTP for the legitimation of their discipline in order to substantiate its scientific and technical nature.[35] In parallel to a multitude of styles and tendencies in architectures, there were various understandings of a corporativist city or explicitly Fascist urban planning. A "corporativist city" was claimed in 1934 by the Lodovico Belgioioso (1909-2004) and Gian Luigi Banfi (1910-45) in the journal *Quadrante* as "an element of the full ensemble of cities, organized and framed in the Corporativist life of the nation"

---

35 For IFHTP and the foundation of INU cf. Wagner 2018; for Quadrante cf. Rifkind 2012.

(Belgioioso 1934: 40; Rifkind 2012b: 264). A propagandist exhibition in Vienna showcased "Italian urbanism under the fascist regime" ("Urbanistica italiana in regime fascista") from a more traditional perspective in 1937 ([Civico] 1937a).

In a national context, in contrast, the majority of theorists of urban design connected their specialized texts to fascist propaganda. In the journal *Urbanistica*, organ of INU, Vincenzo Civico followed national and international efforts of urban planning in his column "Notiziario urbanistico" in various examples. Civico, as he himself remarked in an article (Civico 1937b: 467), was the editor of the exhibition catalog for Vienna ([Civico] 1937a). That exhibition, curated under the patronage of the ministry for propaganda, systemized urbanism in subcategories of "traffic and roads", "redevelopment" (*risanamento*), "[historical] monuments", "new quarters", parks and "green", "public buildings", "new and reconstructed cities" (in this case after natural disasters) and "cities of the empire" (of the colonies and Italianized areas).[36] The text links most of the categories explicitly to the historical cultural heritage.

According to the catalogue ([Civico] 1937a: 26), "monumental enhancement" (*valorizzazione monumentale*) often dominated the preparation of urban development plans (*piani regolatori*) in fascist Italy.[37] This reflected Gustavo Giovannoni's central claim for historical monuments which demanded, in his view, a 'distance of respect' around them. New buildings and architectural conditions were not supposed to change their historical environment (*ambiente*), that is certain assumed architectural characteristics such as "style", [...] "color", [...] "decoration" and "building technique" (Giovannoni 1918; reprinted in Zucconi 1997a: 112).[38] By extending that idea to an urban scale in his book *Vecchie città ed edilizia nuova* ("Old Cities and New Building") (Giovannoni 1931), Giovannoni advocated for an urban planning that respected important urban structures or

---

36 Chapters in the catalogue were entitled: "Il traffico e la viabilità", "Il risanamento", "I monumenti", "I nuovi quartieri", "Il verde", "Gli edifici e i servizi pubblici", "le città nuove e quelle ricostruite", "le città dell'Impero".

37 "L'amore, la scienza, l'arte degli urbanisti, degli archeologici, dei cittadini tutti, portano il loro appassionato contributo all'opera di valorizzazione monumentale, che domina spesso nelle sistemazioni di piano regolatore [...]."

38 "Vi possono quindi rientrare le distanze da lasciare come 'zona di rispetto', tra la nuova fabbricazione ed i monumenti le norme riguardanti la mole e la statura degli edifici nuovi in confronto dei vecchi, tutto lo schema edilizio del tracciato di piazze e di strade. Ma non di minore importanza sono, sostituire od a non alterare l'ambiente, le condizioni architettoniche individuali di stile, di colore, di ornato, della fabbricazione che rientra nella 'prospettiva'."

buildings and "grafting new urban quarters on an old trunk" (Giovannoni 1931: 184),[39] a concept which he had developed while planning the Roman extension quarter of Garbatella together with Piacentini.

Urban redevelopment

The examples mentioned in the catalog for city transformation in the Fascist era show three different ways of dealing with historic urban fabric: First, historic districts can be excluded from major structural redevelopments. Second, new, more or less integrated structures can replace the old urban fabric, and third, it can be partially renewed, maintaining most important historic buildings or features of the urban structure such as street traces. Both preservation and restructuring followed editing strategies for cities: certain areas were 'enhanced' for representing a (glorious) past. Others, often more impoverished areas, were eliminated, thus erasing social misery from central urban quarters. Despite Civico's affirmation that the state had built new healthy quarters, e.g. in Brindisi ([Civico] 1937a: 20), in reality citizens inhabiting these quarters were often expelled to the periphery, in Rome to the so-called *Borgate ufficiali di Roma*, as shown by Fernando Salsano (2010), Luciano Villani (2012) and Milena Farina (2017) for Rome. Lower social classes, who lived in poor quarters, were feared by the regime for rebelling against the system. For Bari's old town, which was initially meant to be torn down completely except for the churches, a connection between antifascist left-wing citizens and the demolishing plans has been drawn (Mangone 2003: 317-318). Similar observations were made for contemporary German *Sanierungen* (redevelopments) (cf. Petz 1990) of poor quarters, e.g., in Hannover (cf. Zalewski 2016). In such cases, physical change in the city resulted in social editing.

An essential part of the national policy in modernization was the expansion of the railway and road systems. Existing quarters should obtain the same road access as new quarters (cf. [Civico] 1937a: 6). Therefore, renewing the road system was a decisive motor of urban editing. Introducing new streets into the existing city lead to the destruction of the old urban fabric. Civico advocated for the preservation of historical urban cores where geographically possible. He suggested laying new roads through (slum) areas with adverse hygienic conditions (*borgate*) and only a small number of listed buildings (ibid: 6-7). As Alberto Coppo shows in his chapter in this book, Pietro Aschieri (1889-1952) proposed for Brescia a system of new roads that aimed to balance between the widening and opening of streets and a simultaneous staging of significant historic buildings (e.g., by

---

39 "L'innesto dei nuovi quartieri sul vecchio tronco."

opening vistas), according to theoretical approaches of Aschieri's former teacher Giovannoni. While Aschieri struggled for continuity in a historic appearance of Brescia, the urban development plans for Rome (1931) and Moscow (1935) focused more on a change in scale in order to shape new monumental avenues for the two capitals, as Anna Vyazemtseva explains in her comparative chapter on Rome and Moscow in this book. In those plans, historic monuments were used and combined with new monumentality gained by wide streets and large-size buildings.

Civico required that Italian urbanists had to bring, "light and healthiness into dense old quarters," while concurrently conserving an urban unity wherever possible and preserving significant historic buildings (*edilizia monumentale*) ([Civico] 1937a: 14).[40] He specifically named Gustavo Giovannoni's strategy of a thinning out of the dense urban fabric (*diradamento*) and described that strategy as an "ideal method" (*metodo ideale*), defining it as an "urban restoration" (*restauro urbano*). According to Civico, *diradamento* was reserved for quarters without significant redevelopment needs due to hygienic reasons (*risanamento*) and without substantial requirements for enhancing the traffic situation. Furthermore, the method should be applied only to quarters with such a significant, "historical and monumental content," that its architecture would enforce natural respect to the pickaxe (*piccone*) (all citations ibid: 14-15).[41] Due to these restrictions, Civico's word use of, "ideal method," to describe thinning could be interpreted here in a slightly critical sense. While he named Rome (Rioni del Rinascimento), Bari, Bergamo, Fiume, Siena and Treviso as successful examples for a thinning, he calls the strategy "in numerous other cases […] insufficient" for solving hygienic problems (ibid: 15). Among the 18 examples enumerated for a redevelopment of historic urban fabrics in Italian cities (Ancona, Brescia, Brindisi, Como, Ferrara, Firenze, Foggia, Forlì, Lecce, Napoli, Palermo, Parma, Reggio Emilia, Sassari, Savona, Terni, Trento, Trieste) is the new piazza Vittoria in Brescia that eliminated according to Civico a whole "sordid" (*sordido*) quarter (ibid: 20). While Civico

---

40 P. 14: "Gli urbanisti italiani hanno avuto pertanto da svolgere un tema di altissimo interesse e di altrettanta difficoltà: riportare luce e salute nel fitto agglomerato dei vecchi quartieri, conservare ad essi, dovunque possibile, l'unità urbanistica, salvare, sempre, l'edilizia monumentale, patrimonio d'inestimabile valore."

41 P. 15: "Questo metodo si presta ad essere attuato quando non concorrano, oltre quelle del risanamento, anche forti ragioni di traffico, quando l'ubicazione dei quartieri malsani, nell'insieme della città, sia tale da consentirne una certa autonomia di vita; quando, soprattutto, il contenuto storico e monumentale sia tanto notevole, da imporre naturalmente rispetto al piccone."

described the new piazza in Brescia as "monumental", adorned with "grandiose buildings" (*grandiosi palazzi*), other examples were praised for new road accessibility, for a staging and better presentation of historical monuments or, in the case of Florence (Firenze), for their "typical urban layout" (*tipica orditura urbanistica*) (ibid: 21). The chapters of Bari (Christine Beese) and Bergamo (Sandro Scarrocchia) in this book discuss realized examples for a thinning of the urban landscape. Nicoloso explains in his book chapter the opening and insertion of more or less homogenous new structures made under the supervision of Marcello Piacentini for Brescia and Trieste.

CONCLUSION

While historical monuments and architecture had become the focus of a national transformation program following Italy's unification in the nineteenth century, the chapters of this book show how this process was renewed and strengthened after the First World War. Architecture was used to evoke historical myths as bases for a nationalist and then specifically Fascist 'renaissance' of historic grandeur and cultural leadership. Monument preservation was exploited to fill those myths with supposedly authentic experiences and to serve as backdrops for spectacles and a revived popular culture. These experiences of townscapes as scenographic surroundings for tourists, for outdoor political events and the new medium of film were all part of urbanism that staged monuments within an idealized environment (*ambiente*) and invited people to take pride in newly-founded state institutions by connecting the appearance of their buildings with well-known edifices. By analyzing examples from various cities and regions, this book shows how a range of disciplines contributed to shaping historic urban landscapes in an artistic, yet simultaneously politicized way.

Architecture played a crucial role in creating and designing connections between past and present. The same was the case for the field of restoration (*restauro*) and preservation, which was used to ostentatiously create connections to a glorious past and profit politically from a revival of that culture. Both architecture and *restauro* spoke to *italianità* and *romanità*. Urban planning incorporated both fields as an overall renewal strategy, reaching from cities to the whole territory.

Architects and monument conservationists regarded townscapes and cities as agglomerations of cultural heritage. This high estimation of urban heritage lead in some cases to the acceptance of whole areas as worthy for being preserved – a comparatively proactive view of heritage conservation at that time. City transformation turned to an "urban restoration". Though, what initially figured as a sensible scheme of careful thinning (*diradamento*), often led to the creation of homogeneously idealized historic urban landscapes. Current studies collected in this book are uncovering these modifications of history and expose hidden forms of urban editing, thus helping us understand how old towns and history were being produced during the fascist *Ventennio*.

Local, regional and national transformations of historical (urban) landscapes were set gradually under the guidance of fascist professional associations, and used by fascist propaganda during the interwar period. The attempt at appropriating history infused monument preservation with the construction of myths. By recalling an image of historic buildings, new architecture out of the catalog of "other modernity" helped to revive and perpetuate that myth.

A research premise of this book is to consider architecture and monument preservation (respectively restoration) as parts of the same strategy of representing a renewed, but culturally, deeply anchored Italy. The purpose of this approach is to develop a more comprehensive view of the architectural culture in interwar Italy by combining research that is often relegated to two separate fields.

This book leaves out the fields of archeological research and excavations in the period described because of its focus on architectural history. For Rome, observations of the combination of archeology, political representations, garden architecture, and urban planning have been thoroughly researched (cf. Beese/Dobler 2018). It would be interesting to extend the argument of this book to other fields such as regional planning or garden culture.

If we look at historical urban landscapes in Italy's cities, we need to consider that through the staging of monuments and complementary new architecture we might look today at antique, medieval, renaissance or baroque elements through the lens of fascist understanding and exploitation of history and tradition. This book offers examples of that effect. By observing the results of this well-researched field in architectural history, we can take a critical look at our own time and building practices in a historic surrounding. We see how subjective our view of a supposedly "characteristic" way of building can be and how easily restoration can lead to a falsification of history to speak to the present.

Nota bene: A glossary explaining technical terms and institutional names has been provided at the back of the book. The first mention of a glossary term in an essay is emphasized in each case by italics.

REFERENCES

Albrecht, Katrin (2017): Angiolo Mazzoni: Architekt der italienischen Moderne, Berlin: Reimer Verlag.
Architettura e arti Decorative (1931): "Pagine di vita sindacale: Relazione ufficiale al consiglio nazionale del Sindacato Fascista degli Architetti." In: Architettura e arti Decorative 10/1931, pp. 633-640.
Bauer, Franz J. (2009): Rom im 19. und 20. Jahrhundert: Konstruktion eines Mythos. Regensburg: Pustet.
Baxa, Paul (2017): Roads and Ruins: The Symbolic Landscape of Fascist Rome, Toronto Buffalo London: University of Toronto Press.
Beese, Christine (2016): Marcello Piacentini: Moderner Städtebau in Italien, Berlin: Reimer Verlag.
Beese, Christine/Dobler, Ralph-Miklas (ed.) (2018): L'urbanistica a Roma durante il ventennio fascista. Roma: Campisano Editore SrL.
Benedetti, Sandro (1998): Piacentini, il Tema, il Luogo: La sede della 'Divina Sapienza'. In: Sandro Benedetti/Mariano Apa (eds.), La Cappella della Divina Sapienza nella città universitaria di Roma, Rome: Gangemi Editore, pp. 57-76.
Benedetti, Sandro (2004): "Un'altra modernità." In: Mario Pisani (ed.), Architetture di Marcello Piacentini : Le opere maestre, Rome: CLEAR, pp. 7-17.
Benedetti, Sandro (2010): "Marcello Piacentini: 'Il mio Moderno'." In: Marina Docci/Maria Grazia Turco (eds.), L'architettura dell'"altra" modernità: Atti del XXVI congresso di storia dell'architettura, Roma, 11-13 April 2007, Rome: Gangemi Editore, pp. 62-79.
Bodenschatz, Harald (ed.) (2011): Städtebau für Mussolini, Berlin: DOM Publ.
Borsi, Franco (1986): L'ordine monumentale in Europa, 1929-1939, Milan: Edizioni di Comunità (Dt. [1987]: Die monumentale Ordnung: Architektur in Europa, 1929-1939, Stuttgart: Hatje).
Calza Bini, Alberto (1933): "Relazione al Consiglio Nazionale del Sindacato Fascista Architetti, Milano, 15 settembre 1933." In: Architettura 12/1933/10, pp. 662-666.
Capomolla, Rinaldo/Mulazzani, Marco/Vittorini, Rosalia (eds.) (2008): Case del Balilla: Architettura e fascismo, Milan: Electa.
Casciato, Maristella (2004): "I concorsi per gli edifici pubblici, 1927-36." In: Ciucci/Muratore 2004b, pp. 208-233.
Cederna, Antonio (2006): Mussolini urbanista: Lo sventramento di Roma negli anni del consenso. 3rd. ed., Venezia: Corte del fontego.

Ciucci, Giorgio (2002 [1989]): Gli architetti e il fascismo: Architettura e città, 1922-1944, Turin: Einaudi.

Ciucci, Giorgio (2004a): "Gli architetti e la guerra." In: Ciucci/Muratore 2004b, p. 476-501.

Ciucci, Giorgio/Muratore, Giorgio (eds.) (2004b): Storia dell'architettura italiana: Il primo novecento, Milan: Electa.

[Civico, Vincenzo, ed.] (1937a): Italienische Stadtebaukunst im faschistischen Regime. Urbanistica italiana in Regime fascista. Wien Nov. Dez. 1937. Roma: Societa editrice di Novissima. [Published in conjunction with an exhibition of the same title, organized by the Ministero della Cultura Popolare together with the Istituto Nazionale di Urbanistica, the Österreichische Gesellschaft für Städtebau and Secession Wien, presented in Vienna, November 1937–December 1937].

Civico, Vincenzo (1937b): Le grandi sistemazioni dell'Urbe e la mostra della nostra urbanistica a Vienna nella Stampa austriaca e in quella italiana. In: Roma: Rivista di studi e di vita romana; organo ufficiale dell'Istituto di Studi Romani 15/12, pp. 466-470.

Colavitti, Anne Maria (2018): Urban Heritage Management: Planning with History, Cham: Springer.

Colonna, Flavia/Costantini, Stefania (ed.) (1994): Principi e metodi della storia dell'architettura e l'eredità della "Scuola Romana," Roma: Università degli Studi di Roma "La Sapienza", Dipartimento di Storia dell'Architettura, Restauro e Conservazione dei Beni Architettonici.

De Bernardi, Alberto/Guarracino, Scipione (eds.) (2003): Dizionario del fascismo, Milan: Bruno Mondadori.

Docci, Marina/Turco, Maria Grazia (ed.) (2010): L'Architettura dell'"altra" Modernità: Atti del XXCI Congresso di Storia dell'Architettura; Roma, 11-13 April 2007. Roma: Gangemini.

Dombrowski, Damian (ed.) (2013): Kunst auf der Suche der Nation: Das Problem der Identität in der italienischen Malerei, Skulptur und Architektur vom Risorgimento bis zum Faschismus, Berlin: Lukas Verlag.

Enss, Carmen M./Vinken, Gerhard (2016): Produkt Altstadt: Historische Stadtzentren in Städtebau und Denkmalpflege, Bielefeld: transcript.

Estermann-Juchler, Margrit (1982): Faschistische Staatsbaukunst: Zur ideologischen Funktion der öffentlichen Architektur im faschistischen Italien, Cologne: Böhlau.

Etlin, Richard A. (1991): Modernism in Italian Architecture, 1880-1940, Cambridge/Mass.: MIT Press.

Farina, Milena/Villani, Luciano (2017): Le borgate del fascismo: Storia urbana, politica e sociale della periferia romana, Melf: Libria.

Fontana, Vincenzo (1999): Profilo di architettura italiana del Novecento, Venice: Marsilio.

Fraticelli, Vanna (1982): Roma, 1914-1929: La città e gli architetti tra la guerra e il fascismo, Roma: Officina Edizioni.

Gentile, Emilio (2001): Le origini dell'ideologia fascista, 1918-1925, Bologna: Il Mulino.

Gentile, Emilio (2005 [2001]): Il culto del littorio: La sacralizzazione della politica nell'Italia fascista, Rome/Bari: GLF Ed. Laterza.

Gentile, Emilio (2007 [2005]): Fascismo: Storia e interpretazione, Rome/Bari: GLF Ed. Laterza.

Gentile, Emilio (2008 [2007]): Fascismo di pietra, Rome/Bari: GLF Ed. Laterza.

Ghirardo, Diane Yvonne (1980): "Italian Architects and Fascist Politics: An Evaluation of the Rationalist's Role in Regime Building." In: Journal of the Society of Architectural Historians 39/2: pp. 109-127.

Giovannoni, Gustavo (1916): "Gli architetti e gli studi di architettura in Italia." In: Rivista d'Italia, 19/1916/2, pp. 161-196.

Giovannoni, Gustavo (1918): L'ambiente dei monumenti: Relazione per A.a.c.a.r, Roma.

Giovannoni, Gustavo (1921): Prolusione inaugurale della nuova Scuola Superiore d'Architettura in Roma letta il 18 dicembre 1920, Rome: Tipografia Armani.

Giovannoni, Gustavo (1929 [1925]): Questioni di architettura nella storia e nella vita: Edilizia, estetica architettonica, restauri, ambiente dei monumenti, Rome: Biblioteca d'arte.

Giovannoni, Gustavo (1931): Vecchie città ed edilizia nuova. Torino: Unione tipografico - Editrice Torinese.

Giovannoni, Gustavo (1932): "Cronaca: La conferenza internazionale di Atene pel restauro dei monumenti." In: Bollettino d'Arte, III ser. XXV/9 (March): pp. 408–420.

Gresleri, Glauco/Gresleri, Giuliano/Culotta, Pasquale (eds.) (2007): Città di fondazione e plantatio ecclesiae, Bologna: Compositori.

Hökerberg, Håkon (ed.) (2018): Architecture as propaganda in twentieth-century totalitarian regimes: History and heritage. Firenze: Edizioni Polistampa.

Insolera, Italo (1976): Roma moderna: Un secolo di storia urbanistica, 1870-1970. 7th ed. (1st ed. 1962), Torino: Einaudi.

Insolera, Italo (2001): Roma fascista nelle fotografie dell'Istituto Luce. Roma: Ed. Riuniti.

Kallis, Aristotle A. (2014): The Third Rome, 1922-1943: The making of the fascist capital. Basingstoke: Palgrave Macmillan.
Kershaw, Ian (2016): To Hell and Back: Europe, 1914-1949, London: Penguin.
Kirk, Terry (2005): The Architecture of Modern Italy, 2 vols. New York: Princeton Architectural Press.
Kirk, Terry. 2006. "Framing St. Peter's: Urban Planning in Fascist Rome." In: The Art Bulletin 88/4, pp. 756-776.
Kostof, Spiro (1973): The Third Rome, 1870-1950: Traffic and glory. University Art Museum: Berkeley.
Lamberini, Daniela (2003): Teorie e storia del restauro architettonico, Firenze: Ed. Polistampa.
Lasansky, Diana Medina (2004a): "Urban editing, historic preservation, and political rhetoric: The Fascist redesign of San Gimignano." In: Journal of the Society of Architectural Historians 63/3, pp. 320–353.
Lasansky, D. Medina (2004b): The Renaissance perfected: Architecture, spectacle, and tourism in fascist Italy, Buildings, landscapes, and societies. 4. University Park, Pa: Pennsylvania State Univ. Press.
Lazzaro, Claudia/Crum, Roger J. (ed.) (2005): Donatello among the Blackshirts: History and Modernity in the Visual Culture of Fascist Italy. Ithaca, N.Y.: Cornell University Press.
Leonhard, Jörn (2014): Die Büchse der Pandora: Geschichte des Ersten Weltkriegs, Munich: C. H. Beck.
Leonhard, Jörn (2018): Der überforderte Frieden: Versailles und die Welt, 1918-1923, Munich: C. H. Beck.
Mack Smith, Denis (2004 [1981]): Mussolini, Milan: BUR (Orig.: Mussolini, London: Weidenfeld & Nicolson).
Mangone, Fabio (2003): "La costruzione della 'grande Bari' negli anni del fascismo, tra ricerca d'identità e omologazione." In: L' architettura nelle città italiane del XX secolo, edited Vittorio Franchetti Pardo, 316–325. Milano: Jaca book.
Marcucci, Laura (ed.) (2012): L'altra modernità nella cultura architettonica del XX secolo: Progetto e città nell'architettura italiana, Rome: Gangemi Editore.
Mariani, Riccardo (1987): E 42: Un progetto per l'"Ordine Nuovo", Milan: Edizioni di Comunità.
Millon, Henry A. (1965): "The role of history of architecture in Fascist Italy." In: Journal of the Society of Architectural Historians 24/1: pp. 53–59.
Monzo, Luigi (2017): croci e fasci: Der italienische Kirchenbau in der Zeit des Faschismus, 1919-1945. 2 vol. PhD diss., Karlsruhe Institute for Technology.

Mras, George P. (1961): "Italian Fascist Architecture: Theory and Image." In: Art Journal 21/1: pp. 7–12.
Münkler, Herfried (2013): Der Große Krieg: Die Welt 1914 bis 1918, Berlin: Rowohlt.
Mussolini, Benito and Emil Ludwig (1932): Mussolinis Gespräche mit Emil Ludwig, Berlin: Zsolnay.
Neri, Maria Luisa (ed.) (2011): L'altra modernità nella cultura architettonica del XX secolo: Dibattito internazionale e realtà locali, Rome: Gangemi Editore.
Nicoloso, Paolo (1999): Gli architetti di Mussolini: Scuole e sindacato, architetti e massoni, professori e politici negli anni del regime. Milano: F. Angeli.
Nicoloso, Paolo (2003): Urbanistica. In: Dizionario del fascismo, Vol. II, edited by Victoria de Grazia. Torino: Einaudi.
Nicoloso, Paolo (2004 [1999]): Gli architetti di Mussolini: Scuole e sindacato, architetti e massoni, professori e politici negli anni del regime, Milan: F. Angeli.
Nicoloso, Paolo (2004): Una nuova formazione per l'architetto professionista, 1914-28. In: Ciucci/Muratore 2004b, pp. 56-73.
Nicoloso, Paolo (2008): Mussolini architetto: Propaganda e paesaggio urbano nell'Italia fascista, Turin: Einaudi.
Nicoloso, Paolo (ed.) (2012): Progetti e opere per fare gli italiani fascisti, Udine: Gaspari Editore.
Nicoloso, Paolo (2018): Marcello Piacentini: Architettura e potere; Una biografia, Udine: Gaspari Editore.
Palozzi, Saverio (ed.) (1936): Il nuovo stile littorio: I progetti per il Palazzo del Littorio e della Mostra della Rivoluzione Fascista in Via dell'Impero, Milan/Rome: S.A. Arti Grafiche Bertarelli.
Pane, Andrea (2018): "Camillo Boito consulente ministeriale per il restauro dei monumenti, 1879-1914." In: Camillo Boito moderno, Vol. II, ed. Sandro Scarrocchia, pp. 579–615. Milano/Udine: Mimesis Edizioni.
Patetta, Luciano (1972): L'architettura in Italia, 1919-1943: Le polemiche, Milan: Clup.
Payne, Stanley G. (2006 [2001]): Geschichte des Faschismus, Vienna: Tosa (Orig. [1995]: A History of Fascism, 1914-1945, Madison: University of Wisconsin Press).
Pensabene, Giuseppe (1933): "Il libro giallo dell'architettura italiana: VI Conclusioni." In: Il Tevere, January 7.
Petz, Ursula (1990): "Urban renewal unter National Socialism: practical policy and political objective in Hitler's Germany." In: Planning Perspectives 5/2 (May 1990): pp. 169-187.

Pfammatter, Ueli (1996 [1990]): Moderne und Macht: Italienische Architekten, 1927-1942, Braunschweig/Wiesbaden: Vieweg.

Piacentini, Marcello (1922): "Nuovi orizzonti nell'edilizia cittadina." In: Nuova Antologia 57/1922, pp. 60-72.

Piacentini, Marcello (1931): "Difesa dell'architettura italiana." In: Il Giornale d'Italia, May 2. (Reproduced in Mario Pisani [ed.] [1996]: Marcello Piacentini. Architettura moderna, Venice: Marsilio, pp. 168-173).

Pisani, Mario (ed.) (1996): Marcello Piacentini: Architettura moderna, Venice: Marsilio.

Portoghesi, Paolo/Mangione, Flavio/Soffitta, Andrea (eds.) (2006): L'architettura delle case del fascio: Catalogo della Mostra "Le Case del Fascio in Italia e nelle Terre d'Oltremare," Florence: Alinea.

Rifkind, David (2012a): "'Everything in the state, nothing against the state, nothing outside the state': Corporativist urbanism and Rationalist architecture in fascist Italy." In: Planning Perspectives 27/1: pp: 51–80.

Rifkind, David (2012b): The battle for modernism: Quadrante and the politicization of architectural discourse in Fascist Italy, Premio James Ackerman per la storia dell'architettura. Vicenza: CISA.

Salsano, Fernando (2010): "La sistemazione degli sfrattati dall'area dei Fori Imperiali e la nascita delle borgate nella Roma fascista." In: Città e storia 5: pp. 207-228.

Sarfatti, Margherita G. (1926): Dux, Milan: Mondadori.

Silva, Umberto (1975): Kunst und Ideologie des Faschismus, Milan: Fischer Verlag (Orig. [1973]: Ideologia e arte del fascismo, Milan: Mazzotta).

Sica, Paolo (1978): Storia dell'urbanistica: Il novecento, Roma/Bari: Laterza.

Sommer, Michael (2016): Römische Geschichte: Von den Anfängen bis zum Untergang, Stuttgart: Reclam.

Spiegel, Daniela (2010): Die Città Nuove des Agro Pontino im Rahmen der faschistischen Staatsarchitektur, Petersberg: Imhof.

Spiegel, Daniela (2015): Urbanism in Fascist Italy: All Well and Good? In: Harald Bodenschatz/Piero Sassi/Max Welch Guerra (eds.): Urbanism and Dictatorship: A European Perspective, Basel/Berlin/Boston: Birkhäuser, pp. 43-58.

Thoenes, Christof (1995): "'La grande era bramantesca non è chiusa': L'architettura italiana del Rinascimento nella visione del fascismo." In: Storia Contemporanea XXVI/3 (June): pp. 441–449.

Tragbar, Klaus (2009): „Dante und der Duce: Zu den politischen Motiven der Umgestaltung historischer Städte in der Toskana." In: Aram Mattioli/Gerald Steinacher (eds.): Für den Faschismus bauen. Architektur und Städtebau im Italien Mussolinis, Zürich: Orell Füssli, pp. 189–210.

Tragbar, Klaus (2010): „Das schwarze Mittelalter. Zur Umgestaltung historischer Städte in der Toskana während des Faschismus." In: Volker Herzner/Jürgen Krüger (eds.): Mythos Staufer: Akten der 5. Landauer Staufertagung 1.-3. Juli 2005, Verl. der Pfälzischen Ges. zur Förderung der Wiss., pp. 183–192.

Tragbar, Klaus (2012): Die Erben Vitruvs: Schlaglichter zum Beruf des Architekten in Italien im 19. und 20. Jahrhundert. In: Winfried Nerdinger (ed.): Der Architekt: Geschichte und Gegenwart eines Berufsstandes. Munich: Prestel, pp. 195-204.

Vannelli, Valter (1992): "Isolamento del Campidoglio: preesistenze e trasformazioni degli anni Trenta." In: L'Architettura delle Trasformazioni urbane, 1890-1940, edited by Gianfranco Spagnesi, pp. 289-294. Roma: Centro di Studi per la Storia dell'Architettura.

Vidotto, Vittorio (ed.) (2015): Esposizione universale Roma: Una città nuova dal fascismo agli anni '60. Roma: De Luca Editori d'Arte, Exhibition catalog Museo dell'Ara Pacis.

Vidotto, Vittorio (ed.) (1998): La memoria perduta: I monumenti ai caduti della Grande Guerra a Roma e nel Lazio. Roma: Argos.

Villani, Luciano (2012): Le borgate del fascismo: Storia urbana, politica e sociale della periferia romana, Milan: LediPublishing.

Wagner, Philip (2018): "Zwischen grenzübergreifender Standardisierung und nationalem Lobbying: Der internationale Kongress für Wohnungswesen und Städtebau in Rom 1929." In: Christine Beese/Ralph-Miklas Dobler (eds.): L'Urbanistica a Roma durante il ventennio fascista (Quaderni della Bibliotheca Hertziana 1), Rome: Campisano Editore, pp. 153-170.

Washburn Child, Richard (ed.) (1999 [1928]): Benito Mussolini: La mia vita, Milan: BUR.

Woller, Hans (2016): Mussolini: Der erste Faschist, Munich: C. H. Beck [It. 2018]: Mussolini, il primo fascista, Rome: Carocci).

Zalewski, Paul (2016): „Kriminologie, Biologismus, Stadtsanierung: Hannovers Altstadt, 1932–39." In: Produkt Altstadt: Historische Stadtzentren in Städtebau und Denkmalpflege, edited by Carmen M. Enss/Gerhard Vinken, pp. 107-122, Bielefeld: transcript.

Zucconi, Guido (1997a): Gustavo Giovannoni: Dal capitello alla città con un regesto degli scritti a cura di Guiseppe Bonaccorso, Como and Milano: Jaca Book.

Zucconi, Guido (2014): "Gustavo Giovannoni: A Theory and a Practice of Urban Conservation." In: Change Over Time 4/1: p. 77–91.

Zucconi, Guido (1997b): L'invenzione del passato: Camillo Boito e l'architettura neomedievale, Venezia: Marsilio.

Tradition, Architecture, Homogenization

Piacentini and Unitary Architectural Directions for Italian Cities

Paolo Nicoloso

For Marcello Piacentini, the beauty of the ancient city did not come so much from single architectural works but from the urban environment as a whole. There is a need to overcome architectural individualism and search for a unity of composition in order to achieve this beauty. This essay examines some of the projects in which the architect pursued a unitary architectural direction. It also highlights how this architectural strategy supported the need on the part of the Fascism regime to give parts of the city an image that was representative of its power.

AMBITIONS OF A "BUILDING DICTATOR"

"The beauty of cities is the greatest weapon of the power of the people." These are the words of Marcello Piacentini (1881-1960) in an interview in March 1929. But, in his view, the "beauty of the city" depended on the figure of an architect who was capable of managing all urban constructions. "I long for a building dictator in Rome, a person who has, like the ancients, the ability and knowledge to take responsibility for ordered things" (Simeoni 1929). Needless to say, he considered himself the best person for the role. These statements did not go unnoticed by Benito Mussolini (1883-1945), who kept the interview in his confidential correspondence.[1]

Piacentini believed that it was only through this architectural leadership that it was possible to find the "sense of the city". A city understood not as a sum of

---

1 Archivio centrale dello Stato (ACS), Segreteria particolare del duce, carteggio riservato, 1922-1943, b. 103, Roma.

individual monuments, but as an extended architectural environment, a collection of buildings lined up around streets and squares.

The concept of a strongly interventionist management of architecture was not new to Piacentini. In 1913, he had already authored an essay in which he invoked a "restriction of artistic freedom" so as to prevent incompetence and bad taste from spoiling "the character and features of the city" (1913: 30-36). Later, in 1922, reaffirming word for word his 1913 thesis, he called for "impersonality" in architecture, something which is necessary to achieve the "unity of views and directions", typical of the great artistic epochs (1922: 67).

But in 1929, these affirmations, in support of an interventionist management, took on a more precise, concrete meaning because they seemed to support the regime's dictatorial turn. Four years after the speech to the House on 3 January 1925, Mussolini had gradually imposed a dictatorship upon the country. After a crisis of consensus following the *Matteotti assassination*, the regime was gaining popular support, strengthened by the reconciliation with the Catholic Church, having signed the *Lateran Treaty* in February 1929.

Piacentini's power had grown in a context that was more favourable to the regime. A few days before the interview, he had been nominated by Mussolini as a member of the Royal Academy of Italy. At this time he was undoubtedly the most famous architect in Italy and also the most influential. Since Mussolini's ascent to power, Piacentini had built some of the regime's most important public works: the Arco della Vittoria in Bozen, and the Casa Madre dei Mutilati, the Teatro dell'Opera and the Stadio Nazionale in Rome. He had also started the Arco della Vittoria in Genoa and the Ministero delle Corporazioni building in the capital (Nicoloso 2018: 61-115).

All of these were individual works. In the 1929 interview, it was clear that the city as a whole, made up of squares and streets, was his subject of interest. In the following years, Piacentini had several opportunities to measure himself up against an urban dimension of the project. He started to apply what he called the "unitary directions" in architecture, first in parts of a city; in Brescia, Rome, Genoa, Turin, Trieste and Milan, and then in a satellite city, in the so-called E42, the Mussolinian city.[2] He then sought to extend these "unitary directions" to the entire capital.

---

[2] For more on the unitary directions cf. "S. E. l'arch. Marcello Piacentini", 1936.

PIAZZA DELLA VITTORIA IN BRESCIA

During the period in which he called for a "building dictator", Piacentini was involved in the design of Piazza della Vittoria in Brescia. He was initially to be a part of the jury of the competition for the city's local strategic plan. Pietro Aschieri's group had won the competition, followed by Luigi Piccinato's group in second and Alfredo Giarratana's in third, but the mayor Pietro Calzoni decided to hand over responsibility for drafting the plan to Piacentini. Once the local strategic plan had been quickly approved, the mayor also commissioned Piacentini with the design of Piazza della Vittoria (Maifrini 1988; Robecchi 1998). Calzoni's justification for his choice was the fact that the architect "enjoys the trust of the national government" (Nicoloso 2018: 114).

Figure 1: Marcello Piacentini, Piazza della Vittoria in Brescia, 1932

Photograph taken from the journal *Architettura*, December 1932, p. 69

Piacentini designed a square from scratch, on the site of the old Peschiere district. His intention was to create a square that drew on Italian tradition, one with an irregular perimeter that was connected to other squares in the city, made up of fourteen buildings that were all different in terms of size and architectural structure.

Ultimately, the square did not look as though it was designed by a single architect but by many different ones. In fact, in February 1929, Piacentini asked Pietro Aschieri (1889-1952), Luigi Piccinato (1899-1983) and Alfredo Giarratana (1890-1982) – the first, second and third placed architects in the competition – to work with him on the design of the square. Piacentini's idea was to direct and coordinate the designs made by his colleague, so as to gain unitary architectural criteria in spite of the diversity of the proposals. The working group, however, was not able to come to an arrangement and Piacentini continued alone. He did not give up on the objective of obtaining a diversity of composition, designing different architectural solutions, nor on the aim of providing unitary direction to the complex.

The new square was created in a very short time and even with obvious references to the Italian tradition, it was a symbol of modernity and a model to be repeated elsewhere. In place of the old dilapidated neighbourhood stood a bright square, lined by lavish buildings. It was a fine expression of the will of Fascism to modernize the country and give a new face to Italian cities. It was the Fascist forum desired by the regime to mark its power over the city. Inaugurating the square on 1 November 1932, Mussolini declared himself pleased because be in front of these "superb buildings [...] words are superfluous, because the buildings speak the facts".

THE CITTÀ UNIVERSITARIA IN ROME

Piazza Vittoria in Brescia was not yet finished when, in April 1932, Piacentini was called by Mussolini to design another piece of another city: the Città Universitaria in Rome (Nicoloso 2006). But in the capital, he was asked to share his role with seven other architects and to put into place something similar to the working group that had failed in Brescia. Among the seven architects, four – Giuseppe Pagano (1896-1945), Giuseppe Capponi (1893-1936), Giovanni Michelucci (1891-1990) and Aschieri – belonged to the "rationalist" group. Aschieri, as seen above, was part of the failed working group in Brescia.

Figure 2: Marcello Piacentini, Città universitaria in Roma, 1935

Photograph taken from the journal *Architettura*, special issue, December 1935, p. 5

But why did Piacentini call upon the rationalists? A year before, there had been a controversy stemming from the "II Esposizione Italiana di Architettura Razionale", which divided Italian architects into 'rationalists' and 'traditionalists'. Piacentini wanted to mend the rift and re-found the image – built ad hoc by Pier Maria Bardi (1900-99) – which saw him as the head of the anti-rationalist group. This is why he called a group of architects, present at the rationalist exhibition, to design the new "University City" under his direction.

Ten years after taking power, the Città Universitaria was the largest architectural venture undertaken by the regime to date. It was to provide an image of what Italian architecture was in the age of Mussolini. And the regime did not want to offer an image of a disunited architectural culture, divided in two.

It is interesting to note that Piacentini initially did not exclude the use of an arch in the design, and he called on architects to not object to the proposal. But an arch did not appear in the final design. It is likely that there was much discussion about the proposal between the architects, especially Piacentini and Pagano. And it seems as though the arch was not seen as indispensable in order to show the Italianism of the architecture.

In choosing the collaborators, the regime's propaganda highlighted the different geographical provenance of the various architects, in an effort to show the unity of Italian architecture, in spite of regional differences. Pagano was from Trieste, Gio Ponti (1891-1979) from Milan, Michelucci from Florence and Gaetano Rapisardi (1893-1988) from Sicily. This was all true. But we also know that, in reality, the latter worked in Piacentini's studio.

Just as in Brescia, the Città Universitaria was built around a main square. Piacentini had designed the plan and the rectory. The individual faculties were assigned to the seven architects. The unitary direction was obtained through the use of common elements, such as windows, which were unified through the crowning frames and cladding, which was generally made from travertine and clinker bricks. Each architect had to give up on something. There was a degree of impersonality needed to produce harmonious architecture and achieve a unitary direction.

Roberto Papini (1883-1957) understood Piacentini's sense of the operation with great clarity. The critic wrote that, in Rome, under the Piacentini's guidance – "a coordinator of minds" – a miracle was accomplished: a dozen architects, all different by mentality, training and origin, had "perfectly tuned into a unity of style", each one proudly bringing their own contribution to modern Italian architecture (Papini 1935).

PIAZZA DELLA VITTORIA IN GENOA

While the Città Universitaria project was concluding in the mid 1930s, Piacentini was busy in Genoa designing a new square and coordinating the work of other designers. He had been busy with the layout of the Spianata del Bisagno, the site of the future Piazza della Vittoria, since 1923, when he won a competition organised by the council. But nothing came of that competition. However, he won another competition in 1939 to build a monument to Victory on the same square (Cevini 1989: 139-157).

A prominent figure in 1931 after being called to judge the city plan, Piacentini returned to the limelight with Piazza della Vittoria in 1934, when the mayor, Carlo Bombrini, took him on as an architectural consultant. The goal was to give architectural unity to the seven buildings positioned around the perimeter of the square; the eighth building was the Nafta building (editor's note: Nafta Società Italiana del Petrolio e Affini, today Palazzo ENI/Ente Nazionale Idrocarburi), completed in 1934 (ibid: 147).

In May 1935, Piacentini presented the proposal for the INPS (Istituto Nazionale della Previdenza Sociale) building. This was the model building around which all the others had to stand up to. Then came the twin buildings, positioned just next to the INPS building: they were built by the Garbarino and Sciaccaluga company and the design of the facades was entrusted to Piacentini himself.

Two other twin buildings were built on the opposite side of the square, next to the Nafta building. Here, the design was entrusted to Beniamino Bellati (1895-

1953), but under Piacentini's supervision, whose choices included the covering materials (Spesso/Brancucci 2016: 84).

There were the two last buildings at the southern end of the square: the Cassa di Risparmio building and the Angiolini building. There was a competition held in 1936 for the former, won by Bellati, in which the architect "wanted to follow the general aesthetic criteria determined by the architect Piacentini" (Cevini 1989: 152). Opposite the Cassa di Risparmio was the Angiolini building, designed by the engineer Giuseppe Tallero. It was the last to be built and it was consistent with the unitary architectural guidelines imposed by Piacentini. Much like the case of the Città Universitaria in Rome, Piacentini had designed some buildings and assigned others to colleagues, obtaining formal control over the entire complex. As in Brescia, Mussolini inaugurated the new square in May 1938, with his architect at his side.

VIA ROMA IN TURIN

The design of Piazza Vittoria in Genoa was contemporary to the restoration of Via Roma in Turin, the road that connects Piazza Carlo Felice with Piazza Castello. Work on the first section, from Piazza Castello to Piazza San Carlo, started in 1930. In 1933, a competition was launched for the second section, from Piazza San Carlo to Piazza Carlo Felice, but it was not a great success.

At this point, the project was handed over to the local council's technical sector. Here, mayor Ugo Sartirana (1901-65) joined Piacentini, to give an "organic and unitary" composition to the works ("La ricostruzione del secondo tratto di via Roma a Torino", 1939: 342). The project drawn up by the council, with Piacentini's advice, was approved in August 1935.

The area of the works, originally divided into four large lots, was divided into sixteen lots. Piacentini provided the design of the facades facing Via Roma, "indicating the general scheme of the spaces, heights, rhythms and recurrences" (ibid: 344). He designed the architraved portico, extended along the entire route, made up of columns measuring 7 metres in height. He also designed the palaces on the new small square behind the churches of Santa Cristina and San Carlo.

The buildings on Via Roma and on the small square behind the two churches provided the architectural model for the other structures to be built in the sixteen blocks affected by the works on the second stretch. Individual lots were entrusted to the architects Alberto Ressa, Mario Passanti, Ottorino Aloisio, Giuseppe Momo, Vittorio Bonadé Bottino, Giovanni Chevalley and Annibale Rigotti, to name but a few.

Under Piacentini's supervision, the buildings were all designed together and then delegated to the individual architects. This ensured a "disciplined and peaceful collaboration between several architects, with a unitary vision of the entire road". Each brought "their own contribution to a great urban unity" (Sessa 1995: 516). Eventually, Piacentini would say that he coordinated the work of 48 professionals in Via Roma, including engineers and architects (Nicoloso 2018: 213).

Figure 3: Marcello Piacentini, Via Roma in Torino, 1939

Photograph taken from the journal *Architettura*, June 1939, p. 358

This time, Mussolini was absent at the inauguration in October 1937. Piacentini was in the front row, next to the Fascist party secretary Achille Starace (1889-1945), Mayor Sartirana and the finance minister Paolo Thaon di Revel (1859-1948).

CITTÀ VECCHIA IN TRIESTE

While working in Genoa and Turin, Piacentini opened up another building site in Trieste. The plan for the demolition and reconstruction of the Città Vecchia was a response to the design of a new Fascist face for the city. The new forum would be overlooking the remains of the ancient Roman theatre and the newly built *casa del fascio*. Next to that would be the Assicurazioni Generali building. This new construction would determine the architectural direction of the other buildings (Nicoloso 2005).

The mayor Enrico Paolo Salem (1884-1948) had decided that this building would "give its tone to the buildings that would later be built along the road and its nearby blocks". He had also constrained the sale of land for construction of the building under special conditions. Among these was that the project should be entrusted to a "renowned architect" (Barillari 2003: 607). Who better than Piacentini to fill that role?

On 17 April 1935, Salem went to Rome to meet Piacentini. We can assume that the purpose of the meeting was the design for the Assicurazioni Generali building in Trieste and the architecture of the adjacent buildings.

The scheme that had already been tested in Rome, and which was currently being implemented in Genoa and Turin, was re-proposed. The architecture of a building, in this case the Generali building, served as a model for the others and determined the unitary character of the architectural context. This was confirmed by the design of the Banco di Napoli, which stood next to the Generali building. Salem's requests were extremely explicit. In July 1935, he wrote that "it is particularly important to me that the Palazzo del Banco is in harmony with Piacentini's design, which has already been presented in detail and which I have approved". Hence the invitation to the Banco di Napoli to "make contact with Piacentini" (Paoletti 2005: 202). In October, the mayor approved a variation on the design, appreciating the choice of placing pilasters on the upper part of the facade, based on Piacentini's model of the building.

PIAZZA DUOMO IN MILAN

In the same period, Piacentini was also involved in the design of the south side of Piazza Duomo in Milan. In 1933, he was called to be part of the commission appointed to define the size of the square (Reggiori 1947: 139). The following year, he was part of the jury for the competition for the Torre Littoria, to be built next to the Duomo, which ended in a stalemate. Then, in 1936, as a consultant to the council, he came up with two proposals for the south side: a bolder one – consisting of the demolition and complete reconstruction of the facade – and a more restrained one, with a partial reconstruction. Finally, in January 1937, together with Gustavo Giovannoni (1873-1947) and Ugo Ojetti (1871-1946), he was invited to

Milan by Giuseppe Bottai (1895-1959) to define the perimeter of the construction of the south side of Piazza Duomo and the new Piazza Diaz.

On this basis, the mayor Guido Pesenti announced the competition for the completion of Piazza Duomo, placing Ojetti on the jury. The competition ended in November 1937 and the jury met in December. The projects disappointed the commission and Ojetti wanted to cancel the competition.

This decision was influenced by what was taking place at E42 in Rome, from ongoing competitions – which will be discussed later – to the classical trend that was gaining steam. Ojetti knew that the events in Rome could determine a general stylistic change in Italian architecture and therefore considered it useful to wait until the results were known. In his view, the restoration of Piazza Duomo was "an issue of great national interest" and any decision on this matter had to be approved by Rome (Nicoloso 2012: 104-109).

After Mussolini's decision to press ahead with a second competition, Piacentini was called to replace Ojetti. Giovanni Muzio's group, the favourite, won, as is well known. But the story did not end here. Piacentini would have continued to have control over the design by the Muzio group. In early September, the mayor made him a special consultant of the council with the task of providing "assistance in drawing up the plans" for Piazza Duomo (Nicoloso 2018: 220).

Piacentini also had an important role in the design of the tall building in Piazza Diaz. As previously mentioned, in January 1937 the architect had designed the new perimeter of the square. In particular, he had considerably enlarged the southern front. This choice favoured the lot on which the building was to be built, and that was precisely the lot where Piacentini was architectural consultant.

Designing that tall building effectively meant designing the south front of Piazza Duomo. In fact, the building was perfectly visible from the square. In particular, for those looking at the Galleria Vittorio Emanuele, the tall building made up the background perspective of the Arengario, designed by Giovanni Muzio (1893-1982). For this reason, Piacentini carefully studied the prospectus, coming up with more proposals. The goal was to give the two buildings – his and Muzio's – a unitary architectural character given that they were visually connected, despite being distant from each other.

E42 IN ROME

Finally, E42 (editor's note: Esposizione Universale di Roma 1942, today part of the residential and business district EUR), the "Mussolinian city" that had to indicate the definitive style of the age of Mussolini, having to hand down the image of Fascism to posterity. E42 was the most important case of this unitary architectural policy. Appointed superintendent of architecture in December 1937, Piacentini was the director of the entire architectural operation. Here, that which was tried out in the Città Universitaria and in other cities, as mentioned above, was repeated on a larger scale.

Controls over the designs to obtain unitary directions came about, for example, through competitions. They were far from impartial and allowed Piacentini to choose the winners, even when he was not part of the jury. Present in the competitions for the Palazzo della Civiltà Italiana and for Piazza Imperiale, he had valid allies in Arnaldo Foschini (1884-1968), Muzio, Enrico Del Debbio (1891-1973) and Marcello Canino (1895-1970) in the two competitions for the Palazzo dei Ricevimenti e dei Congressi and the Palazze delle Forze Armate.

Once the competitions ended, controls were made by the architecture office, led by Gaetano Minnucci (1896-1980), but under Piacentini's supervision. Here all of the winning designs were redesigned, with substantial changes being made. Some examples are the Palazzi delle Forze Armate by Mario De Renzi (1897-1967) and Gino Pollini (1903-91), where the pillars were replaced by classical columns with entases (Muntoni 1996: 318), and the Palazzo della Civiltà Italiana by Ernesto 'Bruno' La Padula (1902-68), where Piacentini redesigned and reducing the number of the arches, modified the dimensions, strengthened the corner pillars and increased the upper band at the top of the building.[3]

Unitary directions were also obtained on directly assigned projects, as in the case of the Church of Saints Peter and Paul by Foschini, the building for the Mostra della Romanità by the Aschieri group, for the Porta Imperiale by Muzio, Mario Paniconi (1904-73) and Giulio Pediconi (1906-99) and for the Mostra del Ministero dei Lavori Pubblici by Luigi Vagnetti's group.

Piacentini spoke about the efforts of this wide and intense directing task to his friend Ojetti: "If you only knew the struggles! Around 80 external architects, and about 40 internal architects and engineers, or employees: each of them with their own little brain and character, all on a background of jealousy." There were days in which he felt "torn to shreds" (Nicoloso 2018: 228). But Piacentini knew that the stakes were enormous: E42 could be the beginning of something much bigger, which went way beyond the satellite city itself. It should have provided the imprint for the nation's architecture for decades to come (Nicoloso 2008: 227-270).

---

3   See Piacentini's design in Casciato/Poretti 2002: 16.

THE *VARIANTE* OF THE ROME MASTER PLAN IN 1941

E42 was coordinated with other significant works aimed at shaping both Mussolini's Rome and Imperial Rome. Examples of this can be found in the plans for Via della Conciliazione by Piacentini and Attilio Spaccarelli (1890-1975), for Corso Rinascimento by Foschini and for Largo Augusto Imperatore by Vittorio Morpurgo (1890-1966): three works linked by a "compact unitary character" ("Urbanistica della Roma mussoliniana", 1936: 6). Palazzo del Littorio by Foschini and Del Debbio also falls under this umbrella. Additionally, the transformation of Angiolo Mazzoni's design for Termini station was a clear demonstration of how E42 was the architectural model for the capital. Here too, as is known, Piacentini offered advice in the design of the facade.

Figure 4: Angiolo Mazzoni, project for Termini Station in Rome, 1939

Photograph taken from the journal *Architettura*, special issue, December 1939, p. 83

But above all, unitary architectural directions were applied to the *Variante* to the Master Plan of 1941, drafted under the direction of Piacentini. Here the architect made use of the collaboration of a large number of colleagues to whom he entrusted the design of various areas. Among them were Piccinato, Del Debbio, Domenico Filippone (1903-70), Eugenio Fuselli (1903-2003), Concezio Petrucci (1902-46) and Giorgio Calza Bini (1908-99), all under Piacentini's subjection (Nicoloso 2018: 250). Some were instructed to draw up plans of central areas, including Piazza Venezia, the new Piazza della Stazione Termini and the Piazza del Pantheon; others worked on connecting areas between E42 and the city and E42 and the sea.

Piacentini's firm desire to impose strict controls on building in the city appeared in the *Variante*. According to the architect, buildings should no longer have singular and individual characters, responding to the tastes of the various owners and architects, but will be aligned according to a strict pre-established order, in a general, united harmony. Buildings will no longer be constitute a detached unit, instead they will be a sub-unit of greater unity, such as the road or the square (Piacentini 1941).

The perspective in which Piacentini arose was that of a "building dictator", a position he already desired in 1929 and which he was now waiting to receive. "I should have been named *Aedile* of Rome, but everything is blurred," he wrote in February 1943 (Piacentini 1943). Mussolini never officially gave Piacentini the title that he so coveted. But this does not mean that he never, at least in part, actually carried out the tasks of the role.

REFERENCES

Barillari, Diana (2003): "Architettura e committenza a Trieste: Piacentini e le Assicurazioni Generali." In: Archeografo Triestino, 63, pp. 595-618.
Casciato, Maristella/Poretti, Sergio (eds.) (2002): Il Palazzo della Civiltà Italiana, Milano: Motta.
Cevini, Paolo (1989): Genova anni '30: Da Labò a Daneri, Genova: Sagep.
Maifrini, Mariarosa (1988): "Tecnici e amministrazione: I piani di Brescia tra le due guerre." In: Giulio Ernesti (ed.), La costruzione dell'utopia: Architetti e urbanisti nell'Italia fascista, Roma: Edizioni lavoro, pp. 303-324.
Muntoni, Alessandra (1996): "Progetto per i palazzi delle Forze Armate all'E42." In: Vittorio Gregotti/ Giovanni Marzari (eds.), Luigi Figini, Gino Pollini, Milano: Electa, pp. 83-95.
Nicoloso, Paolo (2005): "Architetture per la città fascista, 1933-1939." In: Paolo Nicoloso/Federica Rovello (eds.), Trieste: Guida all'architettura, Trieste: Mgs, pp. 47-57.

Nicoloso, Paolo (2006): "Piacentini e Mussolini nella Città universitaria di Roma, 1932-1935." In: Giuliana Mazzi (ed.), L'Università e la città, Bologna: Clueb, pp. 231-245.

Nicoloso, Paolo (2008): Mussolini architetto, Torino: Einaudi.

Nicoloso, Paolo (2012): Architetture per un'identità italiana, Udine: Gaspari.

Nicoloso, Paolo (2018): Marcello Piacentini: Architettura e potere; Una biografia, Udine: Gaspari.

Paoletti, Raffaella (2005): "Banco di Napoli" In: Paolo Nicoloso/Federica Rovello (eds.), Trieste: Guida all'architettura, Trieste: Mgs, pp. 201-203.

Papini, Roberto (1935): "Architetture, se Dio vuole italiane." In: L'Illustrazione italiana November 3, pp. 862-864.

Piacentini, Marcello (1913): "Estetica regolatrice nello sviluppo urbano." In: Rassegna Contemporanea April 10, pp. 30-36.

Piacentini, Marcello (1922): "Nuovi orizzonti dell'edilizia cittadina." In: Nuova Antologia 57/1199, p. 60-72.

Letter by Marcello Piacentini to Melis (1941, 29 October). Fondo Marcello Piacentini, b. 197.8. Biblioteca di Scienze Tecnologiche, Università degli Studi, Firenze.

Letter by Marcello Piacentini to Vittorio Cini (1943, 11 February). Fondo Cini, busta 1, f. 7. Archivio Centrale dello Stato (ACS), Roma.

Reggiori, Ferdinando (1947): Milano, 1800-1943, Milano: Edizioni del Milione.

"La ricostruzione del secondo tratto di via Roma a Torino." In: Architettura June 1939, pp. 339–373.

Robecchi, Franco (1998): Brescia Littoria: Una città modello dell'urbanistica fascista, Brescia: La compagnia della stampa.

"S. E. l'arch. Marcello Piacentini preside della Facoltà di architettura dell'Università di Roma." In: Architettura: Supplemento sindacale 15 February 1936, pp. 13-14.

Sessa, Giovanni (1995) "Via Roma nuova a Torino." In: Agostino Magnaghi/Mariolina Monge/Luciano Re (eds.), Guida all'architettura moderna di Torino, Torino: Lindau, pp. 507-517.

Simeoni, Alberto (1929): "L'architettura del tempo fascista e l'edilizia moderna: Intervista a Marcello Piacentini." In: L'Impero March 31.

Spesso, Marco/Brancucci, Gerardo (2016): Le pietre liguri nell'architettura di Genova: L'età del fascismo, Milano: Angeli.

"Urbanistica della Roma mussoliniana / Urbanisme de la Rome de Mussolini / Städtebau des mussolinischen Rom / Town Planning of Mussolinian Rome." Special issue, Architettura XV/December 1936, Milano: Treves, p. 6.

The Concept of Tradition in the Theoretical and Aesthetic Debate from the 1920s to the Second Post-War Period

Cettina Lenza

The essay investigates the several and often mutable meanings related to the term "tradition" in the field of aesthetic reflection, along with the theoretical debate that has developed in Italy since the interwar period at the margins of architecture and the large urban transformations. The theme of tradition is examined according to three prevailing meanings: as permanence, as continuity and as identity. It quotes the opinions of various authors, including the members of Gruppo 7, Gustavo Giovannoni and Marcello Piacentini, while also taking into consideration the lesser known contribution made by Salvatore Vitale.

In a critical glossary of the architecture of the first half of the 20th century, the term "tradition" would have a considerable place, especially in relation to its dialectical counterpart, i.e. "modernity"; together they form a central dichotomy in the disciplinary debate. The importance assigned to the two antagonistic sides – or at least considered so by many authors – has been very different and mostly in favour of modernity. This is also probably due to a historiographical approach that, tending to interpret the 20th century history in terms of progress, has favoured all that was inclined towards innovation and considered everything outside of this process as 'resistant residue'. Since the 1990s, however, increasing numbers of critical contributions have modified the aforementioned disequilibrium, showing how the so-called 'losers' were those who shaped the construction of the European city between the two wars, not only lining up in their favour a quantitative advantage over the 'winners', but rightfully marking the last qualified border before the spread of the suburbs in the second half of the century (cf. Pigafetta/Abbondandolo/Trisciuoglio 2002). Moreover, numerous studies, especially monographic ones, have contributed to a 'compensation' towards figures left overshadowed, or even excluded from, the great historiographic reconstructions. In the end, the same opening dichotomy between modernity and tradition has been questioned by those who have identified a third way, an "other modernity" or "a different deep-rooted Modernity" (Benedetti 2005: 432), thus proving the difficulty of establishing clear distinctions.

Even if there is no longer prejudice towards the topic of tradition, analysing it is not simple. Like modernity, the concept of tradition is both inclusive and ambiguous, covering distinct and sometimes even distant meanings, with it therefore becoming, in its semantic shifts, a marker of significant differences in purpose and thought in contemporary architectural research. In addition, the time frame through which the question of the relationship between tradition and modernity remains essential, appears not only wide, from the first to the second post-war period, but also marked by profound transformations of the historical scenario, that inevitably influence a modification of the values conveyed.

In the impossibility of proposing an overview, even if brief, of the publications of that time, favouring the writings with a more evident theoretical or critical nature, which are furthermore well known, the concept of tradition will be categorized according to different meanings which, though not alternative, with their different 'dosages' allow to distribute separately the voices that take part in the debate.

TRADITION AS PERMANENCE

The thesis of the *permanence* of tradition can be considered a field of intersection with the modernists. In this regard, the reference to four articles written by the collective of architects known as "Gruppo 7" and published in *Rassegna italiana politica, letteraria e artistica* (directed by the writer and art critic Tomaso Sillani) from December 1926 to May 1927 is mandatory, also considering that from this less specific editorial context they were brought back to the centre of the disciplinary debate thanks to Pietro Betta, who became director of the Turin based magazine *L'Architettura Italiana* in March 1926, where the initial program of young architects was publicized on February 1, 1927: "Il Gruppo 7 di Milano e l'architettura nuova". In the third article in March of that year, entitled "Impreparazione – Incomprensione – Pregiudizi", many misunderstandings associated with the topic of tradition were denounced:

So many are the voices risen in defence of tradition, and so many have been the controversies, for and against, about it, that we are made to wonder whether, after all, we have not too often *misunderstood* this word, or whether we have lost sight of *its true meaning*. (Il Gruppo 7 1927b: 249)[1]

The essential misunderstanding concerned the equivalence between the past and tradition: "The great lesson of our past continues to be misunderstood. The mask of tradition helps to hide any insincerity", concealing the structural frame of reinforced concrete with the application of previous styles (ibid: 249).[2] However, subsequent to their first article, they affirmed: "We do not want to break with tradition: it is tradition that transforms itself, acquires new aspects that few people can recognize" (Il Gruppo 7 1926: 852).[3] Unlike the linguistic internationalism of industrial buildings, architecture preserves in every country, together with absolute modernity, a national character: the spirit of tradition "in Italy, it is so deep that, apparently and almost mechanically, the new architecture cannot fail to preserve a typical mark *of our own*" (ibid: 854).[4] Thus, appealing to the spirit rather than the forms, and invoking the transformation of tradition rather than its rebirth, they had ended up identifying it in that "classical substratum" that has always been among us.

The positions expressed reflect a more general cultural mood which tended to nourish an aesthetics founded on permanent and absolute values. This was confirmed by Carlo Belli and his search for a new classicism that, after the breaking

---

1 "Tante sono le voci sorte in difesa della tradizione, e tante le polemiche che prò o contro di essa si sono avute, che vien fatto di chiedersi se, in fondo, non si sia troppo spesso *equivocato* su questa parola, o se ne sia perso di vista il *vero significato*." (Emphasis in original).

2 "[…] La grande lezione del nostro passato continua ad essere *fraintesa*. La maschera della tradizione serve a nascondere ogni insincerità: e di una grande insincerità è materiata molta parte della moderna architettura da noi. Si continua così a *nascondere* metodicamente lo scheletro in cemento armato degli edifici, con applicazioni più o meno disordinate degli stili antichi." (Emphasis in original).

3 "Noi non vogliamo rompere con la tradizione: è la tradizione che si trasforma, assume aspetti nuovi, sotto i quali pochi la riconoscono".

4 "Da noi in particolare, esiste un tale substrato classico, lo spirito (non le forme, il che è ben diverso) della tradizione è così profondo in Italia, che evidentemente e quasi meccanicamente la nuova architettura non potrà non conservare un'impronta tipicamente *nostra*. E questa è già una grande forza; poiché la tradizione come si è detto, non scompare, ma cambia aspetto." (Emphasis in original)

experiences of the avant-garde, was able to return to art its Greek-classical dimension, without falling into the cult of the past: "Our classicism [...] is not expressed in the imitation of past models but arises from the creation of new archetypes. Establishing and not restoring. [...] Greece inspires us but does not suppress us" (Belli 1992 [1959?]: 98).[5] However, if for Belli it was probably due to a cultural affinity with the members of Gruppo 7, thanks also to his friendship with Gino Pollini, who likewise came from Rovereto, an autonomous precedent of the articles of Gruppo 7 and their thesis about a modern classicism was the essay by Salvatore Vitale, "Elogio dell'architettura", that appeared in the *Rivista d'Italia* on January 15, 1926. A librarian by profession but an art critic out of passion, Vitale, who moved from Catania to Rome in the 1910s, dealt with more general questions about contemporary aesthetics, prompted by his reading of the writings of the philosopher Benedetto Croce. However, he deviated from the latter's thinking, for whom art is one and special aesthetics cannot be admitted, enunciating instead the distinctive peculiarities of architecture. These would consist in an inner space – an early affirmation for those years – in its "constructive spirit", compared to the imitative arts, like painting and sculpture, and over all in "its static, and, at the same time, real nature" (Vitale 1926: 47), which distinguished architecture from the other arts which tend to dissolve over time, like music and poetry that are actualized every time in their performance.[6] This led to its "outdated" nature in relation to the sensitivity of modern civilization that was expressed by the exaltation of movement, in the delirium of power, in the fever of action, as revealed by the transatlantic liner, the new symbol of architecture, that represents a thunderous monument that moves on the waves, an expression of the attempt to make space mobile or to cancel it with speed. However, for Vitale,

> all this, in the end, deceives, but does not satisfy the restless modern soul. The sense of measure and order is too innate in the very idea of beauty [...] so that, definitively, the human soul can be silenced in the aesthetic contemplation of effort without stopping, of action without limits and without purpose. (Ibid: 51)

Thus, this sensitivity would be a "temporary moment of the Spirit", not the definitive aesthetic conception of an era: in fact Vitale identifies "the warning signs of

---

5   "Il nostro classicismo [...] non si esplica nella imitazione dei modelli passati ma si manifesta con la creazione di nuovi archetipi. Instaurare e non restaurare. [...] la Grecia ci ispira, ma non ci sopprime".

6   "Per questo suo carattere statico, e, insieme, reale, l'architettura appare, quindi, assolutamente distante dalla mentalità moderna, e distaccata da essa".

new tendencies, of new efforts, of a new aspiration to order, to calm and quite beauty, to the measure, to the sense of limit, of purpose, of proportions, of rhythm, to the classical ideal, in short" (ibid: 51).[7] Ultimately, it was from architecture that the reaction and overcoming of today's unrest could emerge, returning once again to lead, as "the mother of all the arts", artistic research towards a goal of unity, order and harmony (ibid: 56).[8]

The thesis of the article on an imminent return to a classical ideal, which received positive feedback from Gustavo Giovannoni, as highlighted by a postcard found among Vitale's private papers (cp. Lenza 2010a: 43), was developed in Vitale's book *L'estetica dell'architettura. Saggio sullo sviluppo dello spirito costruttivo*, published in 1928 in the series "Biblioteca di cultura moderna" by Laterza. The book was reviewed positively by Marcello Piacentini in *Architettura e Arti decorative* in August of the same year, who recommended reading it, then it was repeatedly quoted by other architects, such as Plinio Marconi and Agnoldomenico Pica, who were both important voices of the debate at that time. However, the most significant approval came from Edoardo Persico, the influential Neapolitan critic, who in November 1934, in an article in the Milan magazine *Domus* entitled "Punto ed a capo per l'architettura", stated his disappointment over architecture-related publications, pointing out, among the few exceptions to a "bibliography of ignorance", the volume of Vitale, considered a "not groundless essay on the development of this art from the Greeks to our days" (Veronesi 1964: 304; Persico

---

7   "Ma tutto ciò, in fondo, illude, ma non appaga l'inquieta anima moderna. Troppo il senso della misura e dell'ordine è connaturato all'idea stessa del bello [...] perché l'anima umana possa acquietarsi definitivamente nella contemplazione estetica dello sforzo senza freno, dell'azione senza limiti e senza scopo [...]. Può costituire, dunque, l'arte moderna soltanto un momento transitorio dello Spirito, l'indice della stanchezza d'una civiltà esausta, o, come si vuole, il segno della rinascita d'una civiltà giovane, ma non può rappresentare mai la concezione estetica definitiva di un'epoca. E, infatti, non mancano i presagi ammonitori di nuove tendenze, di nuovi conati, di una nuova aspirazione all'ordine, alla bellezza calma e tranquilla, alla misura, al senso del limite, dello scopo, delle proporzioni, del ritmo, all'ideale classico, insomma".

8   "E l'architettura, l'arte più completa, più realizzatrice, più capace di darci questa realtà nuova veramente umana, ideale insieme e concreta, riprenderà, allora, il suo rango di *madre di tutte le arti*, rappresenterà il coronamento definitivo della rinascita spirituale, e ci darà finalmente uno stile." (Emphasis in original)

1934).⁹ Here Vitale, entering more directly into the disciplinary debate, probably had to refer to the articles of Gruppo 7, especially in the final part of the book, where he concluded his historical excursus on the conceptions of space from Greek architecture to the contemporary with an "Epilogo", but added a "Prologo" aimed at outlining the future directions of architecture, trying to assign a theoretical foundation and a development perspective to a rationalism in its beginning. The prefigured result was a "new classicism", in which the "framed" technique of reinforced concrete, after its "archaic" phase – thus defined also in the fourth article of Gruppo 7 (1927c), – would have developed an original style, as the expression of a new aesthetics entrusted to permanent values. This was confirmed by the judgment about Le Corbusier, which was similar to the one formulated by Gruppo 7 (cf. Gruppo 7 1927a: 136),¹⁰ denying his futurist label to define him as

a rationalist, and in a way even a traditionalist, since rationalism [...] inevitably ends up leading back to classicism, which is the patterns and canons fixed by long tradition and accepted by common consensus, by the logic of generations. (Lenza 2010b: 162; Vitale 1928)¹¹

Thanks to the equivalence established between the rational and classical, there is therefore no contrast between modernity and tradition, provided that the classical is not reduced to the academic and superficial recovery of forms taken from the ancient era, but identifies itself in the search for permanent values, reinterpreted by modernity.

This school of thought survived the vicissitudes suffered by the *Movimento Italiano per l'Architettura Razionale* (MIAR), that was founded after the first Italian exhibition of rational architecture organized in Rome in 1928 by Adalberto Libera and Gaetano Minnucci and gathered together many young architects, not only from Rome, but also from Milan, Turin and Genoa, and that dissolved after

---

9 "All'infuori delle polemiche, Salvatore Vitale ha pubblicato, presso Laterza, un'*Estetica dell'architettura* che contiene un saggio non immotivato sullo svolgimento di quest'arte dai Greci fino ai giorni nostri."

10 "L'errore maggiore fu di considerarlo [Le Corbusier] come una specie di futurista, mentre invece egli è, in fondo, un tradizionalista."

11 "È facile, quindi, constatare come la qualifica di futurista attribuita al Le Cobusier sia totalmente errata; egli è, invece, un razionalista, ed in certo senso addirittura un tradizionalista, poiché il razionalismo [...] finisce necessariamente per ricondurre al classicismo, cioè agli schemi ed ai canoni fissati dalla lunga tradizione e accolti, per comune consenso, dalla logica delle generazioni."

the Roman exhibition of 1931 due to the contrasts with the official academic culture. Such a position reappears in those exponents of Gruppo 7 who converge in the *Raggruppamento Architetti Moderni Italiani* (RAMI), such as Sebastiano Larco and above all Carlo Enrico Rava. In the RAMI manifesto published in May 1931 in several newspapers, in addition to stigmatising a persistent frozen tendency "in the passive repetition of forms belonging to previous eras", distance was also established to those "tendencies derived from international forms and concepts [which] are opposed to our tradition, our historical architectural supremacy, our spirit, our needs and to the political climate in which we live"; instead, "the importance of our classical tradition as formative of the modern creative spirit" was defended (Cennamo 1976: 432-433).[12] However, the most interesting developments are from Rava, who would claim precedence (cf. Brunetti 1998: 209-210) by having translated the classical ideal into the meaning of "Latin spirit" and "Mediterraneità".[13] The thesis was developed in a series of eight articles that appeared from January to November 1931 in *Domus*, aimed at identifying Mediterranean features in the best modern architecture of each country, ranging from North African colonies to Mexico or to California and Florida, in order to understand, among so many aspects, the unity of a fundamental Latin concept. A Latin spirit was found by Rava in German "independent rationalism" as well as in many works by Le Corbusier, despite his "uncompromising rationalism", thanks to their "sense of eurhythmy and classical proportion [...] which is its greatest value, and rebels against any constraint of dogmas" (Rava 1931a: 39);[14] Le Corbusier reveals that he too fails to shake free "of this eternal Latin spirit who returns to invade

---

12 "Queste tendenze derivate da forme e concetti internazionali sono contrarie alla nostra tradizione, alla nostra storica supremazia architettonica, al nostro spirito, alle nostre necessità, al clima politico in cui viviamo. [...]. Convinti che mai come in questo momento sia vivo in noi quel sentimento di continuità del presente nel passato che opera [...] come forma dinamica e vitale e per il quale ogni modernità viene ad avere la sua ragion di essere [...], affermiamo l'importanza della tradizione nostra classica come formativa del moderno spirito creativo che [...] risolve ed attiva i problemi nuovi d'ordine pratico, economico e costruttivo come forme architettoniche che per questo certamente saranno rispondenti all'ambiente e al clima politico creato dal Fascismo."

13 Mediterraneity, or Mediterranean-quality.

14 "[...] nella pratica, gran parte delle costruzioni di Le Corbusier rivelano un senso insopprimibile dell'euritmia e della proporzione classica, senso tutto latino, che ne costituisce il maggior pregio, ed è ribelle ad ogni costrizione di dogmi".

Europe" (ibid: 44).[15] Moreover, an ideal aspiration towards the South is found – rather forcibly – in the latest architecture in Austria or Sweden, demonstrating how much this alleged "Latin spirit" was far from a specific geographical or historical connotation. Finally, contradictions are not lacking, when the same Mediterranean-inspired ideal is proposed in support of a national supremacy, with Rava's invitation to rediscover, after the healthy "rationalist cure" (Rava 1931b: 40),[16] the intimate essence of a truly Italian architecture in a native tradition, found in many vernacular "minor architectures" of the Tyrrhenian coast, in Capri, Amalfi or on the Ligurian Riviera.

In favour of this possible conciliation between tradition and modernity, the magazine *Domus* went on to take sides, not only with an editorial by Gio Ponti of 1932 aimed at debunking the "common belief that modernity means the mortification of tradition" (Ponti 1932: 133),[17] but above all with the evocative comparisons between Giotto's frescoes and the architectures of Adalberto Libera and Mario Ridolfi proposed by Giovanni Michelucci (1932a), or Michelucci's graphic reinterpretations of two Tuscan farmhouses, and interpreting them as "'brand new' shapes, those that the inattentive audience defines as Nordic or [...] 'German', have also roots among us, in our clear and peaceful home tradition and are developments of the functional logic of these examples" (Michelucci 1932b: 460).[18]

A dual path is thus traced: on the one hand with a focus on the spontaneous rural house that is able to provide new archetypes to modern architecture, which was represented in Giuseppe Pagano's exhibition at the Triennale of 1936; on the other, with the myth of a Mediterranean classicism which, nourished by Greek canons and neo-Platonic ideals, endorses the refined purism of rationalist

---

15 "[...] di questo spirito latino, che affiora nei contesti nordici come un'ideale aspirazione verso il sud, di questo spirito latino di cui Le Cobusier non riesce a disfarsi, di questo eterno spirito latino che torna ad invadere l'Europa (e non per nulla, lo spirito nordico tende a rifugiarsi in Russia), siamo noi i depositari fatali e secolari".

16 "La 'cura razionalista' ha ormai portato le sue benefiche conseguenze, anzi, appunto con queste, ha esaurito il suo compito e quindi minaccia di diventare presto un ingombro."

17 "È opinione comune che modernità significhi mortificazione della tradizione."

18 "Poiché viva è sempre fra il pubblico la discussione sui caratteri della nuova architettura, ci piace presentare due esempi di case coloniche, delle quali è stato rifatto lo schema disegnativo, a dimostrare come 'nuovissime' forme, quelle che il pubblico poco attento definisce nordiche o per essere più precisi 'tedesche', hanno pure radici da noi, nella chiara serena nostrana tradizione e della logica funzionale di questi esempi sono lo sviluppo."

geometries, as it still surfaces in the "Programma di architettura" published in 1933 in *Quadrante* magazine. The ambiguous category of 'Mediterraneity', divided between the search for absolute forms and national characters, represents the new face of tradition, able to offer "a passport" to modernity (Danesi 1976: 21),[19] facilitating travel between different ideological and cultural shores, and replacing the perpetuity of classic arches and columns with a rationalist 'grammar' as a new interpretation of a permanent "Mediterranean spirit".

TRADITION AS CONTINUITY

Although it seems impossible to establish clear distinctions, the notion of *continuity* offers a different approach to the topic of tradition, far from the search for constants identified in the classical ideal and from the abstractness of the participants of the First Exhibition of Rational Architecture, as Marcello Piacentini wrote in 1928 in his article in *Architettura e arti decorative*, inviting the young Italian rationalists to organize a new exhibition, "but with obliged themes, with well-defined locations" (1928: 562).[20]

Shifting the topic of tradition from a 'metahistorical' plane to one that takes into account the role of history and context is a specific contribution of Gustavo Giovannoni. In 1929 he published the entry "Architettura" in the *Enciclopedia Italiana*, which included a paragraph dedicated to *La tradizione italiana* that, significantly, preceded the paragraph dedicated to *L'architettura moderna*, perhaps to accentuate the latter's dependence on the course of tradition: it is necessary to "prove the vitality of our tradition, which, as in the past has shaped the most diverse needs and structures, so it can assimilate modern needs and structures and give them at least tentative expression" (Giovannoni 1929: 77).[21] According to Giovannoni, the discussion about tradition was linked to a concept of history as a continuity of artistic expressions, in the sense of a transmission of experiences and

---

19 "In complesso la 'mediterraneità' [...] era sufficientemente collegata ai miti ufficiali da poter costituire un porto sicuro o una trincea, un passaporto di cui i nostri artisti in difficoltà cercarono di munire se stessi e le proprie opere [...] [nella] conquista di una terra di nessuno sita fra la tradizione e le modernità [...]."

20 "Chiudo permettendomi di dare ai giovani razionalisti un suggerimento. Un altr'anno tentino ancora una nuova mostra, ma con temi obbligati, con ubicazioni ben precisate."

21 "E tanto può e deve farsi [...] col provare la vitalità della nostra tradizione che, come in passato ha dato forma alle esigenze e alle strutture più diverse, così può assimilare le esigenze e le strutture moderne e dar loro almeno provvisoria espressione."

forms following a course of slow but uninterrupted evolution. In Italy, this continuity, which represents the real essence of tradition in the meaning of *tradere* or transmission through generations, would be determined partly by geographical features, even in the variety of climates and materials of different regions, and partly through a spiritual element that lies in the human race: "This constancy of reasons and this continuity of programs have therefore constituted a true tradition in each of [Italy's] regions" (ibid: 76).[22]

The break in this continuity is not attributed by Giovannoni to either the constructive innovations or the social transformations occurring in the new century, but rather to the early 19th century. A similar conviction had already been clearly expressed in Giovannoni's Opening Lecture at the School of Architecture in Rome, given on December 18, 1920, *L'architettura italiana nella storia e nella vita*, in which he denounced "the coldness of neo-classicism" as "artificially interrupting the logical development" of architecture, which, thus "weakened", could not be prepared to face "the great modern problems" because, quoting Nietzsche's words, "when the thread of evolution is broken, even the best-skilled artist is able to perform only ephemeral experiments" (Zucconi 1997: 133; Giovannoni 1925).[23]

Giovannoni probably invoked the young architects of RAMI and their moderate or 'reasonable' rationalism when, in *Nuova Antologia* of August 1, 1931, he outlined the only two possible ways that could lead to an "Italian architectural style of our time, agile and alive, embraced by everyone as a language not detached from tradition, but not alien to real needs": namely, "starting from existing patterns and shapes to renovate them", or studying the solutions offered by new technical possibilities and adapting them. He was inclined towards the first method, since

it consisted in reviving what is permanent and vital in the Italian architectural tradition [...] resuming the interrupted path, re-joining ourselves to the last periods of unity and stylistic

---

22 "Questa costanza di ragioni e questa continuità di programmi hanno pertanto costituito una vera tradizione in ciascuna delle sue regioni."

23 "I grandi problemi moderni si sono avanzati tumultuando con una rapidità rivoluzionaria e con una impressionante vastità. [...] A tutta questa vita nuova, l'architettura non era e non poteva essere preparata. L'aveva infiacchita il gelo del neo-classicismo con l'interromperne artificiosamente il logico sviluppo e per l'architettura più che per qualunque arte può applicarsi la giusta sentenza del Nietzsche che 'quando il filo dell'evoluzione è spezzato, anche l'artista meglio dotato non riesce che a compiere degli esperimenti effimeri'."

loftiness, assimilating the new results, solving the topics of new life by grafting into the old trunk vigorous and daring sprouts,

as demonstrated by "works that are both modern and traditional, useful and responsive to the environment". He warned that "abandoning this continuity would weaken a powerful Italian vital force, it would be a waiver of our thoughts and feelings" (Giovannoni 1931: 339)[24] and invited the rationalists to a "realistic revision" according to which, considering the true needs of our country compared to those imported from other places or as a result of a fashion coming from magazines,

Italian materials, our wall stones, terracotta, marbles, wrought irons certainly would be re-evaluated, and proportions and forms that do not harmonise with our climate (such as floors that are too low and huge windows, wider than they are tall, without shutters) would be abandoned. (Ibid: 340)[25]

---

24 "Allo stile architettonico italiano del nostro tempo, agile e vivo, accolto da tutti come un linguaggio, non avulso dalla tradizione, ma non estraneo alle esigenze reali, si potrà forse arrivare con un movimento convergente, ravvisando, non elidendo, gli sforzi fatti in questi ultimi anni: da un lato partendo dagli schemi e dalle forme esistenti e rinnovandoli, dall'altro studiando le possibilità nuove e ambientandole.[...] io sono per il primo dei due metodi e di esso vedo più direttamente il contributo che consiste nel ravvivare quello che v'è di permanente e di vitale nella tradizione architettonica italiana [...] riprendendo l'interrotto cammino, riannodandosi agli ultimi periodi di unità e di elevatezza stilistica, assimilando i nuovi portati, risolvendo i temi della vita nuova con l'innestare al vecchio tronco germogli vigorosi ed arditi. Sono convinto che l'abbandonare tale continuità fiaccherebbe una possente forza viva italiana, sarebbe rinunzia di un nostro pensiero e di un nostro sentimento[...]. Credo anche che sia doveroso il riaffermare che su questa via si sono da noi nell'ultimo decennio raggiunti risultati veramente interessanti e confortevoli in opere che sono insieme moderne e tradizionali, utili e rispondenti all'ambiente."

25 "Il compito dei razionalisti italiani può essere non meno importante: dovrebbe riconoscere anzitutto quali siano le vere esigenze positive del nostro paese distaccandole da quelle importate da condizioni di altri luoghi o da una moda priva di significato ed in tale revisione realistica verrebbero senz'altro rivalutati i materiali italiani, le nostre pietre da muro, le terrecotte, i marmi, i ferri battuti, e verrebbero abbandonate proporzioni e forme che (come quelle dei piani troppo bassi e delle invetriate enormi, più larghe che alte, prive di persiane) non si confanno al nostro clima."

Two corollaries arose from this call to 'continuity' with the past. The first concerned the role assigned to historical studies. In the opening speech held at the First National Congress of the History of Architecture in Florence (29-31 October 1936), Giovannoni explicated his idea of architecture as "the most continuous and significant expression that has gone through the centuries", as a process of progressive transformation in which, in the direct transmission from father to son, from teacher to pupil,

> every generation carried a light ferment of evolution, every exuberant energy created in the common language some new accent, but slow was the path in the transition from one style to the other. [...] While now, after the nineteenth-century period that has truly interrupted all continuity and stopped every vibration of architectural Art, the new demands of urban life, of modern institutions and the search for comfort and hygiene, the new means and new possibilities of construction have created the material substrate of a new style, but not yet the new architectural style. (Atti del I Congresso Nazionale di Storia dell'Architettura 1938: VII)[26]

In order to find the right way in what Giovannoni defined a "treacherous sea", "only historical experience can serve as a compass and an astrolabe"; hence "the importance of the rebirth of the History of Architecture studies", not to copy ancient forms, but rather to be used "as a guide to research new architectural expressions". Since the spontaneous evolutionary transmission of traditional forms had been interrupted, it would be necessary to resort to historical knowledge which, replacing the previous natural process, could impart to the ongoing attempts

---

26 "Non minore è l'importanza del risorgere degli studi di Storia dell'Architettura nei riguardi degli ardui e urgenti problemi che si riferiscono alle espressioni architettoniche modernissime. Fino ad un secolo fa i concetti di costruzione e d'Arte che facevano capo all'Architettura si trasmettevano naturalmente e direttamente, come principi stabili, di padre in figlio, da maestro a scolaro. Ogni generazione recava bensì un lieve fermento di evoluzione, ogni esuberante energia creava nel linguaggio comune qualche nuovo accento, ma lento era il cammino nella transizione tra uno stile e l'altro [...]. Invece ora, dopo il periodo ottocentesco che ha veramente interrotto ogni continuità e fermato ogni vibrazione di Arte architettonica, le esigenze nuove della vita urbanistica, delle istituzioni moderne, della ricerca di comodità e di igiene, ed i mezzi nuovi e le possibilità nuove della costruzione, hanno creato il substrato materiale di un nuovo stile, ma non ancora il nuovo stile architettonico. [...] A questi compiti altissimi la Storia dell'Architettura italiana, cioè della manifestazione più continua e significativa che abbia attraversato i secoli, non è ancora preparata."

"a logical unity and a continuity with tradition, without which there will never be an architectural style, but a sequence of ephemeral fashions" (ibid: VI-VII).[27]

In this conception of tradition, it is possible to understand, on the one hand, Giovannoni's stylistic predilections, which, more than demonstrations of a lingering historicism, express the program to knot again the interrupted course of tradition, with a "free interpretation, almost a continuation of the Baroque and Neoclassical types that are closer to our needs and to our civilization than others" (1929: 76);[28] on the other, the operational and planning function assigned to the History of Architecture: as already affirmed in his speech at the Preparatory Congress of Naples in 1934, *Mete e metodi nella Storia dell'architettura italiana*, "Once again the experience of the past will act as a ferment to germinate new life" (Atti del I Congresso Nazionale di Storia dell'Architettura 1938: 283).[29]

The second corollary regarded the relationship with the urban environment. Even Giovanni Muzio, in his review of *L'architettura a Milano intorno all'Ottocento*, published in 1921 in the magazine *Emporium*, criticized "the chaotic and disordered new streets where buildings alternate bizarre and contrasting", writing that "architecture, an eminently social art, must above all be continuous in its stylistic features, to be susceptible to diffusion and to creating, with the entirety of the buildings, a harmonious and homogeneous whole" (Muzio 1921: 258).[30]

---

27 "Due anni or sono [...] io ebbi a esporre i criteri e le finalità del nostro lavoro, che si compendiano nella unità di ordine e di metodo da seguire nella Storia dell'Architettura affinché essa riprenda il posto dominante che le spetta e che le è necessario come presidio agli studi storici ed artistici, come guida alla ricerca di nuove espressioni architettoniche. [...] In questo mare infido, solo la esperienza storica può servire da bussola e da astrolabio [...]. Ed ecco la Storia dell'Architettura che dalla cognizione dei fatti attinenti ai singoli monumenti può assurgere [...] [a] imprimere ai tentativi una logica unità ed una continuità con la tradizione, senza di che non si avrà mai uno stile architettonico, ma una successione di mode effimere."

28 "Nel momento attuale, tendenze forse più serie e più sane sono quelle della libera interpretazione, quasi della continuazione, dei tipi barocchi o neoclassici, più degli altri vicini alle nostre esigenze e alla nostra civiltà."

29 "Ancora una volta l'esperienza del passato servirà di fermento al germinare della vita nuova."

30 "Oggi ancora a noi sembra necessaria una reazione alla confusione ed all'esasperato individualismo dell'architettura odierna, ed il ristabilimento del principio di ordine per il quale l'architettura, arte eminentemente sociale, deve in un paese anzitutto essere continua nei suoi caratteri stilistici, per essere suscettibile di diffusione e formare con il complesso degli edifici un tutto armonico ed omogeneo. Tutti, a nostro avviso,

In 1913, before Muzio, in a famous article about the Renaissance district in Rome, Giovannoni had recommended a harmony between old and new also in a stylistic sense, specifying:

> I would not be misunderstood in this reference to the architectural tradition. It does not mean that the new facades of the buildings must be cold copies of pre-existing works [...] but every city has its own artistic 'atmosphere', it has a sense of proportions, colour, shapes, which has remained as a permanent element through the evolution of the various styles, and we cannot neglect it. (Giovannoni 1913: 59)[31]

The result is the theory of *ambientismo*,[32] a word already introduced in a 1918 report on the possibility of extending protection from the isolated monument to its context, to preserve its conditions of light and perspective (cf. Giovannoni 1918),[33] then republished in *Questioni di architettura nella storia e nella vita* in 1925 with the title "L'ambiente dei monumenti". Here, the *ambientismo* is identified as an antidote to the "very serious dangers towards old monuments and the conditions of harmony required for them", where "the continuity which naturally ensured such harmony was interrupted" (Zucconi 1997: 113; Giovannoni 1925).[34] In the theory of contextualism, which Piacentini shared with Giovannoni at first, the topic of continuity is expressed in formal and aesthetic terms. In the extensive review dedicated to Piacentini in *Emporium* in 1930, Antonio Nezi recalled architecture to the need of contextualizing the building in place and time:

---

preferiranno alle caotiche e disordinate vie nuove dove gli edifici si alternano bizzarri e contrastanti, il calmo e riposante ambiente di una vecchia strada dell'ottocento."

31 "[...] in questo richiamo alla tradizione architettonica non vorrei esser frainteso. Esso non vuol dire che i nuovi prospetti debbano essere fredde copie di opere preesistenti [...] ma ogni città ha una sua 'atmosfera' artistica, ha cioè un senso di proporzioni, di colore, di forme, che è rimasto elemento permanente attraverso l'evoluzione dei vari stili, e da esso non si deve prescindere"

32 Commonly translated as 'Contextualism'.

33 About this writing, cf. Pane 2007.

34 "Tutto ciò [...] rappresenta una serie di pericoli gravissimi nei riguardi dei vecchi monumenti e delle condizioni di armonia per essi richieste. Interrotta quella continuità che assicurava naturalmente tale armonia, è necessario che, dove intervengono le ragioni monumentali, queste richieggano alcuni vincoli, pur non rigidi e ristretti, di carattere stilistico."

Now contextualize does not mean to build *as* those who have preceded us, but to put ourselves in the same spiritual conditions when they prepared in turn to work in the context of the most ancient tradition. In this way, it is possible to add more and more rings to the chain of architectural continuity without breaking its unity. (Nezi 1930: 85)[35]

In other words, the practice of contextualism is the search for "an aesthetic continuity in relation to the past", as well as a "harmonious fusion with the characteristics of the natural landscape" (ibid: 90).[36]

TRADITION AS IDENTITY

The concept of tradition as *identity* reveals, unlike the previous ones, neither an ascent to permanent principles nor a relationship with history and context, but it refers to a homogeneous community, which is intended as a repository of the collective memory and as a vehicle of its transmission.

If the topic of identity is always present under the debate of these years, not without political hues and claims of nationalistic supremacies that degenerate even into the cult of race, in architecture it requires a series of distinctions. The first concerns the formal and ideological construction of this identity. It must therefore be recognised how Piacentini had attempted to propose a national modernity against the academic tendency that aligned with the ideal of the imperial Roman world. In *Architettura d'oggi* in 1930, he declared: "this respect for the past is holy", but "evolution is too often denied and the term Italian is confused with that of ancient, not always in good faith; in the same manner in which any attempt at modernity is considered foreign" (1930: 62).[37] In 1933, in the famous controversy with Ugo Ojetti about the arches and columns during the construction of the University City, in the newspaper *La Tribuna,* Piacentini came back strongly to affirm

---

35 "Ora ambientare non significa costruire *come* i precedenti, ma porsi nelle loro stesse condizioni di spirito allorché si prepararono ad operare a loro volta nell'ambiente della più antica tradizione. Così è possibile aggiungere anelli ad anelli alla catena della continuità architettonica senza spezzarne l'unità." (Emphasis in original)

36 "[...] ambientarsi non significa solo fare opera di continuità estetica rispetto al passato, ma pure di fusione armoniosa con le caratteristiche del paesaggio naturale."

37 "[...] questo rispetto per il passato è santo, nessuno lo contesta, ma spesso lo si esagera, o, meglio, non lo si comprende esattamente. Si nega troppo spesso la evoluzione e si confonde, e non sempre in buona fede, l'appellativo di italiano con quello di antico; nella stessa maniera che si vuol far passare per straniero ogni tentativo di modernità."

an "Italian identity of today", invoking, in order to defend his modernism, an "other way" of being Italian compared to a Roman ideal meant in a superficial and rhetorical sense, and rejecting the notion of "being worthy just because we are the descendants of the ancients" (1933: 3).[38]

In fact, bringing back the identity of tradition outside the myths of the past was compatible with the cultural line of Fascism. This was also demonstrated by Giovanni Gentile, who advocated for the affirmation of a "national genius" not projected into remote ages but rooted in the present. In his speech at the Lyceum of Florence in 1936, *La tradizione italiana*, the philosopher returned to the features of tradition, encouraging his audience "not to rave about abstract depictions of magnitudes belonging to a concluded history" (1936: 34).[39] Moreover, for Gentile, Italians who wanted to look for "their effective and living tradition, thanks to which they can and must say they are Italian" (ibid: 32),[40] could not stop in ancient Roman times, but must go on into a history that included the flowering of cities such as Venice or Florence in the Middle Ages, that continued with Humanism and the Renaissance to be revived in the 18th century, after the arrest caused by the Counter-Reformation, and triumphed in the process of 19th-century unification. Whatever the case, "tradition is not really the heritage of the past, like an escutcheon discovered in the ruins of a destroyed castle, and then reassembled, restored and repainted" (ibid: 12);[41] rather, tradition "that is the strength and the moral foundation of a national consciousness is not a faded past even if glorious, but remains a living present that operates in the actuality of the spirit" (ibid: 14).[42] In conclusion, "Italy is within us, today" (ibid: 17).[43]

---

38 "Noi pretendiamo di essere italiani in altro modo: con la coscienza di essere *oggi* qualcuno e di contare qualche cosa anche noi, e non valere soltanto perché siamo i discendenti degli antichi." (Emphasis in original)

39 "Custodire gelosamente il carattere di questa tradizione, [...] non vaneggiare in astratte raffigurazioni di grandezze appartenenti a una storia conchiusa."

40 "[...] quando gli italiani vogliono sinceramente e seriamente guardarsi in seno, e cercarsi nella loro effettuale e vivente tradizione, per cui possono e devono dire di essere italiani [...]."

41 "la tradizione non è propriamente l'eredità del passato, quasi blasone razzolato tre le macerie di un castello distrutto, e poi ricomposto, restaurato e ridipinto."

42 "La tradizione [...] che è la forza e il fondamento morale di una coscienza nazionale, non è un passato ancorché glorioso ma tramontato, bensì un vivo presente operante nell'attualità dello spirito."

43 "L'Italia è dentro di noi, oggi".

Another necessary distinction regarded scale, the assimilation of identity to a national or regional condition, and therefore the conferring on it of a unitary or plural nature. In 1930, Piacentini observed that, unlike Nordic and imported modernism, "our modernism reattaches to the whole evolution of our architecture and reflects nature and regional traditions" (1930: 57).[44] However, he warned against placing too much emphasis on the differences: "The efforts of the various regions will have to be channelled into one path, and the architects will have to work harder together to achieve the creation of a modern national art" (ibid: 63-64).[45] In short, the search for a "modern and Italian architecture" (Piacentini 1939: 240)[46] had to be based on homogeneity, able to overcome the eclectic multiplicity of the 19th century and to distance itself not only from the "deadly toxin" of the rejected internationalism (ibid: 239),[47] which was foreign to the Italian culture and climate, but also from localism.

The interest in structural features, building types and local materials, although sporadically emerging through the strands of the national architecture, prompted by autarchic needs or by folkloric impulses deriving from the *Strapaese* movement, was expressed after the World War II, in response to a different spiritual need and to the relationship with the torn fabrics of historical cities, which re-proposes – in a tangible coexistence – the conflict between tradition and modernity. Once again, Salvatore Vitale gave voice to this topic, publishing *Attualità dell'Architettura. Ricostruzione urbanistica e composizione spaziale* again with Laterza in 1947, partly recalling articles that had already appeared in *La nuova città*, the magazine founded by Michelucci in 1945. Recognizing the recent lesson of organic architecture, Vitale dissociated himself from the 'excesses of rationalism' in favour of a 'humanized' architecture that was more sensitive to its inclusion in the urban as well as social context and warned against the uniformity of cosmopolitanism and the anxiety for innovation at any cost, expressing the desire for greater proximity to local conditions and cultures. In addition, he criticized the principle of a single national identity and inflected the topic of tradition into the plural, trying to join the spirit of individual communities: in Italy, "architecture has had such a prolific vitality in past centuries that, actually, more than a single

---

44 "Il nostro modernismo [...] si riattacca a tutta l'evoluzione della nostra architettura e rispecchia l'indole e le tradizioni regionali"

45 "Gli sforzi delle varie regioni dovranno incanalarsi su di un'unica via, e gli architetti affiatarsi maggiormente per giungere alla creazione di un'arte moderna nazionale."

46 "Vogliamo un'architettura moderna e italiana".

47 "[...] si tratta di liberarci di questo tossico mortale che è l'*internazionalismo*" (emphasis in original).

tradition, we can and must speak about various traditions that have brightly developed around the great centres of the peninsula", expressed in "those great regional currents that had, each of them, their own independent development, kept alive and operative, with their characteristic appearance, up to our days". There is no shortage of operational ideas:

the regional architecture that was born from the more or less conscious adaptation to the environment provides limitless models that could be taken up today, with undeniable benefit, because they still respond, in a fitting way, to the spirit of the new architecture and they display very successful solutions to some particular problems about which it labours. (Lenza 2010b: 210; Vitale 1947)[48]

Undoubtedly, "our very rich treasure of forms today makes the dialectic game, through which the synthesis between past and present can be made more difficult and complicated"; however,

it will be this full heritage of traditions, with its great variety of such rich and different reasons and themes, with its wide possibility of being enlivened by new aesthetic experiences and modern construction methods, that tomorrow will give Italy the ability to distinguish its own architecture in an original way and, perhaps, the pride to create a truly new style, as the first in Europe (ibid: 211-212).[49]

---

48 "[...] in Italia, [...] l'architettura ha avuto nei secoli passati una vitalità così feconda che in realtà, più che di tradizione unica si può e si deve parlare di varie tradizioni che si sono luminosamente sviluppate attorno ai grandi centri della penisola. L'unità nazionale dello stile architettonico inizia, da noi, assai tardi, soltanto col Bramante, ma, anche dopo, questa unità ha continuato a rifrangersi di diversi colori, come un prisma, riflettendosi in quelle grandi correnti regionali che hanno avuto, ciascuna, un proprio sviluppo autonomo e si sono mantenute vive ed operanti, col loro aspetto caratteristico, fino ai nostri giorni. [...] l'architettura regionale, nata dall'adattamento più o meno consapevole all'ambiente, presenta infiniti modelli che potrebbero essere ripresi, oggi, con innegabile utilità, poiché rispondono ancora, in modo congeniale, allo spirito della nuova architettura e presentano soluzioni felicissime di alcuni problemi particolari intorno a cui essa si affatica."

49 "[...] è stato proprio questo nostro ricchissimo tesoro di forme che ha servito finora da freno, col suo provvidenziale richiamo alla tradizione, all'affermarsi in Italia di una architettura eccessivamente spregiudicata ed estremista, ma è anche esso che rende, oggi, più difficile e complicato il giuoco dialettico attraverso cui si potrà realizzare la sintesi tra passato e presente [...]. E sarà, perciò, questo dovizioso patrimonio di

This attempt to widen the restricted formal dictionary of rationalism was misunderstood in an anti-modern way by Bruno Zevi, who, in his harsh review published in *Metron*, accused Vitale of embodying "one of many quick-change intellectuals who believe they serve culture with these vague norms that help to kill or blur every living course, justifying all compromises, all stylistic cocktails" (1948: 77).[50] Vitale replied with a passionate letter, which was again published in *Metron* with Zevi's rejoinder, and was also sent to Vincenzo Fasolo and Giovanni Michelucci, from whom Vitale hoped to obtain clear support.

However, to redeem those themes that, with some ambiguity, Vitale had tried to reintroduce, Ernesto Nathan Rogers intervened with much more effectiveness. It is thanks to Rogers that ongoing attention has been given to tradition (cf. Lenza 2010c, 2014), from his early article in *L'Ambrosiano* in 1938, where he declared it as a third way, in contrast to both rationalism and culturalism, specifying: "Tradition is neither the arch nor the capital, neither the horizontal nor the vertical, but it is the way of understanding all of these means in their meaning of essence" (1997 [1938]: 39),[51] up to his book of 1961, *Gli elementi del fenomeno architettonico*, in which the last chapters are dedicated to "L'elemento della tradizione" and to the "Nuovo significato di 'tradizione'". Between the two, there is the successful 1953-54 season of *Casabella*, not by chance entitled "Continuità": here Rogers defined "historical consciousness; that is the true essence of tradition [...] Dynamic continuation and not a passive recopying" (Rogers 1997 [1953-1954]: 93),[52] and recalled the "responsibility towards tradition" and the necessary relationship between contemporaneity and environmental pre-existences. Continuity, and therefore history; responsibility, and therefore ethics; the relationship with the culture of the place, and therefore identity: everything converges in Rogers, and, purified of ideological incrustations as well as protected from formalistic drifts, tradition reaches its most authentic dimension.

---

    tradizioni, colla sua grande varietà di motivi e di temi così ricchi e diversi, [...] che potrà dare, domani, all'Italia la capacità di distinguere in modo originale la propria architettura e, forse, il vanto di creare essa, per la prima in Europa, uno stile veramente nuovo."

50 "uno degli infiniti trasformisti che credono di servire la cultura con queste precettistiche vaghe che servono a uccidere o a sfocare ogni indirizzo vivo e a giustificare tutti i compromessi, tutti i cocktails stilistici."

51 "la tradizione non è [...] né l'arco né il capitello, né l'orizzontale né la verticale, ma è il modo d'intendere tutti questi mezzi nel loro significato di essenza."

52 "*Continuità* [...] significa coscienza storica; cioè la vera essenza della tradizione [...] Dinamico proseguimento e non passiva ricopiatura." (Emphasis in original)

REFERENCES

Atti del I Congresso Nazionale di Storia dell'Architettura. 29-31 ottobre 1936-XV (1938), Firenze: Sansoni.

Belli, Carlo (1959?): "Origini e sviluppi del 'Gruppo 7'". In: La Casa: Quaderni di architettura e di critica 6, pp. 176-197.

Belli, Carlo (1992): Interlogo: Cultura italiana tra due guerre, Milano: Sapiens.

Benedetti, Sandro (2005): "Marcello Piacentini: Tradizione e/o 'altra' modernità." In: Paolo Bertozzi /Agnese Ghini/Luca Guardigli (eds.), Le forme della tradizione in architettura: Esperienze a confronto, Milano: Franco Angeli, pp. 428-442.

Brunetti, Fabrizio (1998 [1993]): Architetti e Fascismo, Firenze: Alinea.

Cennamo, Michele (ed.) (1976): Materiali per l'analisi dell'architettura moderna: Il M.I.A.R., Napoli: SEN.

Danesi, Silvia (1976): "Aporie dell'architettura italiana in periodo fascista: Mediterraneità e purismo". In: Silvia Danesi/Luciano Patetta (eds.), Il razionalismo e l'architettura in Italia durante il fascismo, Milano: Electa, pp. 21-28.

Gentile, Giovanni (1936): La tradizione italiana, Firenze: Sansoni.

Giovannoni, Gustavo (1913): "Il 'diradamento' edilizio dei vecchi centri. Il quartiere della Rinascenza in Roma". In: Nuova Antologia, 48/997, pp. 53-76.

Giovannoni, Gustavo (1918): "Sul significato della parola 'prospettiva' usata nella legge sulla conservazione dei monumenti", Roma: Calzone.

Giovannoni, Gustavo (1925): Questioni di architettura nella storia e nella vita: Edilizia, estetica architettonica, restauri, ambiente dei monumenti, Roma: Soc.ed. d'arte illustrata.

Giovannoni, Gustavo (1929): "Architettura". In: Enciclopedia Italiana di Scienze, Lettere ed Arti, Roma: Istituto dell'Enciclopedia Italiana Giovanni Treccani, *s.v.*

Giovannoni, Gustavo (1931): "Problemi attuali dell'architettura italiana". In: Nuova Antologia, LXVI/1425, pp. 325-342.

Il Gruppo "7" [Ubaldo Castagnoli/Luigi Figini/Guido Frette/Sebastiano Larco/ Gino Pollini/Carlo Enrico Rava/Giuseppe Terragni] (1926): "Architettura". In: Rassegna italiana politica letteraria e artistica, XVIII/CIII, pp. 849-852.

Il Gruppo 7 (1927a): "Architettura (II): Gli stranieri". In: Rassegna italiana politica letteraria e artistica, XIX/CV, pp. 129-137.

Il Gruppo "7" (1927b): "Architettura (III): Impreparazione – Incomprensione – Pregiudizi". In: Rassegna italiana politica letteraria e artistica, XIX/CVI, pp. 247-252.

Il Gruppo 7 (1927c): "Architettura (IV): Una nuova epoca arcaica". In: Rassegna italiana politica letteraria e artistica, IX/CVIII, pp. 468-472.
Lenza, Cettina (2010a): "Introduzione". In: Cettina Lenza, Salvatore Vitale: L'estetica dell'architettura e altri scritti. Bologna: Compositori. pp. 15-76.
Lenza, Cettina (ed.) (2010b): Salvatore Vitale: L'estetica dell'architettura e altri scritti, Bologna: Compositori.
Lenza, Cettina (2010c): "Il nodo della tradizione". In: Anna Giannetti/Luca Molinari, Continuità e crisi: Ernesto Nathan Rogers e la cultura architettonica italiana del secondo dopoguerra, Firenze: Alinea, pp. 3-13.
Lenza, Cettina (2014): "Rogers, il progetto moderno e i termini incerti della teoria". In: Andrea Maglio, La traccia e la memoria: Tradizione e continuità, Napoli: Istituto Italiano per gli Studi Filosofici, pp. 205-230.
Michelucci, Giovanni (1932a): "Contatti fra architetture antiche e moderne". In: Domus: L'arte nella casa V/51, pp. 134-136.
Michelucci, Giovanni (1932b): "Fonti della moderna architettura italiana". In: Domus: L'arte nella casa, V/56, pp. 460-461.
Muzio, Giovanni (1921): "L'architettura a Milano intorno all'ottocento". In: Emporium LIII/317, pp. 241-258.
Nezi, Antonio (1930): "Artisti contemporanei accademici d'Italia: Marcello Piacentini". In: Emporium LXXI/422, pp. 83-108.
Pane, Andrea (2007): "Il vecchio e il nuovo nelle città italiane: Gustavo Giovannoni e l'architettura moderna". In: Alberto Ferlenga/Eugenio Vassallo/Francesca Schellino (eds.): Antico e Nuovo. Architetture e architettura, Padova: Il Poligrafo, pp. 215-231.
Persico, Edoardo (1934): "Punto ed a capo per l'architettura." In. Domus: L'arte nella casa, VII/83, pp. 1-9.
Piacentini, Marcello (1928): "Prima internazionale architettonica". In: Architettura e arti decorative VII/12, pp. 544-562.
Piacentini, Marcello (1930): Architettura d'oggi, Roma: Paolo Cremonese.
Piacentini, Marcello (1933): "Gli archi, le colonne e l'italianità di oggi: Marcello Piacentini risponde a Ugo Ojetti". In: La Tribuna 2 febbraio 1933, p. 3.
Piacentini, Marcello (1939): "Evoluzione architettonica". In: Le Arti 1/3, pp. 239-240 and plates.
Pigafetta, Giorgio/Abbondandolo, Ilaria/Trisciuoglio, Marco (2002 [1997]): Architettura tradizionalista: Architetti, opere, teorie, Milano: Jaca Book.
Ponti, Gio (1932): "Morte e vita della tradizione". In: Domus: L'arte nella casa V/51, p. 133.

Rava, Carlo Enrico (1931a): "Panorama del razionalismo: Svolta pericolosa; Situazione dell'Italia di fronte al razionalismo europeo". In: Domus: L'arte nella casa, IV/37, pp. 39-44.

Rava, Carlo Enrico (1931b): "Specchio dell'architettura razionale: VI. Conclusione". In: Domus: L'arte nella casa IV/47, pp. 34-40.

Rogers, Ernesto Nathan (1938): "Un architetto di quasi trent'anni". In: L'Ambrosiano 15 July 1938, XVII/167, p. 5.

Rogers, Ernesto Nathan (1953-1954): "Continuità". In: Casabella-continuità 199, pp. 2-3.

Rogers, Ernesto Nathan (1997): Esperienza dell'architettura, ed. Luca Molinari, Milano: Skira.

Veronesi, Giulia ed. (1964): Edoardo Persico: Tutte le opere, 1923-1935, Milano: Edizioni di Comunità.

Vitale, Salvatore (1926): "Elogio dell'architettura". In: Rivista d'Italia XXIX/1, pp. 32-56.

Vitale, Salvatore (1928): L'estetica dell'architettura: Saggio sullo sviluppo dello Spirito costruttivo, Bari: Laterza.

Vitale, Salvatore (1947): Attualità dell'architettura: Ricostruzione urbanistica e composizione spaziale, Bari: Laterza.

Zevi, Bruno (1948): Review to Salvatore Vitale: "Attualità dell'Architettura", Laterza, 1947. In: Metron 26-27, p. 77.

Zucconi, Guido ed. (1997): Gustavo Giovannoni: Dal capitello alla città, Milano: Jaca Book.

Urban Transformations

Transformations in Architectural and Urban Culture in the Sant'Ambrogio Area of Milan between the World Wars

Cecilia De Carli

In the 1920s and 1930s in Milan, the area surrounding the Basilica di Sant'Ambrogio witnessed a profound transformation, with even greater implications for urbanism than for architecture. The *Bando di concorso per lo studio di un progetto di piano regolatore e d'ampliamento per la Città di Milano*, which was promoted by the City Council in 1926 on the initiative of Cesare Albertini (1874-1951), then head of the Ufficio Tecnico, appeared to announce a competition for ideas. On the day of the deadline for the tender, April 21, 1927, twenty-four projects had been presented. Doubtless they demonstrate the way the (prevalently Milanese) architects and engineers applied their culture to the urban phenomenon and the planning of its future (Portaluppi/Semenza 1927; "Forma Urbis Mediolani" [1927]; Alpago Novello/De Finetti/Muzio 1930; Albertini 1931, 1934. Bibliography: Reggiori 1947; De Finetti 1969; Franchi/Chiumeo 1972; Grandi/Pracchi 1980; Vercelloni 1988; Ciucci 1989; Vercelloni/Rumi/Cova 1994).

The first prize was awarded to the project submitted by the architect Piero Portaluppi (1888-1967), a bold and eclectic experimenter, who had collaborated with the architect Marco Semenza. The second prize was awarded to a group of enthusiastic architects who for over five years had identified with the Novecento movement, which aimed for the same "return to order" that characterized the European art scene in the period between the World Wars and which mostly meant a return to humble crafts.

This second project resulted from the collaboration of Giovanni Muzio (1893-1982) and the Club degli Architetti-Urbanisti, which included Alberto Alpago Novello (1889-1985), Giuseppe De Finetti (1892-1952), Tomaso Buzzi (1900-81), Ottavio Cabiati (1889-1956), Guido Ferrazza (1887-1961), Ambrogio Gadola

(1888-1971), Emilio Lancia (1890-1973), Michele Marelli, Alessandro Minali (1888-1960), Piero Palumbo, Gio Ponti (1891-1979) and Ferdinando Reggiori (1898-1976). Their motto was "Forma urbis Mediolani", and they were influenced by the teachings of Ugo Monneret de Villard (1881-1954) and Gaetano Moretti (1860-1938). Indeed, their plan bore the same heading as a project that had been promoted by the Soprintendenza ai Monumenti and Monneret de Villard himself, whose mission was to reconstruct the plan of Roman and Medieval Milan, by seeking out the historical axes and orientations that were permanently embedded in the city's fabric.

In the area surrounding Sant'Ambrogio, starting in 1924, Muzio was given the opportunity both to work on one of the city's most iconic locations, a place rich in symbols and allusions, and to design the appearance of a new and important institution, the Università Cattolica del Sacro Cuore.

Figure 1: Monumento ai caduti and Università Cattolica, Milano

Photograph: Archivio Muzio, 1930

Between 1924 and 1928, alongside Alpago Novello, Buzzi, Cabiati, and Ponti, Muzio created the Monumento ai Caduti di Milano (Fig. 1) in the area adjacent to the Basilica di Sant'Ambrogio (Piacentini 1925; Reggiori 1927; Cardarelli/Reggiori 1936: 1-10; Irace 1994; Massarini 2005), placing it along the axis on which he would subsequently align the entrance to the Università Cattolica.

The *Coemeterium ad Martyres*, which had been discovered in the Sant'Ambrogio area in the 19th century, provided the ideal justification for Muzio's monument, which drew a connection between the martyrs resting in that ancient burial ground, and the city's World War I martyrs.

The monument's octagonal plan recalls that of the Church of the Holy Sepulchre in Jerusalem, as well as the Paleochristian Mausoleum of Theoderic in Ravenna; both of these buildings belong to the architectural typology from which the octagonal plan of the Ambrosian baptismal font also derived, highlighting the close ties between death and resurrection, and between the death and rebirth of Christ. The Tower of the Winds in Athens, which is thought to date to 50 AD, may constitute an even more ancient precursor.

Even the monument's cladding, polished Musso marble which contrasts with the basilica's brickwork, appears to suggest the concept of rebirth with its white luminescence. Moreover, the same material was also used for the Columns of San Lorenzo, so it may also be seen as a reference to Roman craftsmanship. The memorial's octagonal tower includes a portico in its lower section: the eight arches, whose number alludes to the city's eight gates (Ticinese, Tosa, Comasina, Orientale, Nuova, Vercellina, Giovia, and Romana), are adorned with friezes, architraves, and tympana topped with pine-cones, symbolizing eternity. Each arch corresponds to an internal niche; the one at the center is dedicated to Milan's patron saint, Ambrose, whose presence is invoked by a majestic, 16-foot bronze statue created by Adolfo Wildt (1868-1931). The third entrance is dedicated to the Venezia Tridentina region: Antonio Maiocchi's marble sculptures depict the liberated cities (Trento, Rovereto, Riva, Bressanone, Merano, and Bolzano) and Silvio Zaniboni's salamander symbolizes the sacred fire.

Above the portico section, the octagon's diameter decreases, and its exterior is adorned with Salvatore Saponaro's Neoclassical friezes depicting a sequence of windows and winged victories in flight. The memorial is then crowned by a cone-shaped roof, topped by a lantern. Inside, twisting around an imposing central column, a spiral staircase of striking beauty and plasticity leads to the Sala dei Cimeli and the Famedio. Its ascending movement is enhanced by mosaic semi-columns and niches depicting cistae alluding to Romano-Hellenistic classicism. The monument is surrounded by a twenty-three-foot gate with railings designed by Alessandro Mazzucotelli (1865-1938), leaving enough space for a large courtyard at the front. This courtyard was meant to display two equestrian sculpture groups by Libero Andreotti, and indeed the plaster maquette for one of these was present at the inauguration held on November 4, 1928, on the occasion of the tenth anniversary of the war victory. However, neither was ever made into its final bronze version.

Though the construction of the Monumento ai Caduti constitutes a significant chapter in the transformation of the area surrounding Sant'Ambrogio, the work that led to the transformation of the convent of Sant'Ambrogio into the seat of the

Università Cattolica was an even grander and more important event. During the Napoleonic era, the convent had been turned into a military hospital, but the Royal Decree of September 10, 1923 established that state property that did not properly fulfill this function could be offered in exchange. The Università Cattolica thus made the request to purchase the building in order to use it as its headquarters.

It was here that Father Agostino Gemelli (1878-1959), who had been a physician alongside Ludovico Necchi (1876-1930) in the military hospital before joining the Church and becoming a Franciscan, found the *genius loci* that embodied his plan: to reintegrate the Catholic world into public life by demonstrating the Church's capacity for stimulating cultural discourse, as it had when the stones of the ancient Ambrosian monastery were first assembled.

Gemelli evidently saw the establishment of the Università Cattolica in the same site as the ancient monastery as an event whose significance transcended that of the university itself. Likewise, the work Muzio carried out (with the assistance of the engineer Pierfausto Barelli) to convert the monastery into a university constituted a testing ground for the advancement of an approach to urban architecture whose lofty aim was to restore the entire discipline of architecture to its institutional duties. Giovanni Muzio joined the firm of Pierfausto Barelli (1887-1963) and Vittorino Colonnese as a draftsman at the same time that they began planning the famous Ca' Brütta on the corner between Via Moscova and Via Principe Umberto, now Via Turati (1919). Father Gemelli had already requested the intervention of the Barelli-Colonnese firm for the building in Via Sant'Agnese, the first seat of the Università Cattolica del Sacro Cuore between 1920 and 1921. Given the challenge to provide a new institution with a physical venue, Muzio deeply intuited its civil and religious significance, and, facing the prospect of intervening in a building designed by Donato Bramante (1444-1514) himself, reflected on whether it made any sense to return to the past, and whether it was possible or even opportune to restore classicism in a manner that was not pure mimicry.

The works to convert the monastery of Sant'Ambrogio into the seat of the Università Cattolica lasted from 1928 to 1949.

This was no small challenge for the young architect, as it meant intervening in the most famous example of a Romanesque basilica in Lombardy; extraordinary and extensive competence were required, and many problems would undoubtedly arise.

Muzio's idea was, first and foremost, to arrange the entire structure around Bramante's cloisters, which would therefore function as the core of the complex, as he explained at a conference held in Venice in 1932:

Here, two cloisters, identical squares measuring sixty meters on each side, one Doric, the other Ionic [...]. The whole fabric, including its porticos, corridors, and halls, is symmetrical, perfect, and very grand; it was completed in the eighteenth century, but the way it was planned and laid down was so perfect and well thought out that all those who were put in charge of the work had no choice but to faithfully follow the original directives.[1]

According to Muzio's interpretation, the original monument provided the rule; and indeed, the entrance to the new university building coincides exactly with the axis of the Doric cloister, thus creating a telescopic effect that guides the viewer toward an ideal understanding of the building's spatial order. However, Muzio's project did not solely focus on the restoration of the cloisters and associated structures. What makes his interventions interesting is the way they relate to the construction of the university complex itself: from the creation of an entrance building by demolishing two houses on the same site, which in turn led to the construction of a whole system of buildings (chapel, library, assembly hall, boarding houses, and classrooms) through a sequence of operations that followed different but related rationales. The project therefore involved restorations, transformations, juxtapositions, additions, completions, and new constructions. Together, these actions aimed at the reconstruction of a fabric; the re-composition of a fragment of city elevated by an ideal; the production of an university campus *ante litteram*; and the recreation of that "civil magnificence" that was as admired as it was welcoming of experimentation.

The project for the fabric began with the demolition of the two houses at 7 and 9 Piazza Sant'Ambrogio (now Largo Gemelli), and the reconstruction of the residential and office building in line with the Via Santa Valeria, at a distance of 20 meters from the Caserna Garibaldi standing opposite, so as to clear the view onto Sant'Ambrogio's apse. Characterized by a double architectural order whose module is a free-standing arch flanked by pilasters within which the windows are neatly arranged, the new building is completely clad with exposed bricks – a choice that derives in part from the nearby presence of the basilica, in part from Muzio's wish to differentiate the new interventions from the 16th-century

---

[1] "Qui due chiostri quadrati uguali di sessanta metri di lato, l'uno dorico e l'altro jonico [...]. Tutta la fabbrica nel giro dei portici, dei corridoi, delle sale è simmetrica, perfetta e grandiosissima: continuò a completarsi sino nel '700, ma l'impostazione e il tracciato erano così perfetti e congegnati che tutti i continuatori ne dovettero seguire strettamente le direttive." Muzio, Giovanni: 1932. "Architetti e architetture in Lombardia," p. 9. This is a pamphlet that includes the text Muzio presented at a conference held in Venice in 1932; it may be accessed in the Archivio Muzio in Milan.

plasterwork, and not least from the bricks' cohesiveness in relation to the reinforced concrete that composed the building's structural frame. Inside the building, in contrast to the rigor of its exterior brickwork, the grand entrance is made of white granite; it is also dis-symmetrical with respect to the building, being placed on the axis of the Doric cloister located beyond it, which connects to it through an open brick portico. Placed above the entrance, which is flanked by four columns, we find the balcony, the central niche featuring a tympanum and framing the bronze sculpture of Christ the King, the step tower that bears the name of the university, the clock, and the aedicula for the bell. The dominant positioning of the sculpture, which is the work of Giannino Castiglioni (1884-1971), makes a decisive contribution to the architecture's composition and volumetry, and functions as a companion piece of Adolfo Wildt's statue of Saint Ambrose in the Monumento ai Caduti.

Within the transitional landscape that began to emerge from these interventions, I would like to note two key aspects of Muzio's work: the restoration of the cloister, which included the liberation of the arches from the obstructions added when the monastery was converted to a military hospital; and the transformation of the entrance on the ancient monastery's facade, which was not suited to the soon-to-be university. Specifically, Muzio had the ancient entryway incorporated into the side of the chapel of the Sacred Heart. In some way, then, its function as an entryway was preserved, but, in its almost surgical transplant into the body of the chapel, it can also be said to have been sacralized, providing the new structure with an alternative pathway for processions.

Between 1933 and 1934, in order to implement Gemelli's idea of making the university into a small citadel of learning even for those who came from afar, Muzio created its men's boarding houses immediately to the east of the entrance building, on the other side of the street that would eventually become Via Ludovico Necchi (Reggiori 1935; Cardarelli/Reggiori 1936: 39-44). The Augustinianum boarding house featured 100 rooms for lay students, while the Ludovicianum offered fifty rooms for clerical students; thus while their facades and height were the same, the two buildings differed in depth. The two long buildings, both placed in the interior of the block and oriented perpendicular to the street, meet in a lower structure that overlooks it. This lower structure's sequence of arches and its exposed brick cladding echo the language of the monastery complex opposite, while the boarding houses, rectangular blocks divided into five levels, express a more rationalistic architectural language that is the logical consequence of the practical function they must fulfill.

In April 1938, having completed the design of the men's boarding houses, Muzio began his work on the women's boarding house, the Marianum, on the corner of the Via Santa Valeria and the Via Ludovico Necchi. Construction began in April 1938, and the building was inaugurated on November 22 of the same year, the Feast Day of Santa Cecilia. The five-level structure, whose longer side overlooks the Via Ludovico Necchi and continues the line of the facade of the Augustinianum-Ludovicianum before twisting into an "L" shape onto Via Santa Valeria, is an important element in the backdrop to the university's entrance building and the monumental Neoclassical complex of the Caserna Garibaldi. The building is predominantly Rationalist in style. The choice of materials, the arrangement of the spaces and their relation to each other, and in particular the use of concrete-framed glass panels for the stairwell at the center of the structure, demonstrate the freedom of the architect's 'linguistic' choices, which took into account all available factors in a constant redefinition that included contemporary ideas.

Proceeding through the architectural landscape of Sant'Ambrogio along the Via Santa Valeria, a further new element in the transformation process comes into view: the seat of the Società Filatura Cascami Seta (Fig. 2), designed and realized by the architect Piero Portaluppi between 1920 and 1924. Portaluppi was one of the most emblematic figures defining the cultural climate that characterized the period between the World Wars. A student of Gaetano Moretti, he was in touch with Camillo Boito (1836-1914), Luca Beltrami (1854-1933), Aldo Andreani (1887-1971), and Ludovico Pogliaghi (1857-1950), and he rapidly acquired significant professional and academic standing. He began teaching at the Politecnico Composizione Architettonica in 1935, and served as the dean of the faculty from 1939 to 1963.

Portaluppi's deconstruction of traditional canons, along with his propensity to experiment and to cross-pollinate distinct architectural languages even as he researched past styles, find parallels in the work of Alessandro Sidoli (1812-1855), who, like Portaluppi, also re-evoked Art Deco in his approach.

In a way, the seat of the Società Cascami Seta can be seen as a symbolic stand-in for the textiles it produces. As in his other industrial projects, Portaluppi did not conceive of the workplace as a functional factory in a modern sense, as architects would begin to do just a few years later; rather, he thought of it as a place for reception and habitation. The building, which Portaluppi designed to abut the pre-existing Palazzo Cornaggia and take over its demolished section (once used as stables and storage sheds), presents an ingenuous solution to the terrain's irregularity: specifically, the entire building is structured around the pentagonal reception area, a remarkably effective space from which the corridors leading to the various offices branch off. The facade's classical partitioning, which is both symmetrical and harmonious, is enhanced by an Art-Deco-style ornamentation that tones down the facade's more grandiloquent features. The sense of movement that emerges on the facade through decorations in artistic concrete on Ceppo di Brembate cladding continues into the curvilinear motif of the iron railings, and, inside the building, in the balcony that opens on the double space of the atrium. The combination of these solutions and decorations make this building a miniature masterpiece (Colombo 2003: 18).[2]

Figure 2: Seat of the Società Filatura Cascami Seta, Via Santa Valeria, Milano

Photograph: Archivio Storico Università Cattolica

---

2   For archival sources and biographical information relevant to the architect cf. *Piero Portaluppi: Linea errante nell'architettura del Novecento*, exhibition catalogue, Triennale di Milano, September 19, 2003-January 4, 2004, Milan: Skira.

Proceeding onto the Via Nirone, another structure is encountered that fits nicely within the context sketched so far: it is the Casa Federale del Fascio di Milano (1926-1927), designed by the architect Paolo Mezzanotte (1878-1969). Mezzanotte was a member of the upper crust of society living in the heart of Milan. He studied at the Politecnico, specifically at the Istituto Superiore di Ingegneria, and was awarded the title of architect in 1928, after designing buildings of great importance. He was also appointed to a number of public roles: for example, he was a member of the Commissione per lo Studio del *Piano Regolatore* (1925), and contributed to the Reale Commissione dei Monumenti e Scavi for the Province of Milan (1959).

Figure 3: Casa del fascio, Via Nirone, Milano

Photograph: "Corriere Architettonico", 1927

The Palazzo dei Fasci on the Via Nirone (1926-27) (Fig. 3),[3] which Mezzanotte (Mezzanotte 2015: 95) completed the year before he began work on his most

---

3   More generally, cf. also Portoghesi/Mangione/Soffitta 2006.

famous building, Milan's Palazzo della Borsa, marked the moment when he transitioned from 18th-century-inspired forms to a *longue durée* architecture that, when combined with classical forms, became a metaphor for immutability in the face of the passing of time, not unlike in Muzio's work. Indeed, like Muzio, Mezzanotte demonstrated great wisdom in his choice of material combinations: travertine from Serra di Rapolano (near Siena) alongside granite from Ornavasso and pale bricks from the area near Voghera. Together, these materials established the building as belonging to the same tradition as the Lombard Romanesque; at the same time they aligned it with the Viennese School and the work of Otto Wagner (1841-1918), who advanced modern architecture with his Proto-Rationalist elements and his choice of materials, which Loos would later inherit.

The decorations enhance the elegance of the facade, which is framed by travertine pilasters and articulated by a pediment and niches. The lateral pilasters, which are decorated with obelisks rising above symbolic depictions of weapons and *fasci*, soften the austerity of the brickwork; familiar symbolic motifs are also incorporated into the Palladiana flooring on the ground floor. The latter was made to resemble a large carpet with varied and unobtrusive patterns, not unlike those found in Pompeii. Imagery from ancient mythology such as weapons, the hippocampus, and the eagle, all symbols that have taken on different meanings in different eras, cultures, and contexts, together constitute an iconographic system that resonates with the work of the engraver, etcher, and architect Giovanni Battista Piranesi.

A final example is Gino Chierici's restoration of the Pusterla di Sant'Ambrogio (1938-40) (Amore 2011), another significant instance of the many possible (and often surprising) ways in which ancient and contemporary architecture could be combined. As described by De Angeli d'Ossat, Gino Chierici (1877-1961) was "the most active and admired restorer of his time. His luminous and energetic actions were characterized by clarity of concept, initiative, and scrupolous rectitude, wherever he was called to carry out his duties" (1961). In late 1919, Chierici assumed the directorship the Soprintendenza ai Monumenti di Siena e Grosseto, and, from 1924 onwards, that of the Reale Soprintendenza all'Arte Medioevale e Moderna della Campania; his responsibilities included the preservation of artistic and monumental heritage, the protection of areas of natural beauty, the supervision of works of art housed in private collections, setting guidelines for exhibition galleries, and the compilation of inventories and catalogues of art objects.

Between 1920 and 1959, Chierici published dozens of books, articles, and conference presentations. He used many of these documents as critical reports on his restoration interventions, but some of them were essays on the history of architecture, inspired by his own studies and the discoveries he made during some of his restoration projects. He was active at the time of the publication of the *Athens Charter for the Restoration of Historic Monuments* – the seven-point manifesto adopted at the First International Congress of Architects and Technicians of Historic Monuments in Athens in 1931 – as well as the corresponding *Italian Charter* (1931) and the *Instructions* (1942), up until the 1950s.

In 1935 Chierici came to Milan, where he had the opportunity to work on several important restoration projects, most notably those performed on the San Lorenzo complex, the western facade of the Palazzo Reale, and the churches of Santa Maria delle Grazie and Santa Maria Maggiore a Lomello.

In the fall of 1937, demolition works meant to free up the area surrounding Sant'Ambrogio led to the discovery of the remains of the Pusterla di Sant'Ambrogio, which once marked the entry to the city from the street then known as Via San Vittore. Before this discovery, the only part of the Pusterla that was still standing was the medieval tower that the previous superintendent, Ettore Modigliani, had already decided to free of its surrounding accretions (Reggiori 1938). In January 1938, Chierici notified the Ministry of National Education of the discovery, adding that the Comitato per l'Archeologia e l'Arte in Lombardia, headed by the senator Giuseppe De Capitani d'Arzago (1870-1945), would support the Pusterla's restoration. This in fact took place, and Education Minister Giuseppe Bottai (1895-1959) became involved as well, directly requesting that Chierici go ahead with the project.

In his project report, Chierici wrote:

Planned restoration works include: the reconstruction of part of the left-side tower, so that it may reach the height of the gate; the restoration of the pillars and arches, making partial use of original architectural materials that were recovered through excavations; the cleaning and repair of the exterior ornamentation; and the reconstruction of the right-side tower. Throughout the project, the utmost respect shall be shown for the original components of this great monument. Wherever additions may be necessary to restore some of the gate's essential lines, bricks of a yellowish tint shall be used, in order to make clear the distinction between the original components and the ones that have been reconstructed. (Chierici 1940: 12)

Chierici favored an ideal re-composition of the volume (Fig. 4), even going so far as to place, over the arches, a tabernacle that dated to the same era as the tower and that had been offered to the city by Javotte Bocconi (editor's note: between

1932 and 1957, president of the Università Commerciale Luigi Bocconi). He defended this decision in the following way:

[A]ll of the city gates had similar tabernacles [...] With respect to restoration, we are accustomed to proceeding with the utmost circumspection, and we oppose the 'picturesque' and the 'decorative' when they are achieved through artifice. In this specific case, having concluded that there were as many arguments in favor as there were against, we have added the tabernacle, at least on a trial basis, also in consideration of the fact that it appears to date to the same era, or thereabouts, as the Pusterla, and that in any case it would be placed on the reconstructed part, whose modernity is clear to see [...] A marble inscription inside the tabernacle informs the scholar as to its provenance, as well as the date of the new construction. (Chierici 1940: 20)

Figure 4: Pusterla di Sant'Ambrogio, Milano

Photograph: Giovanni Dall'Orto, 2007

CONCLUSION

The architectural and urban landscape surrounding one of Milan's most ancient monuments is an exemplary microcosm of the transformations that characterized Italian cities in the period between the World Wars. Within it, a number of factors converge that characterize the Novecento movement, the principles of which were transferred from the figurative arts to architecture. The architects' goal was to reconnect the ancient and the modern, and thus to breathe new life into heritage and tradition. Their buildings (a war memorial, the seat of a university, a place of learning and research, the cloisters of an ancient monastery, a place of industry, a space for the Fascist Party to gather and represent itself, and a restored medieval gate) all made vital contributions to society; they also fall along a spectrum of urban solutions, creating a context that is clearly readable with regard to its strengths and weaknesses, and its real and ideal representation.

REFERENCES

Albertini, Cesare (1931): Il Piano regolatore del centro di Milano per la zona a sud, est e nord-est di Piazza del Duomo, Milan.

Albertini, Cesare (1934): Relazione sul progetto di Piano regolatore approvato con legge 19 febbraio 1934, Milan.

Alpago Novello, Alberto/De Finetti, Giuseppe/Muzio, Giovanni (eds.) (1930): Memorie sui progetti per il Piano regolatore di Milano-1928-1929, Milan: Libreria Editrice degli Omenoni.

Amore, Raffaele (2011): Gino Chierici: Tra teorie e prassi del restauro, Naples and Rome: Edizioni Scientifiche Italiane.

Cardarelli, Vincenzo/Reggiori, Ferdinando (1936): Architetture di Giovanni Muzio, Milan and Geneva: Collezione I Grandi Architetti.

Chierici Gino (1940): La pusterla di S. Ambrogio, Comitato per l'archeologia e l'arte lombarda: Milano.

Ciucci, Giorgio (1989): Gli architetti e il fascismo: Architettura e città, 1922-1944, Turin: Einaudi.

Colombo, Dario (2003): Sede per la Società Filatura Cascami Seta (entry). In: Luca Molinari/Fondazione Piero Portaluppi (eds.), Piero Portaluppi: Linea errante nell'architettura del Novecento, exhibition catalogue, Triennale di Milano, September 19, 2003 – January 4, 2004, p. 18. Milan: Skira.

De Angelis D'Ossat, Gioacchino (1961): Gino Chierici, Rome: Atti della Accademia Nazionale di San Luca.

De Finetti, Giuseppe (1969): Milano: Costruzione di una città, ed. Gianni Cislaghi, / Mara De Benedetti/ Piergiorgio Marabelli, Milan: Hoepli.

"Forma Urbis Mediolani" [1927] (project report, no date): Milan.

Franchi, Dario/Chiumeo, Rosa (1972): Urbanistica a Milano in regime fascista, Florence: La Nuova Italia.

Giacomini Miari, Erminia/Mero, Elisabetta (eds.) (2018): Milano attraverso le stampe: I disegni e i graffiti di un architetto del Novecento, exhibition catalogue, Spazio San Celso May 16 – June 6, 2018, Bergamo: SEC.

Grandi, Maurizio/Pracchi, Attilio (1980): Milano: Guida all'architettura moderna, Bologna: Zanichelli.

Irace, Fulvio (1994): Giovanni Muzio, 1893-1982: Opere, Milan: Electa, pp. 91ff including bibliographical and archive references.

Massarini, Flavia F. (2005): "Monumento ai Caduti, Milano, 1926-1928." In: Maria Antonietta Crippa/Carlo Capponi (eds.): Gio Ponti e l'architettura sacra: Finestre aperte sulla natura, sul mistero, su Dio, Cinisello Balsamo: Silvana, pp. 192-197.

Mezzanotte, Gianni (2015): "Proposte negli anni venti per un'architettura fascista: Il primo Centro Federale di Milano; La sede di un Gruppo Rionale; Una casa per Balilla." In: Arte lombarda 175/3: pp. 85-116.

Piacentini, Marcello (1925): "Concorso per il Monumento ai caduti di Milano." In: Architettura e arti decorative 4/9: pp. 410-417.

Piacentini, Marcello (1927): "Il concorso nazionale per lo studio di un progetto di piano regolatore e d'ampliamento per la città di Milano." In: Architettura e Arti decorative VII/3-4, pp. 132-182.

Portaluppi, Piero/Semenza, Marco (1927): Milano com'è ora come sarà: Progetto per il Piano Regolatore della Città di Milano, Milan and Rome: Bestetti e Tumminelli.

Portoghesi, Paolo/Mangione, Flavio/Soffitta, Andrea (2006): L'architettura delle Case del Fascio, Florence: Alinea.

Reggiori, Ferdinando (1927): "Il Monumento ai caduti milanesi." In: L'illustrazione italiana 16 (January): pp. 44-46.

Reggiori, Ferdinando (1935): "I 'collegi' dell'Università Cattolica del Sacro Cuore a Milano." In: Architettura 14/6: pp. 321-330.

Reggiori, Ferdinando (1938): La pusterla di S. Ambrogio, Milan: Esperia.

Reggiori, Ferdinando (1947): Milano, 1800-1943: Itinerario Urbanistico-edilizio, Milan: Edizioni del Milione.

Vercelloni, Virgilio (1988): La storia del paesaggio urbano di Milano, Milan: Officina d'Arte Grafica Lucini.

Vercelloni, Virgilio/Rumi, Giorgio/Cova, Alberto (1994): Milano durante il fascismo, 1922-1945, Milan: Amilcare Pizzi.

Transformation and the Vertical City
Milan's Early Skyscrapers

Scott Budzynski

MODERN MILAN

In *Ascolto il tuo cuore, città*, Alberto Savinio (1891-1952) writes, "As a modern city, Milan is a giant school where everything, including streets, shop windows and rubbish bins have a lesson to teach" (Savinio 1984 [1944]: 158; all Savinio translations into English are by the author).[1] The author arrives in Milan from Venice and introduces the city through his "skyscraper", as he calls it. He is hosted by a friend on the tenth floor of one of Milan's new tall buildings at Piazzale Fiume, today Piazza della Repubblica (cf. ibid: 86).[2] The year is 1943, before the devastating bomb attacks of August (cf. ibid: 383). Writer and painter Savinio – nom de plume for Andrea Francesco Alberto de Chirico, brother of Giorgio de Chirico – engages with a city defined by juxtapositions between new and old in which the new city – the world of the skyscraper – is inserted into the preexisting horizontal city. The city is thus simultaneously a "theater of memory" and a "theater of prophecy", to use the terms of the *Collage City* of Colin Rowe and Fred Koetter (1998 [1978]: 144-145). Savinio narrates the urban space as a chain of associations, experiencing the revelry of the new city induced by its symbolic objects, including the skyscraper. He expresses the fantastical space of the vertical city, which takes on an existence separate from the existing one at a time when the city was undergoing transformations under Milan's latest master plan, the 1934

---

1 "Città aggiornata, Milano è una immensa scuola ove tutto, strade, vetrine, cassette per i rifiuti, impartisce lezioni di cose."
2 "Excelsior! Abito al decimo piano."

Piano Albertini. Evocative architectural objects set into the city, the tall constructions gave rise to fantasies of living in unknown worlds, as Savinio expresses:

> The skyscraper has transformed the life of the Milanese. Clandestine activities take place within these vertical cities of which the horizontal city is unaware as it gently extends out onto its plane with its low houses and closed gardens. Strange writings decorate the windows of my skyscraper. As far as the eye can see I read unknown and wonderful words. (Savinio 1984 [1944]: 98)[3]

The writings which Savinio notes are the names of Milanese companies, such as Tecnomasio Italiano Brown Boveri, whose presence attests to the contribution of advertising in forming the new urban dimensionality of tall buildings (cf. ibid: 98). Attached to the facades of high-rises, words would seem to hover in the night sky of the city, creating an urban dreamscape reminiscent of the complicated spatialities of Cubist images.

From the 1930s on, the skyscraper has been an integral part of Milan's urban planning and development and has served as a representation of Milan as a modern city. It has both provided spatial order and served as a container of urban fantasies. Savinio captures the excitement of the new structures in Milan at a point when the city's continuity would soon be challenged by the wartime destruction, which was also repeatedly understood as an opportunity to more fully realize Milan as an ideal modern city. Savinio, too, felt strangely optimistic walking through the ruins of Milan. He addresses the experience of bomb-struck Milan in a postscript, writing: "I sense that a new life will be born from this death. I sense that a city more strong, rich, and beautiful will emerge from these ruins" (ibid: 396).[4]

Although under tragic circumstances, Savinio continues to experience Milan as transformational object. It is an associative space for modern living and through its destruction it holds the possibility of renewal. Understood in the psychoanalytic

---

3 "Il grattacielo ha trasformato la vita dei milanesi. Misteriose attività si svolgono dentro queste città verticali, che la città orizzontale ignorava, dolcemente stesa nella sua pianura, con i suoi palazzotti bassi e i suoi giardini chiusi. Strane iscrizioni istoriano le finestre del mio grattacielo, e fin dove lo sguardo arriva, leggo parole ignote e magnifiche."

4 "Giro tra le rovine di Milano. Perché questa esaltazione in me? Dovrei essere triste, e invece sono formicolante di gioia. Dovrei mulinare pensieri di morte, e invece pensieri di vita mi battono in fronte, come il soffio del più puro e radioso mattino. Perché? Sento che da questa morte nascerà una nuova vita. Sento che da queste rovine sorgerà una città più forte, più ficca, più bella."

object relational terms of Christopher Bollas, transformational objects are largely psychic in that they generate a sense of environment for deeply subjective experiences of the new (cf. 1989: 27-28). The object relational direction in psychoanalysis generally concentrates on the dynamic between internal and external, or between the real and the imagined (cf. Greenberg/Mitchell 1983: 13-14). Savinio's Milan is both real and imagined; an object generating transformational experiences.

EVOKING THE VERTICAL CITY

The city is an object in so far as it is a mentality holding its population together. Yet, no one vision, Bollas states, can become its reality (cf. Bollas 2009: 56). Urban visions are evoked by the associative power of the city's buildings (cf. ibid).[5] Alberto Savinio experiences the space of the new city as it is evoked by skyscrapers. The vision facilitated by a new vertical scale in large cities developed in the nineteenth century. As Roland Barthes explains, the Eiffel Tower in particular gave a form to the way the city was both seen and imagined by the public: "[...] to perceive Paris from above is infallibly to image a history [...]" (Barthes 1997 [1979]: 11). Seen from above, a city can be composed into a bird's-eye perspective. Urban monuments can be recognized and ordered by the gaze from above. Fantasies of perspective can also be imagined when tall structures are seen from below. They represent new views onto the city for a public, who may never actually experience them from that height. In addition, towering buildings also create new points of reference within the city, often impossible to overlook. Guy de Maupassant often ate lunch at the Eiffel Tower, as Barthes relates, because it was the only place in Paris, where he didn't have to see the tower (cf. ibid: 3). It introduced a new dimension into the cityscape, creating a man-made curiosity, or urban myth, comparable to forms of nature, such as mountains and rivers, to define the urban landscape (cf. ibid: 8).

In this sense, skyscrapers are particularly strong evocative objects with the potential to affect transformation. Evocative objects, as understood by Christopher Bollas, speak of a sense of fantastical anticipation, or a meeting of objects of desire and those of reality (cf. 2009: 92). Evocative architecture is highly medial, its mediation forming sensibilities for the new. Particularly evocative objects, such as

---

5 "When evocative structures are built they will give rise to intense associations in the population."

visionary architecture, strike up feelings of revelry, which Bollas refers to as a type of dreaming:

> Visionary architects intend their structures to suggest dreams to their dwellers, but I shall maintain that all along we know that vivid structures will enter our dreams and affect our dream life. Indeed we might say that just as perspective in fine art was achieved through the architectural effects of Renaissance architecture (the extraordinary influence of Brunelleschi), our dream life is influenced by the perspectives accomplished in the architectural imagination. (Ibid: 64)

Visionary architecture brings dreaming into the urban space, as evocative objects bring their imagined cities into the existing one, changing it and serving as associative devices in the experience of their environments.

Skyscrapers evoke the modern city through their image of verticality, as Cesar Pelli writes, "The skyscraper, by being much taller than the average construction, began to assume (whether or not it was wanted) a public role, that of primary contributor to the silhouette and the image of the city of which it was part" (1982: 137). With the skyscraper, buildings became of the sky, seen above the roofs of buildings that were of the ground. The skyscraper silhouette transformed the city and came to denote the metropolis (cf. ibid). One of the first buildings to truly express the skyscraper image, according to Pelli, was the Woolworth Building in New York City (Cass Gilbert, 1913). It both celebrated and fully utilized its verticality and found an image appropriate to the skyscraper typology, the neo-Gothic (cf. ibid: 138).

Milan's tall buildings ushered it into a world of modern skyscraper cities and defined it as a metropolis. Through the imagination, its tall constructions could take on new dimensions beyond the mere physical ones, enabling tower constructions to be fantastically aggrandized into skyscrapers. The first architectural style to be applied to Milanese high-rise constructions was that of the burgeoning Novecento. First developed after World War I by architects, including Giovanni Muzio, Mino Fiocchi, Emilio Lancia, and Gio Ponti, the style, also referred to as Milanese Novecento, was regarded as quintessentially Milanese and modern, fusing elements of Lombard Neoclassicism with the clear, geometric forms of modernism (cf. Etlin 1991: 165-177). Novecento architecture played a strong role in transforming the city in the 1920s and 30s. It introduced particularly tall structures into the cityscape, such as the first Novecento building, the eight-story Ca' Brutta (Giovanni Muzio, 1919-1923). Soon after the style would appear in the city's first skyscrapers, interchangeably referred to as *grattacieli* (skyscrapers), *torri* (towers), and sometimes *palazzoni* (large buildings, or high-rises). In Milan's context the three intersect, whereby *grattacielo* expresses the fantastical nature of the structures, which called forth dream-like associations of living in the vertical city.

As a quintessentially urban and modern building type, the skyscraper embodied Novecento's themes of the city and a new sense of order. Unlike the Futurists, as Luigi Monzo notes, the Novecento designers did not strive for a radical break with history, but sought to channel creative and humanistic continuities in a modern idiom. The projects of Novecento architects conveyed an aesthetic of uniformity, bringing order into the urban space both through their building and urban planning designs for Milan (cf. Monzo 2015: 86-87). Milan's Novecento skyscrapers reflect the movement's dual interest in tradition and modernity. They fulfill the historical role of urban monuments, functioning as focal points expressing the spirit of their era and establishing order and recognizability in the expanding city. Their geometric patterns and rich surfaces, sometimes including relief sculpture, speak to the essence of a classical tradition in a pared down and updated manner. The skyscraper immediately carried with it images of Chicago and New York. In Milan, however, it could also convey associations with the Torre Filarete of the Castello Sforzesco – the early twentieth century reconstruction of Filarete's Renaissance tower of the Milan fortress – or the spires of the Gothic Duomo di Santa Maria Nascente. The Novecento architects shared the Metaphysical artists' (*Pittura metafisica*) concern of merging modern life with the tone of a lost Arcadian ideal (cf. ibid: 88). A painter of Metaphysical art himself, Savinio gives voice to the immaterial world of the Milanese skyscraper.

SAVINIO'S SKYSCRAPER

Savinio's skyscraper, the one where he is guest during his Milan visit, referred to as "il mio grattacielo" (i.e. my skyscraper), may seem more of a tall building at ten stories tall. But the first skyscraper in America, William LeBaron Jenney's Home Insurance Building (1885), was also originally ten stories high (forty-two meters) and the status of a building as skyscraper is dependent upon the context of time and place (cf. Pelli 1982: 134). And typical of the skyscraper, Savinio's Milan abode is able to evoke fantasies of the city and new urban living. He is very specific about its location, describing it as part of a "herd of skyscrapers grazing on the manicured grass of the Piazzale Fiume" (1984 [1944]: 86).[6] Savinio adds

---

6 "Il mio grattacielo fa parte di quella mandria di grattacieli che pascolano l'erba pettinata del piazzale Fiume. I grattacieli, come i grandi mammiferi del pliocenico, sono erbivori.

that it is not the tallest of them. That would have been the neighboring eighteen-story (sixty-seven meter high) Torre Locatelli (Mario Bacciocchio, 1936-1939; Fig. 1).

Figure 1: Mario Bacciocchi, La Torre Locatelli, 1936-39, Milan

Photograph by the author

Apart from the Duomo, the Torre Locatelli was the highest building in the city from 1939 until 1952, when it was surpassed by the eighty-meter, twenty-two-story Centro Svizzero (Armin Meili, 1949-1952) at Piazza Cavour (cf. Beltrame 2012: 32-33). Savinio's "skyscraper" is most likely the double building complex Case Bonaiti e Malugani (1935-1936, Piazza della Repubblica 5-9; Fig. 2), designed by Giovanni Muzio. Partially framed by the green meridians of the

---

Grande è il mio grattacielo ma non è il maggiore. Altri ci sono più grandi di lui, i quali schierano in altezza quattordici, sedici, diciotto piani. Chi fermerà l'uomo nella sua audace scalata del cielo?"

southwest side of the square along Via Marcora, the complex matches Savinio's description with its rooftop terraces, hanging gardens, pools, and views onto the Bastioni di Porta Venezia (cf. 1984 [1944]: 87-88).[7] Also clearly visible from the complex is the Torre Locatelli, situated on the opposite northern side of the square. Savinio compares the rooftop experience to that of Nebuchadnezzar's Babylon, implicitly calling up associations with the fantastical Tower of Babel, but also specifically using the thought as a digression into the subject of Giuseppe Verdi and his opera Nabucco, and thereby connecting to Milan's opera tradition (cf. ibid).

Figure 2: Giovanni Muzio, Case Bonaiti e Malugani, 1935-1936, Milan

Photograph by the author

In his accounts of Milan's skyscrapers, Savinio conveys the potentiality of the Piazzale Fiume site, which was highly significant for the transformation and expansion of the city and remained so into the economic miracle – renamed Piazza della Repubblica in 1946 – and continues today to be an important nexus between new and old. It was created through the building of Milan's first main train station, Stazione Centrale, in 1864 (Louis-Jules Bouchot), which stood just outside the

---

7   "In cima al mio grattacielo si aprono terrazze e giardini pensile, come nella Babilonia di Nabuccodurussur, che gl'ignari chiamano Nabuccodonosor, e Verdi, per brevità, Nabucco."

still-existing Spanish ramparts, Milan's Renaissance boundary, and constituted a modern entranceway into the city (cf. Morandi 2005: 30). With urban growth and development, the railway system was expanded and moved further out from the city center under the 1912 Pavia-Masera plan, which prompted the demolition of the first main station and its replacement with a new one, the Stazione di Milano Centrale, designed by Ulisse Stacchini and opened in 1931.

Having travelled from Venice to Milan and arriving at the new station, Savinio performs the skyscraper's intended function: to frame the city as a modern metropolis at a moment when the ideal spatial-visual order of Stazione di Milano Centrale and the new tower focal points were developing. Writing on the narcissistic aspect of skyscrapers, Hubert Damisch states: "To travel, to visit foreign lands, is to give oneself the word as representation, to see others as actors" (Damisch 2001: 87). Milan's skyscrapers set a stage for representing the new city, attracting visitors' attention as they entered in from the new main train station. As the Renaissance fortifications vanished, the Milan skyscraper appeared as recognizable image of the city, largely in the Novecento style. Under the 1934 Albertini plan, a large number of Novecento buildings were erected in areas of the city undergoing transformation, such as the Piazzale Fiume and the developing Via Pisani, the axis leading from the new station into Piazzale Fiume, and then further into the urban core (cf. Morandi 2005: 44-47). Many of the buildings, like Savinio's skyscraper and the Torre Locatelli, incorporate clinker, brick, stone plinths and trimming, often in marble (cf. Boriani/Morandi/Rossari 2007:149). Simplistic rectilinear forms are stressed in both buildings coupled together with a tactile surface quality. The marble plinth of Torre Locatelli stands out with its remarkable relief sculptures, depicting allegorical construction scenes. Not far from the highrises stands Muzio's groundbreaking Ca' Brutta (1919-1923), which as the first modern building in Milan had introduced a new monumental scale of apartment dwellings into the urban fabric (cf. Berizzi 2015: 98). It runs along Via Turati with its monumental arch, continuing the Via Pisani-Piazza della Repubblica (Piazzale Fiume) diagonal axis into the historical city and into Gio Ponti's first Palazzo Montecatini (1935-1936) at Largo Donegani.

Looking out from the terrace of his skyscraper, Savinio recognizes a cruciform pattern of skyscrapers stretching out along the Spanish walls from the highest aggregation at Piazzale Fiume towards Porta Nuova to the west and Porta Venezia to the east, and along the Via Pisani axis to the new Stazione di Milano Centrale (cf. 1984 [1944]: 98-99).[8] From his rooftop position, Savinio is not only able to

---

8 "Questi grattacieli che si sono raccolti nel piazzale Fiume, e aprono le braccia di un'immensa croce sugli ex bastioni di Porta Venezia e di Porta Nuova, e dilungano l'asse

gain a new perspective onto the city, he is able to re-compose it through the skyscrapers stretching out between the nineteenth century city gates of the old Spanish walls. At Porta Venezia he would have seen Gio Ponti and Emilio Lancia's twelve-story (forty-five meter) residential tower (Fig. 3), Torre Rasini (1933-1934), built into the remnants of the Bastoni di Porta Venezia.

Figure 3: Emilio Lancia and Gio Ponti, Palazzo e Torre Rasini, 1933-34, Milan

Photograph by the author

In the evocative sense, Savinio creates a mental representation of Milan. He enters into the mentality of the modern city as he experiences Milan's new tall buildings

---

della croce nel viale che conduce alla Stazione, compongono una medesima famiglia di giganti, occhiuti come Argo e impennacchiati del fumo delle loro caldaie di riscaldamento."

as transformational objects (cf. Bollas 2009: 65).⁹ He is simultaneously seeing and creating Milan via its skyscrapers and experiencing the revelry of the new urban space. The old city is still present, but the new city is a world onto its own, at least when seen from the correct perspective. It contrasts the old, rising up next to the nineteenth century city gates along the path of the Spanish walls.

TRANSFORMATION IN THE URBAN CORE

The center too, however was undergoing a modernization given form by tall buildings and Novecento architecture. In the case of Piazza San Babila, situated within the earlier border of the medieval walls, an old city symbol was being obscured by new tall buildings. Savinio writes that the "small old Romanesque Lombard church and the little Doric column in front of it holding up a lion on its capital" were now surrounded by skyscrapers (1984 [1944]: 99).¹⁰ This is a reference to the Basilica San Babila, dating back to the eleventh century, and the facing seventeenth-century Lion Column (Colonna del Leone di Milano), an ancient symbol of the area (cf. Massani 1962: 58). The church stands opposite what is considered Milan's first real skyscraper (Fig. 4) built in 1937, the fifteen-story (59.3 meters) Torre Snia Viscosa (Alessandro Rimini), a mixed commercial and residential tower (cf. Beltrame 2012: 25). Also carried out in the Novecento geometrical style, the high-rise is supported by reinforced concrete and is clad in green Serpentine marble and yellow trachyte stone (cf. Berizzi 2015: 81). Its symmetrical, geometric green and yellow stone cladding, lends it the feeling of an Egyptian monument, heightening its fantastical-mythical character. It was perceived at the time as being a courageous sign of the time of Milan as an industrial city at the avant-garde (cf. Reggiori 1937: 79). Besides representing advances in Milan in the use of reinforced concrete, the building also surpassed the traditional limit of thirty stories for buildings within the historical center (cf. Berizzi 2015: 81; Crippa/Zanzottera 2004: 44).

Located about 750 meters from the Duomo and within the path of the old medieval walls, the Cerchia dei Navigli, the tower resulted from a gutting out, or

---

9   "Taking Winnicott's view that a holding environment is an act of psychic intelligence, then a city is a living form that holds its population. Mentality is the idiom of holding, reflecting the very particular culture of place."

10 "Un'altra famiglia di grattacieli è sorta intorno a San Babila, per umiliare ancor più la chiesetta romanico lombarda, e la colonnetta dorica che la precede, reggendo sul capitello un leone."

sventramento, of the San Babila area, as did other Novecento structures nearby, like Rimini's adjacent building and the Palazzo del Toro (Emilio Lancia, 1935-39), which were carried out in conjunction with the 1934 Piano Albertini (cf. Morandi 2005: 46-47). After World War II, San Babila continued to play a role in Milan's urban planning as a major part of the Racchetta, a modernizing street project, adapted into the 1953 building plan, but never completed (cf. Oliva 2002: 87). Piazza San Babila stands out as a transformational environment of the new city within the city center with the skyscraper Torre Snia Viscosa as a catalyst for its evocation. Savinio describes Torre Snia Viscosa not by its physical presence as a building, but by referring to the lit sign "Snia Viscosa" standing out in the night sky (cf. 1984 [1944]: 102).[11] The building took up the American precedent of the skyscraper as corporate symbol. Torre Snia Viscosa was meant to be a recognizable image of the Italian rayon manufacturer SNIA Viscosa and the managerial and business values it stood for (cf. Crippa/Zanzottera 2004: 44).

Figure 4: Alessandro Rimini, Torre Snia Viscosa, 1935-37, Milan

Photograph by the author

11 "Anche il palazzotto mammelluto di terrazzini neri fregiati di scritte d'oro, ha ceduto il posto a un fratello del grattacielo che gli sta di fronte, il quale accende ogni sera sul suo fastigio l'infocato nome della Snia Viscosa."

As an evocative object, the tall edifice in Milan dates back much earlier than the modern skyscraper. On the imaginary level, towering structures represent a sense of continuity in the city. Savinio imagines the Milan skyscraper as *figlio di Maria*, son of Maria, the title of his chapter thematizing the skyscraper, expressing that "up there, there is air of the gods" (1984 [1944]: 88).[12] Maria is a direct reference to the so-called *Madonnina*, a golden statue of the Madonna, officially titled *Madonna Assunta* (by Giuseppe Perego, Giuseppe Antignani, and Giuseppe Bini), which until after World War II, represented the highest point in the city at 108.5 meters at the top of the Milan Cathedral. The statue was unveiled in 1774 atop the Cathedral's highest spire, which had been carried out between 1765 and 1769 by Francesco Croce (cf. Beltrame 2012: 17). As the highest structure in Milan at the time, the *Madonnina* still mothered over Savinio's skyscrapers. Living at heights nearing those of the golden Mary is expressed by Savinio as a divine experience.

CONCLUSION

When Savinio wrote *Ascolto il tuo cuore, città*, Milan was undergoing expansion and transformation and the skyscraper became a highly symbolic object of Milan as modern city and continued to do so following the war. The transformations were not only physical, but mental. Milan's skyscrapers created a potential space of the new city. Through its skyscrapers, Milan could be associated with international metropolises and their monuments of modernity. Although the high-rises provided an image of future living, they could also call up associations with an historical Milanese trajectory of tall urban objects, specifically the Duomo and the Torre del Filarete of the Castello. Through evocation, the early Milanese high-rises became skyscrapers. They were embedded in dream-like associations of objects of the new, or objects that potentially bring their recipients into the future, while also reflecting the idiom of the city. Situated at diverse parts of the city, they occupied strategic points of urban transformation and expansion. Today, the families of giants of which Savinio spoke have expanded and reached new heights. And as at the time of Alberto Savinio's Milan homage, skyscrapers continue to form a visual spatial interrelationship as a panorama when viewed from the upper floors of other tall structures.

---

12 "Quassù c'è aria da dèi."

REFERENCES

Barthes, Roland (1997 [1979]): The Eiffel Tower and Other Mythologies (R. Howard, trans.), Berkeley: University of California Press.
Beltrame, Massimo (2012): Milano guarda in alto: 50 anni di grattacieli nel capoluogo Lombardo, Milan: LittleItaly.
Berizzi, Carlo (2015): Architectural Guide Milan: Buildings and Projects since 1919, Berlin: DOM Publishers.
Bollas, Christopher (1989): The Shadow of the Object: Psychoanalysis of the Unthought Known, New York: Columbia University Press.
Bollas, Christopher (2009): The Evocative Object World, London: Routledge.
Boriani, Maurizio/Morandi, Corinna/Rossari, Augusto (2007): Milano contemporanea: Itinerari di architettura e urbanistica, Milan: Maggioli.
Crippa, Maria Antonietta/Zanzottera, Ferdinando (2004): Milano si alza: Torri, campanili e grattacieli in città, Milan: Istituto Gaetano Pini.
Damisch, Hubert (2001): Skyline: The Narcissistic City, (J. Goodman, trans.), Stanford: Stanford University Press.
Etlin, Richard (1991): Modernism in Italian Architecture, 1890-1940, Cambridge, MA: MIT Press.
Greenberg, Jay R./Mitchell, Stephen A. (1983): Object Relations in Psychoanalytic Theory, Cambridge, MA: Harvard University Press.
Massani, Giuseppe (1962): Milano: Centro d'Europa e la Lombardia. Italia universal, Vol. II, Rome: Editrice Felix.
Monzo, Luigi (2015): "Im Schatten der Arkade: Italiens architektonischer Aufbruch ins 20. Jahrhundert zwischen Stilleben und urbaner Wirklichkeit." In: Kristin Eichhorn/Johannes S. Lorenzen (eds.), Expressionismus 01/15: Künstlerkreise, Berlin: Neofelis Verlag, pp. 81-94.
Morandi, Corinna (2005): Milan: The Great Urban Transformation (R. Sadleir, trans.), Venice: Marsilio Editori.
Oliva, Federico (2002): L'urbanistica di Milano: Quel che resta dei piani urbanistici nella crescita e nella trasformazione della città, Milan: Hoepli.
Pelli, Cesar (1982): "Skyscrapers." In: Perspecta 18, pp. 134-151.
Reggiori, Ferdinando (1937): "La casa-torre in piazza S. Babila a Milano." In: Rassegna di Architettura 5 (May 1937), p. 79.
Rowe, Colin/Koetter, Fred (1998 [1978]): Collage City, Cambridge, MA: MIT Press.
Savinio, Alberto (1984 [1944]): Ascolto il tuo cuore, città, Milan: Adelphi Edizioni.

The Transformation of Rome and the Masterplan to Reconstruct Moscow
Historical Heritage between Modernity, Memory and Ideology

Anna G. Vyazemtseva

The 1931 master plan for Rome was one of the first big city master plans approved in Europe in the 20th Century. It reflected the aspirations of the fascist propaganda, as well as the new trends of Italian and international urbanism. One of its most interesting aspects was the deep transformation of the historical city center. The works on the new projects for the Italian capital had attracted the attention of Soviet professionals since the 1920s, when Moscow had become the capital (1918) of the new state – Soviet Russia and then USSR. The projects of the reconstruction of Rome elaborated during the 1920s–1930s were reviewed by protagonists of Soviet urbanism and architecture during their work on the new master plan for Moscow. The paper analyzes, in light of architectural polemics and the controversial political situation, this interest and the impact it had on Moscow's new master plan, approved in 1935.

Rome's urban plan has long served as a model for European – including Russian – city planning. We can find "Roman" traces within the urban fabric of Russian cities as early as 1700, above all in Saint Petersburg, where the baroque "trident" became the solution for the establishment of the new capital: the Admiralty.

The trident was still recognized as a good solution in urban planning in the early 20th century. In 1912, Vladimir Nikolaevich Semenov (1874-1960) used it as the basis of his residential project at Prozorovskaja Station (Starostenko 2018) (Fig. 1). The neighborhood, commissioned by Moscow-Kazan Railways, became the first garden city in Russia, and is even mentioned in Manfredo Tafuri and Francesco Dal Co's *History of Modern Architecture* (cf. Tafuri/Dal Co 1976: 178) – one of the first fundamental studies on the international architecture of the 20th century. The trident's creator, Semenov, a prominent young urbanist and member of Raymond Unwin's Garden-City Association, was later to become one of the designers of Joseph Stalin's famous 1935 "Master Plan for the Reconstruction of the City of Moscow" (Generalny plan rekonstrukzii Moskvy 1935) [Fig. 3].

Although Russian professionals and intellectuals of the time viewed classical Rome as a universal model for urban planning and architectural design, they did not think highly of the urban renewal efforts of the Italian Post-*Risorgimento*. Yet after the October Revolution of 1917, when the Soviet capital was moved to Moscow, their interest in contemporary urbanism in Italy began to grow.

Figure 1: Vladimir Nicolaevich Semenov, master plan of Prozorovskaya Station near Moscow. 1912

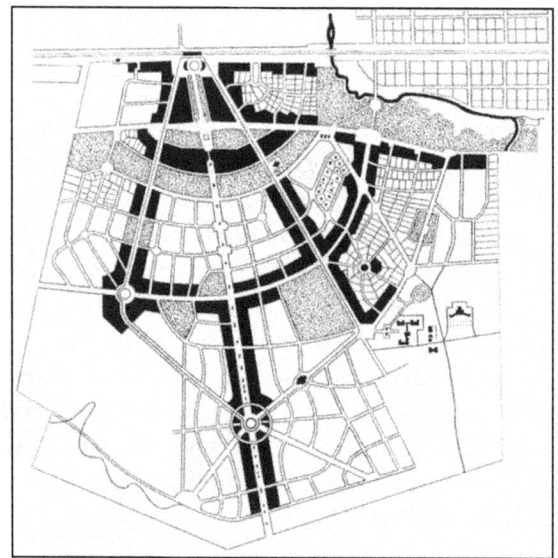

From: Belousov, Smirnova 1980, p. 11

In Saint Petersburg, Ivan Fomin (1872-1936), former champion of neoclassicism, began developing a "red Doric" or "proletarian classical" style (Khan-Magomedov 2011: 181-258). A fellow at the Russian Academy of Arts in Rome in 1910, Fomin had designed the district known as Новый Петербург (Novyj Peterburg / New Petersburg), commissioned by the Italian businessman Riccardo Gualino in 1914 (cf. Cazzola 1971: 34, Gualino 1931: 42-48). After the Revolution, Fomin joined the city-planning commission. Although his district was never completed, the experience had significant impact on his later work.

In Moscow, the commission for the new master plan was organized soon after the city gained its new status as capital. At the committee's helm was Alexey Shchusev (1873-1949), a young but already well-known architect with an expertise in restoring medieval Russian churches. This appears to have been a mandatory skill since early 20th century Moscow retained its historical layout, and was full of medieval monuments, primarily churches. In his project *Новая Москва*

Figure 2: Alexei Shchusev and others, Moscow Master-plan "Novaya Moskva", unrealized, 1923

State Historical Museum, Moscow. Inv. ГО-10304

(Novaja Moskva / New Moscow, Fig. 2), Shchusev tried to adapt the conservative city to its new status while preserving its historical legacy and moving the administrative center northwest (cf. Starostenko 2009).

It is worth noticing that some years earlier, in the 1910s, Shchusev worked in Bari, where he designed the church of San Nicola, as well as a residence for pilgrims (cf. Kejpen-Warditz 2013). In this case, Shchusev's method is easy to deduce: inspired by Russian medieval architecture, he adapted to the context by using local sandstone and mimicking the plan of Bari's historic center. Naturally, Shchusev was familiar with the European tendency of methods of urban renewal that promoted heritage conservation, as formulated by Camillo Sitte (Sitte 1889) and promoted by various urbanists on the continent, including the Italians Camillo Boito and, later, Gustavo Giovannoni.

Shchusev was also among the first members of Semenov's Prozorovskaya housing cooperative, where he acquired a site on which to design a house for his family. His way of reconciling past and present was a response to contemporary European urbanism and was shared by several emerging figures in Italian architecture and urban planning, including Marcello Piacentini (1881-1960). It seems that Piacentini and Shchusev developed a mutual interest in each other's work, one that began in Rome in 1911 during the *Esposizione Internazionale*, where Piacentini contributed as a planner of four pavilions and Shchusev as a participant (cf. Esposizione internazionale di Roma 1911: 299) in the Russian Pavilion, which was designed by Vladimir Shchuko (1878-1939) (cf. Kaufman 1946: 20-22). It was probably on that occasion that Piacentini noticed Shchusev's projects and restorations, which he later mentioned in the first issue of *Architettura e Arti Decorative* in 1921 (cf. Piacentini 1921: 43). Piacentini continued referring to Shchusev's works in his articles until the 1950s (cf. Piacentini 1952).

Shchusev's work on the Moscow master plan began in 1918 and lasted for several years. Meanwhile, despite the difficult international situation, the Soviet professional press published articles on urbanist trends abroad that were useful to the projects designed to construct new Soviet cities. Among these were, in fact, articles on Piacentini's 1925 urban planning project for the rebuilding of Rome. The content of Boris Sakulin's essay "New Forms of Rome" (1878–1952) was published in Коммунальное хозяйство (Kommunal'noe khozajstvo / Municipal government) (cf. Sakulin 1927). Sakulin was one of the urban-planning theorists whose ideas were used in the master plan for "Great Moscow," developed by Sergej Shestakov in 1921-1925, and later applied to the 1935 master plan (Fig. 3).

If the publication of "La Grande Roma" in the journal of the City Administration Kommunal'noe khozajstvo was fairly predictable, a more curious reference to Piacentini's project is the illustrated note in the Sovremennaja arkhitektura (SA)

(Novoje stroitel'stvo v Rime [Inostrannaja khronika] 1926), the constructivist journal run by Moisei Ginsburg (1892–1946) and Aleksandr Vesnin (1883–1959). The note on "the development, under the leadership of the architect Marcello Piacentini, of the project to create an entirely new urban center instead of the narrow streets that we find there now" was published at the peak of the critique against the so-called "academic" architecture.

Figure 3: V. N. Semenov, S. E. Chernyhev, Moscow City Master-Plan, 1935

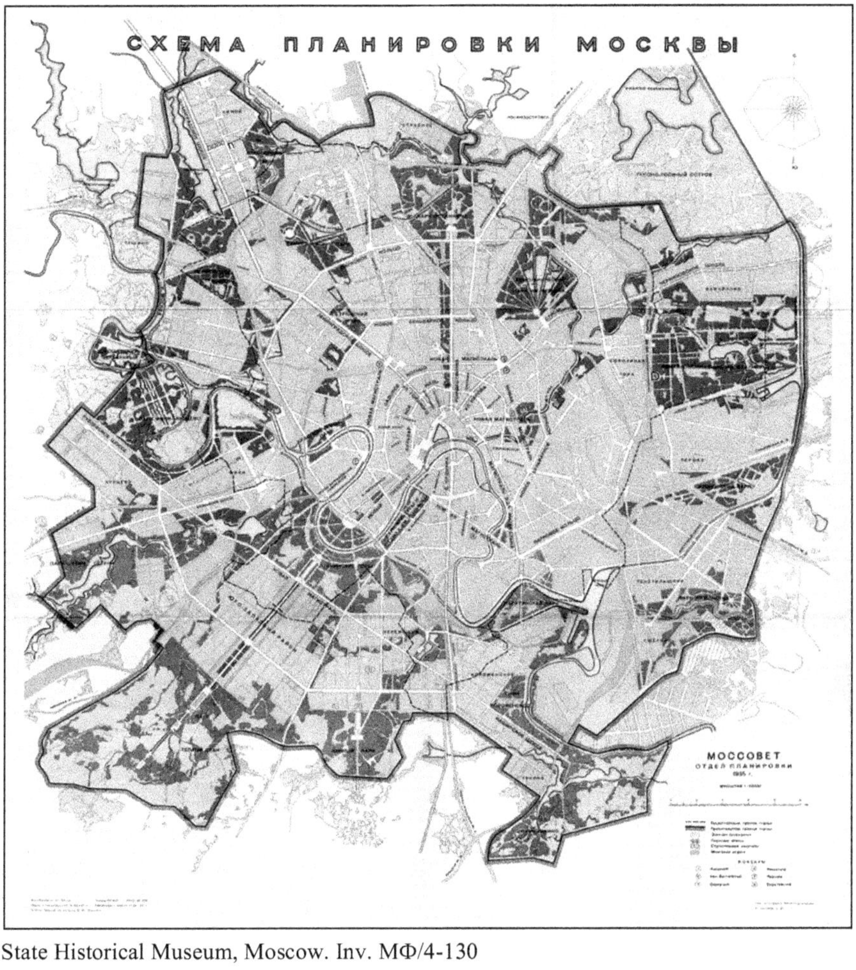

State Historical Museum, Moscow. Inv. МФ/4-130

In 1925, Shchusev's persistent desire to save historical monuments was considered inappropriate for the center of the young Soviet state (cf. Ovsyannikova 2011: 294-296). As N. Popov wrote in *Izvestija* in 1925, "Moscow is not a museum of past olden times, it is not Venice or Pompei. Moscow is not the graveyard of a past civilization, but a cradle of a new rising proletarian culture, based on work and knowledge [...]. Our architecture is a style of labor, freedom and knowledge, and not that of opulence, oppression and superstition" (Popov 1925).

The late 1920s was a time of confrontation of ideas and positions that were still supported and encouraged by state policy. The Pan-Soviet Society of Cultural Connections (Russion acronym VOKS) – established in 1925 – acquired books and magazines on architecture and urbanism for professional institutions, and organized conferences on contemporary urbanism abroad. The selection of texts was relatively diverse. In 1926, the *SA* reviewed Le Corbusier's recently published *Urbanisme* (cf. Korshunov 1926), while Sitte's *The Art of Building Cities* was translated into Russian (cf. Sitte 1925) and reviewed by Shchusev twenty years before the appearance of its English edition (cf. Sitte 1945).

In 1929, the project prepared by Shchusev's studio was criticized for being too traditionalist and "aesthetic" (Khazanova 1980: 20) and consequently rejected. When constructivism – the main trend of modern movement architecture in the Soviet Union – came to dominate, even Shchusev built several buildings that complied with the modernist canon. One of these was *Narkomzem* – the People's Commissariat of Agriculture – which was located not far from Le Corbusier's *Tsentrosoyuz* building (1928–1934) on Myasnizkaya Street in Moscow.

As the modernist trend gained a foothold, publications on Italian architecture and urban planning became more rare, not only because of the ideological contradictions between Soviet and Fascist states, but also because of a lack of interest within the Soviet mainstream for the somewhat conservative Italian building practices of the 1920s, favoring instead avant-garde architecture. However, a group of Soviet architects and engineers did participate in the XII International Congress of the International Federation for Housing and Town Planning (IFHTP) held in Rome in 1929, with the topic "Renovation of the Historical City and Its Adaptation to the Needs of Modern Life" ("Sistemazione delle città a carattere storico per adattarle alle esigenze della vita moderna"). Among those who attended was Moisey Ginsburg (Atti del XII Congresso 1929: 188), the leader of the constructivist movement, editor in chief of the *SA*, and architect of the Narkomfin residence (1928–1930) in Moscow, the first building of the *Unité d'habitation*-type to be erected. The subject of the conference was obviously appropriate to the work of the special urban planning department of *Mossovet*, the municipal administration. During the congress, delegates were able to visit the exhibition of minimalist housing in the working-class neighborhood of Garbatella, as well as the Esposizione Nazionale dell'Abitazione e dei Piani Regolatori (Ciacci 1930) in the *Palazzo delle Esposizioni* in via Nazionale, one of the main streets in central

Rome. The huge exhibition offered much inspiration: new master plans for Italian cities, historical engravings of the *Urbe,* a series of recent projects for its new master plan, including one for the *Governatorato* of Rome, the so-called "1925/1926 *Variante plan*", and two projects by teams of young architects: *Gruppo Urbanisti Romani* – Group of Roman Urban Planners – "GUR" (L. Piccinato, L. Lenzi, G. Nicolosi, R. Lavagnino, E. Fuselli, M. Dabbeni, A. Scalpelli, C. Valle, G. Cancellotti), edited by Marcello Piacentini, and *La Burbera* group (V. Fasolo, A. Limongelli, G. Venturi, P. Aschieri, F. Giobbe, G. Boni, A. Foschini, E. Del Debbio, F. Nori), edited by Gustavo Giovannoni. On display were also projects for individual sites by Innocenzo Costantini and Innocenzo Sabbatini, Cesare Bazzani and Nestore Cenelli.

In 1932, soon after the *Piano Regolatore Generale* was approved in Rome (cf. Governatorato di Roma 1931), the Soviet government called for a closed international competition to which it invited the most prominent figures in modernist urbanism: Le Corbusier, Hannes Meyer, Ernst May, Nicolai Ladovsky and others. Among these was German Krassin (1871-1947), who was mentioned as one of the members of the group at the Roman IFHTP congress of 1929, and who suggested a plan with green "wedges" – parks, gardens and woods – that would "enter" the city from the outskirts (the idea was later adopted in the General Plan of the Reconstruction of Moscow). This proposal may have been inspired by the 1910 Berlin master plan, which gained popularity in subsequent years, but we can also detect the influence of Rome with its green areas – villas and a *passeggiata archeologica* – a green archeological area, that started at Roman Forum in the city center and proceeded to the outskirts, via Appia Antica and then to the *Roman Campagna*.

All the projects presented at the competition were rejected. Some scholars are convinced that the "only true author of the Moscow Master Plan" was Stalin himself, and that all the ideas of urban planners that were adopted, were approved by him (Chmelnizki 2007). The circumstances of the Moscow project were quite similar to those of the contemporaneous competition for the Palace of the Soviets, which was conducted in three phases and won by Boris Iofan (1891–1976), who was Manfredo Manfredi's (1859–1927) Russian disciple at the Academy of Fine Arts in Rome from 1914 to 1916, and worked in the studio of the Roman architect Armando Brasini (1879–1965) while also collaborating with the engineer Giulio Barucci (1891–1955) (cf. Patti 2009).

Most likely, Mussolini's intention to recreate Rome according to his vision gave Stalin no rest. After the 1932 competition, a new commission was placed in charge of the master plan for Moscow, with Vladimir Shchuko at its head. A former member of the Imperial Academy of Fine Arts (and, as we may recall, the designer of the Russian pavilion at the *Esposizione Internazionale* of 1911 in Rome), Shchuko was at that moment working with Boris Iofan on the final project for the Palace of Soviets. In the autumn of 1934, Shchuko, Iofan and Vladimir Gelfreikh (1885–1967), the third co-architect, left for a long trip through Europe – which included a stay in Rome – and to the United States. Although their memoirs criticize contemporary architecture and urban planning, they also reveal their interest in them (cf. Vyazemtseva 2019).

In the 1930s, Soviet interest in the reconstruction of Rome increased. The magazine *Строительство Москвы* – (Stroitel'stvo Moskvy / Construction of Moscow) – published an article called "Urban renewal works in Rome" by Aleksandr Sacchetti (1934), a Soviet translator and Roman law expert of Italian origin. In the article, Sacchetti described the plans for archaeological works in the area of the Capitoline Hill and the Monument to Victor Emmanuel II, as well as the construction of Via del Mare and Via dei Monti according to the General plan of 1931.

Later, the first issue of the magazine *Архитектура за рубежом* (Arkhitektura za Rudezhom / Architecture Abroad), founded in 1935, opened with an article called "The Redevelopment of Rome" by Nazim Nessis (1935). Around that time, the *Архитектура СССР* (Arkhitektura SSSR / Architecture of the USSR) published "The Architectural Planning of Rome", an article by Lazar Rempel (1935a), in which the history of the new urban plan for Rome was described for the first and last time in the Russian language.

1935 also saw the publication of Lazar Izrailevich Rempel's *Архитектура послевоенной Италии* (Arkhitektura poslevojennoj Italii / The Architecture of Postwar Italy) (1935b), the first foreign monograph on Italian architecture of the 1920s and 1930s, generated by the publishing house of the Academy of Architecture. Rempel also worked for a while as deputy editor of the journal *Архитектура за рубежом*, published in 1935–36, for which he wrote a number of articles on modern Italian architecture. A considerable part of his book, however, was dedicated to urban planning, with a focus on Rome.

The journal, like the book, was part of the Academy's project on contemporary Western architecture. According to Rempel's memoirs, in 1935, a team of authors that included the Hungarian art historian Ivan Matza, the German architect and former Bauhaus director Hannes Mayer as well as Rempel himself, was tasked with writing a book on the architecture of post-war Italy. However, as his "mentors were busy with other works" (Rempel 2009 [1992]: 198), the book was written by him alone. In 1936, the Italian journal *Architettura* – published by the *Sindacato Nazionale Fascista degli Architetti*, published a review of Rempel's book, and observed that an evaluation of modern Italian architectural trends by the Soviet author, "would have been interesting" had Rempel not been "completely consumed by his aversion to Fascism" and capable of abstaining from explaining all its flaws through "the scars of Fascism" ("L. I. Rempel: Architettura italiana del dopo Guerra" 1936).

The book was brought to Rome by the Soviet delegation to the XIII International Congress of Architects the year in which it was published. Held in late September 1935, the congress brought together the most important exponents of the professional elite (Fig. 4). The group of the Union of Soviet Architects was represented by Alexey Shchusev, the General Secretary of the Trade Union and the head of the delegation, Karo Alabjan (1897–1959), critic David Arkin (1899–1957), architect Nicolai Kolli (1894–1966), professor and rector of the Academy of Architecture Mikhail Kriukov (1884–1944), constructivist architect Viktor Vesnin (1882–1950) – architect at the time of the People's Commission of Industry and one of the leaders of the Constructivist movement in the 1920s – and Sergey Chernyshev (1881–1963) – the chief urban planner of the city of Moscow. Along with Semenov (the already mentioned author of the first Russian garden city in the 1910s) Chernyshev worked on the General Plan for the Reconstruction of Moscow, approved on June 10, 1935. The booklet on the new master plan for Moscow was also presented at the conference, translated for the occasion into English, French, and German in order to bring it into the spotlight. The Russian delegates evidently wished for it to be compared to the Rome master plan of 1931. Back in Moscow after the Congress, Arkin, a key Soviet architectural critic, wrote his account of the rebuilding of Rome, where he criticized all the demolition that was taking place and concluded with a twist on an Italian adage: "what Barberini did not do, Mussolini did". At the same time, however, the booklet on the Moscow plan reads: "Maintaining the historic image of Moscow is impossible for the city. Moscow is a center of activity and development" (Generalny plan rekonstruktsii Moskvy 1935).

In the late 1930s, Moscow lost not only several of its historical religious monuments, such as churches and monasteries, but also much of its lay heritage, including the 17th century Sukhareva Tower, restored in 1934, and a great part of the medieval wall of the so-called White City, which had been restored in the late 1920s. The removal of these buildings made room for the new squares, avenues and multistory housing complexes adorned with ancient Roman motives, built in the style known as "socialist realism" and proclaimed after 1932, as the main and unique style of Soviet art and architecture. These, in turn, surrounded the monument that now stood at the center of both the city and the state, the Kremlin, a medieval fortress that has since become synonymous with the nation's government. This approach was relatively similar to the one that "liberated Rome from its subsequent layers" (cf. Mussolini 1956 [1924]) and allowed vehicular traffic to run around monumental symbols of the city's great past. The scale of Mussolini's Rome, however, was greatly surpassed: Stalin was determined in his desire to pit his capital against Imperial Rome. Indeed, the new squares and avenues elaborated by the *Mossovet* revealed the inspiration of ancient and baroque Rome (Fig. 4). It is also noteworthy that the heaviest demolitions ordered by Mussolini's regime were conducted only after the Moscow Plan was approved; in fact, some of its projects, including Piazza Nicosia (1936), and Via della Conciliazione (1936-50), were not part of the original 1931 *Piano Regolatore Generale*.

Figure 4: Soviet delegation at the XIII International Congress of Architects, 1935. From left to right: S.G. Chernyshev, D.Je. Arkin, A.V.Shchusev, N. J. Kolli, K.S. Alabjan, V.A.Vesnin, S.V. Krjukov (?)

State Museum of Architecture "A.V. Shchusev", Moscow. Inv.: OCH-3313

To conclude, we can assume that Soviet attention to Italian and especially Roman urban planning between the two world wars was considerable, and that it combined technical and artistic solutions with ideological goals. Interest in these Italian trends was not explicit, however, but covert or hidden behind negative critique. The 1931 *Piano Regolatore Generale* had significant impact on the process leading to the elaboration and approval of the Moscow project. Ideologically motivated, this exchange remained a key phenomenon of urban planning in both nations during the interwar era.

REFERENCES

Atti del XII Congresso internazionale dell'abitazione e dei piani regolatori. Roma, 12-16 September 1929.
Belousov V.N., Smirnova (1980): Vladimir Nicolaevich Semenov, Moscow: Stroyizdat.
Cazzola, Pietro (1971): "Dalla Transiberiana alle automobili". In: 45° Parallelo, marzo-aprile, pp. 34-40.
Ciacci, Francesco (1930): "Il piano regolatore di Roma alla mostra dei P.P. R.R. e delle abitazioni", In: Mostra dei P.P. R.R. e delle abitazioni, Roma 12 September – 15 October 1929, Rome: L'Universale Tipografia Poliglotta.
Esposizione internazionale di Roma (1911): Catalogo della Mostra di Belle Arti, Bergamo: Istituto italiano d'arti grafiche.
Generalny plan rekonstruktsii Moskvy. [Manuscript]. (1935). Nauchno-issledovatel'sky institute teorii, istorii I perspektivnykh problem sovetskoy arkhitektury i ego predshestvenniki, 1934-1991 (Scientific institute of theory, history and problems of the perspective of Soviet architecture and its predecessors, 1934-1991) (RGAE, f. 377, op.1, ed. khr. 2, l. 12). Russian State Archive of Economics, Moscow.
Governatorato di Roma (1931): Piano Regolatore di Roma 1931, Roma-Milano: Treves.
Gualino, Riccardo (1931): Frammenti di vita, Milan: Mondadori.
Kaufman, Sofia (1946): Vladimir Alekseevich Shchuko, Leningrad: Academy of Architecture of USSR Publisher.
Kejpen-Warditz, Diana (2013): Khramovoe zodčestvo A.V. Shchuseva, Moscow: Sovpadenije.
Khan-Magomedov, Selim (2011): Ivan Fomin, Moscow: Gordeev [Хан-Магомедов С. О. Иван Фомин. Москва: Гордеев].
Khazanova, Vigdaria (1980): Sovetskaja arkhitektura pervoj pyatiletki. Problemy goroda budushchego, Moscow: Nauka.
Korshunov, B. (1926): "Urbanism / review". In: "Sovremennaja arkhitektura", 1, p. 37.
"L. I. Rempel: Architettura italiana del dopo guerra. Edizione dell'Academia di Architettura dell'U.R.S.S." (by W.W.), In: Architettura 7, 1936, p. 348.
Mussolini, Benito (1956 [1924]): "Discorso 21 aprile 1924." In: Susmel D. (ed.) Opera omnia di "Novoje stroitel'stvo v Rime (Inostrannaja khronika)" (1926). In: Sovremennaja arkhitektura 1. p. 24.
Nessis, Nikolaj (1935), "Pereplanirovka Rima". In: Arkhitektura za rubezhom 1, pp. 25-30.

Ovsyannikova, Elena (2011): "Tvorchestvo A. V. Shchuseva s istoricheskoj distanzii". In: P. Shchusev: Stranizy iz žizni akademika A.V. Shchuseva, Moscow: S.E.Gordeev.

Patti, Federica (2009): Boris Iofan,1891-1976: Dagli anni romani all'ascesa professionale in Unione Sovietica, Turin: Politecnico di Torino/Politecnico di Milano.

Piacentini, Marcello (1921): "Il momento architettonico all'estero". In: Architettura e arti decorativi I/1.

Piacentini, Marcello (1952): "L'architettura russa". In: Il Globo, 28 December 1952, p. 3.

Popov, N.F. (1925): "Moskva: Ne musej stariniy". In: Izvestija, n. 267, 22 November.

Rempel, Lazar' I. (1935a): "Arkhitekturnaja planirovka novogo Rima". In: Arkhitektura SSSR 1935, pp. 74-79.

Rempel, Lazar' I. (1935b): Arkhitektura poslevojennoj Italii, Moscow: Academy of Architecture of USSR Publisher.

Rempel; Lazar' I. (2009 [1992]): Moi sovremenniki, Tashkent: Izdatel'stvo literatury i iskusstva.

Sakketti, Aleksander (1934): Pereplanirovochnyje raboty v Rime. In: Stroitel'stvo Moskvy 12, pp. 34-36.

Sakulin, Boris (1927): "Novye formy Rima". In: Kommunalnoje khozjajstvo 3–4, pp. 76–78.

Sitte, Camillo (1889): Der Städtebau nach seinen künstlerischen Grundsätzen, Wien: Graeser.

Sitte, Camillo (1925): Gorodskoje stroitel'stvo s tochki zrenuja ego khudozhestvennykh prinzipov. Trans. from. German, Moscow: Moscow Governance Engineering Administration [Зитте Камилло, Городское строительство с точки зрения его художественных принципов. - Пер. с нем. – М.: Упр. Моск. губ. инж.]

Sitte, Camillo (1945): The Art of Building Cities. Translation by Ch. T. Stewart, New-York: Reinhold Publishing Corporation.

Starostenko, Yulia (2009): Metamorphosis of the conception of the urban development of Moscow city-center "central nucleus" of Moscow in 1920-1930s. PhD diss.,. Moscow: Moscow Architectural Institute – MARKHI [Старостенко Ю.Д. Метаморфозы архитектурно-градостроительной концепции развития центра (центрального ядра) Москва 1920-е – 1930-е гг. Канд. дисс. Москва: МАРХИ].

Starostenko, Yulia (2018): The Hospital Town of "the First Garden City in Russia" near Prozorovka: The History of Design and Construction, 1912-1930. In:

Academia: Arkhitektur I stroiltel'stvo 2, pp. 40-49 (in Russian, with abstract in English).
Tafuri, Manfredo/Dal Co, Francesco (1976): Architettura Contemporanea, Milano: Electa.
Vyazemtseva, Anna (2019): Soviet Fascination for Fascist Rome, or The International Style of Regimes. In: Kai Kappel/Erik Wegerhoff (eds.) Blickwendungen: Architektenreisen nach Italien in Moderne und Gegenwart / Shifts in perspective: Architect's travels to Italy in modern and contemporary times. Römische Studien der Bibliotheca Hertziana 45. Munich: Hirmer.

Preserving the Old to Build the Modern
Visions of an Alternative Brescia in the Project by Pietro Aschieri

Alberto Coppo

The competition for the urban development plan of Brescia in 1927 offers an interesting opportunity to analyze Italian architectural culture in the 1930s. The Aschieri Group's project, in particular, allows us to explore 1930s urban transformation in Italy, which was based on ancient heritage as a starting point for city planning. Despite the negative outcome of the competition, Aschieri raises new questions about an alternative development of the city and the role of coeval debates in this process.

On November 27, 1927, the results of the competition for the urban development and expansion plan of the city of Brescia were published. The competition opened on April 21 of the same year, and called for proposals to expand the Lombardy city following the renovation of the railway station. The more difficult task was to find a balance between Brescia's rich historical heritage, offering precious evidence of Roman, Medieval and Renaissance times, and the city's modern development from the beginning of the 20th century. Strong industrial growth, and a strategic location between the centers of Milan and Venice, direct contact with national politics (cf. Kelikian 1986: 201-206) and Brescia's symbolic role within the history of the Risorgimento, gave rise to this urban development plan.

The competition grew out of a long local debate, begun in the 1910s (cf. Robecchi 1998: 79-86) into a national debate, as Brescia's transformation represented the first important "urban laboratory" during the fascism (Ciucci 1989: 29-34). Moreover, this episode clarified the importance of the Roman design school (*Scuola Romana*) for the transformation of Italian historical centers. It is important to recognize the architects involved: two groups, led by Pietro Aschieri

(1889-1952) and Luigi Piccinato (1899-1983) (first and second place in the competition), and the prominent figure of Marcello Piacentini (1881-1960), nominated by the local administration to be the judge of the proposed works. The protagonists of this story are in fact linked to Piacentini: Piccinato is an assistant of the department of *Edilizia Cittadina* (Urban construction) at the Scuola Superiore di Architettura di Roma, chaired by Piacentini; Aschieri is an esteemed colleague, well known by Piacentini since the World War I; Ghino Venturi (1884-1970), also part of the participating Aschieri group (*Gruppo Aschieri*), is one of Piacentini's former staff collaborators (cf. Nicoloso 2018: 98). In the end, Piacentini is considered to be the true leader of the whole affair.

What is important in this competition is not only the solutions advanced by the competitors, but also the subsequent outcomes. An expressive example of this can be found in the construction of Piazza della Vittoria in the historic center, by Piacentini. This serves the needs of local industrialists, as well as propaganda for the restoring "fascist civilization" (Pacini 1932: 652).

The definitive project is the translation of a monumental vision of the urban rehabilitation action that represented, for the time, a powerful icon of the fascist political rule. Showcasing a new sense of space, recognizable as the visual expression of Mussolini's regime, in open comparison with the ancient city squares. However, according to architectural historian Mariarosa Maifrini (1998) and Franco Robecchi (1998), a local historian of Brescia at the beginning of the century, the construction of a new urban center no longer appears as an imposed a priori model from the outside, but as the result of a programmatic action, which is not only composed by scholarly reflections and an unprejudiced realism, but also by timid attempts to imagine an alternative modernity.

The work of Aschieri shows emblematically the fate of the city undergoing such a long and complex project. Starting with the conservation and enhancement of the most important architectural assets, Aschieri, in fact, proposes a brand new building within the new urban center designed by Piacentini, which has a clear rational layout devoid of any formalist concession to monumentality.

ASCHIERI'S AESTHETICS

The competition was part of a national debate on the expansion of Italian cities dealing with the development of functional and regulatory requirements and the maintenance of precise formal identities of its centers.[1] The projects of Aschieri and Piccinato were strongly indebted to the theory of thinning urban fabric (*diradamento*) and represented the possibility of using historical heritage for harmonious urban growth. The ideas of Gustavo Giovannoni (1873-1947) constitute the theoretical core that, starting from precise points – *l'Associazione Artistica fra i Cultori di Architettura*, the periodical *Architettura e Arti Decorative* and the School of Architecture of Rome intended to direct urban transformation, with the precise aim of associating the future of the urban center with the territorial policy of fascism, exercised as control management.

According to Giovannoni, architectural practice was not possible without deep cultural connections. Architectural composition was able to influence both new design and restoration. Starting from this concept, it is possible to read Aschieri and Piccinato's interventions as similar, but at the same time having somewhat different ideas for exporting the model provided by Giovannoni beyond the territorial and ideological boundaries of Rome.

Both projects were markedly driven by a larger architectural vision, supporting an urban setting, but without the global control of a city system. The city is understood as unitary organism and not composed by its parts. This approach can be seen in the numerous drawings presented, in which the three-dimensional design of the city stands out even before the planimetric one. The drawings proposed the ambitious goal of summarizing in a fragile synthesis of identity, every question of an economic, social and political nature. Furthermore, this attention to the historical city prevented demolitions. As a matter of fact, the competition itself encouraged designers to propose invasive measures for hygienic and traffic reasons (cf. Robecchi 1998: 87-89).

Piccinato, however, thinks of urban development according to a dynamic perspective, which envisages a sub-center for each city expansion area. The construction of the modern city was conceived as a continuous addition in an interconnected polycentric system, where there was a strict building policy that lightened the city centre and, at the same time, allowed its modernization with new housing standards.

Piccinato, in fact, following an idea already proposed for the regulatory plan of Padua (1926) and, more programmatically, in the project for the city of Rome (1929, a so-called general variant to the regulatory plan of 1909), knew perfectly

---

1   For a general vision, both of a design and a normative approach, cf. Bottini 2004: 346-371. For a look at the Brescia case understood as a symbol of fascist politics, cf. Etlin 1991: 418-421 and Doordan 1995. For the conduct of the competition, its participants and final conclusions, cf. Marconi 1927.

well that the old center could not contain all the administrative and financial functions. In this second project, presented together with the *Gruppo Urbanisti Romani* (GUR) and Piacentini, he planned to move the administrative center of the capital to the East and to procede with the urban development on a territorial scale, connecting the capital with satellite centers, such as the towns in the "Castelli Romani" area.

Figure 1: Pietro Aschieri, Project of Egidi House, Rome (1927)

Fondo Gustavo Giovannoni, Centro Studi per la Storia dell'Architettura, Rome

The intervention of the Aschieri group instead, despite paying much attention to the new areas of expansion, seems more concerned with defining the city's key points, such as Piazza delle Erbe, Piazza della Loggia and Piazza Duomo, at an architectural level. In doing so, Aschieri revealed his own approach with a strong scenographic character, aimed at constructing an urban space by using perspective representations, and inclined to identify the maintenance of the 'characteristic atmosphere' of the city as the main objective of his project.

The same approach can be seen in his proposal for the reorganization of the bridgeheads of the Vittorio Emanuele II bridge in Rome (1924/1926), and becomes even more evident in the unprecedented expansion proposal of the Egidi house in 1927, still in Rome. The very central location of the building, located on the corner between Piazza Colonna and Via dei Bergamaschi, imposed a historicist solution. The project was not only concerned with inserting a connecting portico with the posterior Piazza di Pietra, but also expanded the road section of Via dei Bergamaschi and redesigned the historical buildings in front of it. The result is a contextualizing solution that intented to harmonize an ordinary transformation with the surrounding buildings, and still maintain an urban framework that resolved both traffic difficulties, by separating the pedestrian traffic from the vehicular traffic, and the issue of architectural decorum (Fig. 1).

This is therefore an intervention that Giovannoni had already done in the nearby Rinascimento district, using the same model advocated in the arrangement of the historic center. This strategy works very well as long as it is applied case by case, but reveals its limits when it is applied to a large-scale urban project, as was requested in Brescia. As we can see in Giovannoni's work, financial resources and time constraints ended up being hard to manage.

All the more reason for Aschieri's project that, we must not forget, provides numerous cuts in the historical urban fabric with the consequent costs of the demolition of old buildings, the settlement of the inhabitants, the acquisition of the empty areas and the construction of new buildings (cf. Benevolo/Bettinelli 1981: 130-149).

DESIGN THROUGH PERSPECTIVE REPRESENTATIONS

Aschieri created the project together with his co-designers Ghino Venturi, Roberto Gennari and Riccardo Pisa, an important local architect. As required by the competition, the aim was twofold: to create a city extension "New Brescia", and to restructure the existing city, in particular the road system (cf. Gruppo Aschieri 1927: 7).

The intervention involved two levels. First, it sets up traffic management along the two main North-South and East-West routes: Via Tartaglia was stretched to connect the northern part of the city with the southern part, thus defining a system that, together with the East-West ridge where the old station was located, is able to keep traffic away from the historical center. Second, new neighborhoods were planned around the city center: to the north the district of Porta Trento, to the east the Ronchi hill and the area of Porta Venezia, to the south the urban district between the historic center and the station, and to the west the new industrial zone. In addition, a garden city district to the southeast and a working-class garden district to the west were added (Fig. 2).

Figure 2: Pietro Aschieri: urban development plan of Brescia, the new city (1927)

Fondo personale dell'autore, Foto Rapuzzi, Brescia

Yet from the attention given to the arrangement of the center within the project report, Giovannoni's concentration emerges on the transformation of historical heritage as the only real engine of any future expansion (cf. Aschieri Group 1927: 25-27). In fact, a further East-West artery is proposed with the enlargement of Corso Goffredo Mameli and Via Trieste and the isolation of the major urban monuments – whose list drawn up by the head of the Sovrintendenza dei Beni Culturali (Superintendence of Cultural Heritage) is among the attached documents of the competition – to strengthen the local identity. The hilly area of the Ronchi, of great interest from a landscape point of view, was connected to the city through a new avenue of access that started right from Piazza delle X Giornate (not realized), where the church of San Faustino in Riposo was freed from surrounding buildings. As proposed by other competitors, considerable demolition was planned in the old Carmine quarters (Contrada del Carmine) and the Pescherie area (Quartiere Medievale delle Pescherie). The goal was to highlight the church of Santa Maria del Carmine and to connect it with a new breakthrough to San Faustino in Riposo to the north and the Palazzo della Loggia. The new square was supposed to be enclosed by the Monte di Pietà Vecchio from North and developed up to the top of via Dante Alighieri, which later evolved into Piacentini's Piazza della Vittoria. Completing the overall picture of these interventions, is the arrangement of the church of San Francesco d'Assisi through the opening of a road extending from the church of Santa Maria dei Miracoli. This operation was followed by the demolition of houses leaning against and upon the Old Cathedral (Duomo Vecchio). As a result, a new street has been constructed from the open space in front of the church of San Lorenzo up to the renovated station, ensuring further access to the center (Fig. 3).

The declared will of the architects (Aschieri group) to protect the ancient heritage from the traffic of modern Brescia is therefore denied in practice by the numerous new roads that were designed and by the expected deep changes. Moreover, the offsetting between Corso Goffredo Mameli and Via Trieste prevents the creation of a continuous crossing and, consequently, puts in doubt the effective utility to reduce traffic congestions.

Figure 3: Pietro Aschieri: the new area in front of San Lorenzo's Church, Brescia (1927)

Fondo personale dell'autore, Foto Rapuzzi, Brescia

It must be recognized that many of these interventions were nothing more than ideas taken by competitors from the municipal technical office, unrealized since the 1910s and 1920s and well known among Brescian designers: in addition to

Riccardo Pisa in the Aschieri group, joining the Gruppo Urbanisti Romani was Mario Dabbeni (1904-1985), son of the architect Egidio Dabbeni (1873-1964), one of the proponents of the city's transformation. Joining the group of Angelo Bordoni (1891-1957) was the engineer and politician Alfredo Giarratana (1890-1982), an associate of the industrialist Giulio Togni, one of the promoters of the competition.

As for the project of the Aschieri group, the underlying ambiguity that accompanied the drawings originated from the basic urban conception which, according to Giovannoni, expected a centripetal development and not, as understood by Piccinato and associates, a polycentric trend. In this sense, the arrangement of Brescia is portrayed as a branched system with its urban identity as the focal points. Curiously, in the drawings, the monuments are free from the surrounding buildings, returning them to their ancient splendor, without showing the new spaces in an historical context. The only representations in this regard concern the suburbs, close to the station or in the industrial area without showing, for example, the square in the old Pescherie area, cited above, or the open space near the church of Santa Maria del Carmine.

The historicism at the core of the project is further confirmed by the design of the new municipal office buildings created near the Palazzo della Loggia. They are designed with the same parietal treatment of the base and with the continuation of the decorative frame in line with Giovannoni's concept of contextualism (*ambientismo*).[2] Moreover, the idea of planning interventions in individual buildings goes back to the project that Aschieri himself developed for the town of Sulmona in 1931. Here too, the historical heritage, understood as a homogeneous area, became the primary element on which to build the new urban reality. Consequently, the scenographic architectural treatment and addition of new administrative buildings in the historic center influenced the future growth of the city. A clear example of this is the *Casa del Fascio* project for Sulmona in front of the Complesso della Santissima Annunziata.

Given these considerations, the opinion expressed by the jury is even more complicated to interpret. Aschieri's project is declared as the winner, not so much for its arrangement of the center, which, despite the attractive views, is not convincing (cf. Turati et al. 1928: 22). The strong point of this proposal is instead constituted by the design of the enlargement of the city, the definition of the new

---

2   By contextualism the paper intends 'ambientismo' as asserted by Richard Etlin (cf. 1991: 116). To understand the importance of this concept for Giovannoni, refer to the relationship between monument and environment in one of his writings (cf. 1931: 26).

neighborhoods and the harmonious connection with the historical nucleus. One of the motivations for this choice can be traced to the very nature of the competition, conceived as a contest of useful guiding ideas. This could only ever act as the drafting of the final plan (cf. Calzoni 1929[?]: 2).[3]

POST COMPETITION

The events that took place after the conclusion of the competition (cf. Nicoloso 2018: 98–99) explain the balance of power between the various promoters of the transformation of Brescia, such as the fascist politician Augusto Turati, Marcello Piacentini and the industrialist Giulio Togni. The jury's report, published in August 1928, showed how the real interest was focused on the transformation of the historic center through the development of attractive areas for investors. Not only that, the existence of a different town planning developed by the local Ufficio tecnico (literally "Technical Office") starting at least from 1925, testified to the wide choice of possible options and the consequent difficulty in developing a unitary project that dealt with the whole territory (cf. Barni 1925).[4]

The competition had also shown the impossibility of finding a formal synthesis among all the proposals already in the pipeline for decades. In addition, it is for this reason that, in all likelihood, the elaboration of a precise and representative intervention, in a central and strategic point, such as the Quartiere Medievale delle Pescherie, already indicated as a "sacrificable" area (Nezi 1932: 292), presented itself as the best guarantee of a transformational success of Brescia.

Moreover, the romantic taste that pervaded some suggestions of the Aschieri project, such as the arrangement of the new station square or the development of the industrial area, represented the limits that Giovannoni's vision set when implementing a building program, or its arbitrary choice of what to keep and what to discard (cf. Zucconi 1999: 153). The presence of such rarefied pragmatism in the thinning of urban structures (*diradamento*) and so defined in Piacentini's action is well understood in the passage between urban compositions designed in the competition and the construction of Piazza della Vittoria. It was no longer a matter of

---

3 The report of the Brescia *podestà*, not dated, but presumably written for approvals in the early months of 1929, clarifies how the entire competition had been conceived as a preparation for the operational plan.
4 The report of the College of Engineers and Architects, already cited by Robecchi (1998: 79-82), contains general indications on possible modifications to the project supported by the Technical Office.

exercising small interventions in the urban context in a surgical manner, but of concentrating, in a single symbolic point, the portrait of a city at the service of new political, economic and administrative functions.

It thus appeared legitimate to rethink the existing city as long as the physical appearance of monumentality was maintained, and architectural elements of historic monuments could be repeated in new buildings. The transformative vision of this approach not only expressed the regime's decision-making policy at its best, but also promoted urban renewal. This formed a new frame of reference free from the fear and limitation of other interventions. Moreover, even if Piacentini himself had previously opposed the disembowelment (*sventramento*) in the plans for Rome in 1916 and 1925, we must not forget that, as suggested by Stockel (cf. 1992: 865), this conservative spirit was also due to the fear that such operations were too burdensome for public administrations. Certainly, the solution of the building consortiums proposed by Giovannoni appeared as too abstract a system to become a credible implementation tool. The thinning theory found its applicability within minor areas, such as in the arrangement of the center of Bari, and in intermediate-level projects, at the scale of a city block, in which it was possible to achieve adequate financing. This theory by Giovannoni could be seen mostly in the practice of restoration. Instead, in terms of urban planning, his major contribution was the concept of considering the entire historical centre as one single monument, from its conservation to its valorization, as defined by national law (cf. Legge n. 1089/1939). Yet the harmonious composition of the spaces was judged by Piacentini as fundamental. Furthermore, he also considered himself an urban planner and held the chair of Edilizia Cittadina (Urban construction) at the Scuola Superiore di Architettura di Roma.

Piacentini – in accordance with the concept of *ambientismo* – applied a certain environmental sensibility to his projects in a second step, when it was necessary to recreate a characteristic environment with new buildings. This is the way in which the Torrione INA (INA tower) should be interpreted – as one of the first Italian 'skyscrapers', as it is typologically inspired by American buildings, but shaped by forms of a medieval civic tower.

From this point of view, it seems extremely interesting that Aschieri, Piccinato and Giarratana are chosen as members of the commission presided by Piacentini to develop, starting from 1928, a new transformation plan for the center of Brescia (cf. Maifrini 1998: 316). This choice could be read as a justification of the competition ranking, as the jury could have determined the three ideal collaborators for the final plan to guarantee the designated designer the presence of trusted and respected colleagues (Aschieri and Piccinato) and a deep connoisseur of the local situation (Giarratana).

Soon the last two were lost due to divergent visions: in particular, Giarratana resigned after unsuccessfully trying to reduce the width of the new square at Via Dante Alighieri. On the other hand, Aschieri's collaboration appears more enduring even if it is not officially accredited. His alleged expulsion must have taken place between 1928 and 1929, when by then the intense project activity in Rome must have drawn his attention away from Brescia, where plannings were increasingly dominated by Oscar Prati (1898-1971), close collaborator of Piacentini who was left in charge (cf. Nicoloso 2018: 98) (Fig. 4).

Figure 4: Pietro Aschieri: Project of INA Tower, Brescia (1929)

Fondo Pietro Aschieri, Accademia Nazionale di San Luca, Rome

Yet, a design by Aschieri himself, kept at the personal fund at the Accademia Nazionale di San Luca (Fondo Pietro Aschieri, FPA 25A, 01f), could reveal new insights. What has always been reported in the official registries as a skyscraper in Brescia, presented by Aschieri in the exhibition of the rationalist movement Movimento Italiano Architettura Razionale (MIAR) in Rome in 1931, is none other than Aschieri's project for the Torrione INA in Brescia. The attribution is supported by the sketches of the porticoed building on the left side, identifiable as the headquarters of Assicurazioni Generali di Venezia. In addition, the writing at the bottom left, "A, 1929", gives credit to a long-lasting collaboration with Piacentini, well beyond the time immediately following the conclusion of the competition.

The modern matrix of the skyscraper, very different from the one realized, therefore represents an alluring proposal from those who had imagined the center of Brescia precisely starting from historicist solutions. Evidently, the date is crucial, since it marks the notorious Aschieri adhesion to a modern language, defining a unique and recognizable style. One should not fail to mention that the designer himself had then reached the awareness that contextualization is not a viable path in the new reality already defined as Piacentini's Brescia, which required representation that did not match the aesthetic and deeply anti-speculative criteria specified by Giovannoni. From the project in 1927 to the Torrione INA, we can clearly see a change of approach in Aschieri's vision. This is even more evident since both projects belong to the same city. There is no longer an intention to redefine a harmonious environment with architecture characteristic of the place. The aim is rather to propose a new identity of the place itself, through a rationalist aesthetic limited to a geometric chiaroscuro design.

CONCLUSION

Aschieri's intervention, therefore, developed over a wide period, from 1927 to 1929. This was fundamental not only for his career, but also for the Italian architectural culture. A period during which, as it is well known, many architects polarized their architectural tendencies in relation to the cultural dominance of the Fascist regime. Aschieri's approach in the city of Brescia clarifies the complexity, which is present in the discipline over the years when the fascist regime had not yet elaborated a clear architectural policy and different designers are confronted with the difficult issue of modernity. Even if Marconi (cf. 1977: 7) considered Aschieri to be a designer of urban spaces, Aschieri had difficulty finding transitions and creating harmony between his architecture and the surrounding context.

The passage from a quiet and respectful contextualism to a search for autonomy of the modern in historical centers often remained unresolved. At the turn of the 1930s, Aschieri's approach moved away from both the Giovannoni matrix and Piacentini's interventionism and precisely for this reason, reveals the complexity of the urban debate in Italy, coeval and subsequent to Aschieri's work.

REFERENCES

Barni, Edoardo (1925): Collegio degli Ingegneri ed Architetti di Brescia: Relazione. Archivio di Stato di Brescia, Rub. XVIII, 9, 2153a. Brescia, Italy.
Benevolo, Leonardo/Bettinelli, Rossana (eds.) (1981): Brescia Moderna: La formazione e la gestione urbanistica di una città industriale, Brescia: Grafo Edizioni.
Bottini, Fabrizio (2004): "Dalla periferia al centro: idee per la città e la city". In: Giorgio Ciucci/Giorgio Muratore (eds.), Storia dell'architettura italiana: Il primo Novecento, Milano: Electa, pp. 346-371.
Calzoni, Pietro (1929[?]): Oggetto n. 1, allegato alla relazione di Marcello Piacentini (Rub. XVIII, 9, 2153). Archivio di Stato di Brescia, Brescia, Italy.
Ciucci, Giorgio (1989): Gli architetti e il fascismo: Architettura e città 1922-1944, Turin: Einaudi.
Doordan, Dennis Paul (1995): "Piazza della Vittoria, Brescia: A case study in Fascism Urbanism". In: Roland Behar (eds.): The architecture of Politics, 1910-1940, Miami Beach: The Wolfsonian Foundation, pp. 22-33.
Etlin, Richard (1991): Modernism in Italian architecture, 1890-1940, Cambridge: The MIT Press.
Giovannoni, Gustavo (1931): Vecchie città ed edilizia nuova, Torino: Utet.
Gruppo Aschieri (1927): Relazione per il piano regolatore di Brescia, Brescia: Tipo-Litografia F.lli Geroldi (BC COM III.000790). Archivio Storico del Politecnico di Milano, Milano.
Kelikian, Alica A. (1986): Town and Country under fascism: The transformation of Brescia 1915-1926, Oxford: Clarendon Press.
Maifrini, Mariarosa (1998): "Tecnici e amministrazione: I piani di Brescia tra le due guerre". In: Giulio Ernesti (eds.), La costruzione dell'utopia: Architetti e urbanisti nell'Italia fascista, Roma: Ed. Lavoro.
Marconi, Paolo (ed.) (1977): Pietro Aschieri architetto, Roma: Bulzoni.
Marconi, Plinio (1927): "Concorso nazionale per il Piano Regolatore della città di Brescia". In: Architettura e arti decorative VII/6, pp. 251-270.

Nezi, Antonio (1932): "L'antico e il nuovo centro di Brescia". In: Emporium LXXI/425, pp. 291-301.

Nicoloso, Paolo (2018): Marcello Piacentini: Una biografia, Torino: Einaudi.

Pacini, Roberto (1932): "La sistemazione del centro di Brescia dell'architetto Marcello Piacentini". In: Architettura XI/10, pp. 649-671.

Robecchi, Franco (1998): Brescia Littoria. Una città modello dell'urbanistica fascista, Brescia: Gangemi.

Stockel, Giorgio (1992): "Risanamento e demolizioni nel tessuto delle città italiane negli anni trenta". In: Corrado Bozzoni, Giovanni Carbonara, Gabriella Villetti (eds.), Saggi in onore di Renato Bonelli, Roma: Multigrafica, pp. 859-872.

Turati, Augusto et al. (1928): Concorso nazionale per lo studio di un progetto di piano regolatore e di ampliamento per la Città di Brescia: Relazione della Giuria, Brescia: Unione Tipo-Litografica Bresciana (Rub. XVIII, 9, 2153a). Archivio di Stato di Brescia, Brescia, Italy.

Zucconi, Guido (1999 [1989]): La città contesa: Dagli ingegneri sanitari agli urbanisti (1885-1945), Milano: Jaca Book.

The Townscape of Bari
A Laboratory of Italian Urbanism during the Early Twentieth Century

Christine Beese

This article presents the main urban principals that affected the plans for Bari, which were marked by a rupture during the 1920s and then by continuity after 1945. Through an examination of the plans of the architects Concezio Petrucci (1930), Pietro Maria Favia (1932) and Marcello Piacentini (1949), differences regarding their concepts of 'tradition' become evident. While Petrucci's design strategies were based on 'ambiental characteristics' (tradition as continuity), Favia sought to implement a model of the fascist metropolis (tradition as identity), and Piacentini tried to apply picturesque design principles (tradition as permanence).

The planning history of Bari provides a context in which to examine Italian concepts of urbanism particularly closely. A municipal piano di risanamento (1892) was replaced by the plans of the architect Concezio Petrucci in 1930. He envisaged the application of Gustavo Giovannoni's principle of *diradamento* along with Marcello Piacentini's teachings of urban design in order to spur the modernization of Bari. Through the appointment of Piacentini (1881-1960) and Giorgio Calza Bini (1908-99) to elaborate a further plan in 1949, the civic council expressed its desire for continuity in terms of both the ideas and the individuals involved. It was only during the 1960s that the idea of the functionalist city affected the Apulian capital.

The case of Bari not only represents the different urbanistic approaches of the first half of the 20th century, but also reveals the importance of several Fascist professionals and institutions on the national scale. Araldo di Crollalanza (1892-1986), the first Fascist mayor (*podestà*) of Bari and then State Secretary of the

Ministry of Public Works, was interested in establishing the city as the new Fascist service center in southern Italy. He therefore kept track of current town-planning trends, as presented for example at *the International Federation of Housing and Town-Planning* (IFHTP) conference in Rome in 1929. In their capacity as members of the *Consiglio superiore per le antichità e belle arti*, Luigi Piccinato and Gustavo Giovannoni (1873-1947) supported Crollalanza's call for an artistic plan; as the head of the recently created Istituto Nazionale di Urbanistica (INU), Alberto Calza Bini (1881-1957; editor's note: father of Giorgio Calza Bini) improved his institution's position as an important player in the field of town planning.

This article presents the main urban principals that affected the plans for Bari which were marked by a rupture during the 1920s and then by continuity after 1945. I will focus on the interferences of local and national events by analyzing the interests of the different players involved, such as politicians, civil servants and architects. Special attention will be given to the different concepts of 'tradition' as used by the architects: tradition as continuity, tradition as permanence and tradition as identity (cf. Cettina Lenzas' article in this volume). By examining the transferral of these theoretical concepts into the practical urban planning of the past generation, the contradictions they implied become visible.

URBAN PLANNING IN THE HYGIENIST TRADITION – BARI FROM THE 19TH TO THE 20TH CENTURIES

The ancient and medieval town of Bari had already seen its first creative extension during the Napoleonic era. The extension area – established in 1813 during the reign of the King of Naples, Napoleon's brother-in-law Joachim Murat (1767-1815), and for that reason referred to as the borgo murattiano – is a typical example of the rigid Beaux-Arts grid, as was also applied in Paris by Haussmann several years later. Soon the extension took on the major political, cultural and economic institutions of the city. This brought about a decline of Bari's historic urban core. In order to tie the old city and its economic activities to the growing traffic system implemented in the borgo murattiano, the first axis crossing the historic town center was planned in 1852. This was eventually followed by a general piano di risanamento in 1892 (Di Bari 1968: 11-14).

The ideal of hygienic and technical progress remained strong in urban planning until the early 20th century (cf. Zucconi 1989). As the proposals by Aldo Forcignanò (architect) and Gaetano Palmiotto (engineer) show, the concept of replacing the historic fabric and its urban tissue with entirely new buildings on a schematic grid pattern was still very much alive in 1926. Of the existing historic fabric, only the two main churches were to be conserved and at the same time isolated as historic monuments (Di Bari 1968: 23-29; Cucciolla 2006: 99-102).

In comparison, the plan put forward by the municipal engineer Arrigo Veccia in 1911 and again in 1924 appears to be quite moderate. Instead of erasing the entire city core, he suggested laying a main commercial road between the Via Sparano and the cathedral of San Sabino. The road would be the location of institutions such as the national post office. Veccia had already been encouraged in 1911 to take into account the 'ambiental characteristics' of the old city core. Despite this, 'risanamento-models' such as the newly opened Corso Umberto I in Naples or the reorganization of the Piazza del Duomo in Milan maintained a firm hold on his philosophy of city planning (Di Bari 1968: 15-22). In keeping with earlier radial city extensions such as those in Vienna or Cologne, Veccia proposed the construction of circular and arterial roads in order to guide the development of the entire city towards the hinterland regions, while at the same time holding the railway system in check. While an industrial zone limited the potential for expansion to the west, the eastern seaside and its scenic value were especially heavily emphasized as an asset to be exploited in future city development (Petrignani/Porsia 1982: 150).

The importance given to the founding of a national post office can be explained by the political ambitions of Araldo di Crollalanza, who was appointed podestà of Bari in 1926. In line with Mussolini's directives, Crollalanza wanted to transform Bari into a new center for the implementation of Fascist rule. According to the commercial and military propaganda of the time, the city was to become a bridge between the Orient and the Occident (La Sorsa 1934: 32). In reality, the economy of Bari became more and more heavily based upon the administration and service sectors over time, with the result that the influence of the city was directed geographically more toward its hinterland (Mangone 2003: 316).

Crollalanza's appointment to Undersecretary and then to State Secretary of the Ministry of Public Works in 1928 and 1930 respectively forced a shift in his attention and energies towards Rome. In the local politics of Bari he was represented by his vice-podestà, Vincenzo Vella. Presumably acting in Crollalanza's name, Vella ordered Arrigo Veccia to keep the medieval urban fabric as intact as possible, to eliminate later annexes, and above all to abandon the implementation of wide streets and rectangular squares (Làera/Riccardi 1988: 265-266). As Làera and Riccardi note, these urbanistic positions were recorded in the final resolution of the 1929 International Federation for Housing and Town Planning conference in Rome, as published by Marcello Piacentini in that same year (Piacentini 1929: 3; cf. Riboldazzi 2009: 109-124; cf. Wagner 2018: 153-170).

During the conference, Gustavo Giovannoni's concept of *diradamento*, of a careful rehabilitation of the old town, received particular attention and was widely shared as a new approach to reconciling the conflict between the preservation of the historic city and the demands of modern traffic. Similar to the situation in Bari, Giovannoni's concept had been elaborated upon in Rome to prevent the cutting of broad paved streets through the historic center of the city, in disregard of the existing urban tissue (Giovannoni 1913: 449-472). Crollalanza, who had opened the Rome conference, presumably instructed Vella to retreat from the hitherto favored Beaux-Arts models and to adopt the latest trends in urban design based on a revaluation of local forms. Under pressure from the Ministry of Communication to realize the central post office in Bari, however, Veccia did not respond to Vella's demands and fought for the immediate implementation of his plan (Làera/Riccardi 1988: 265-266).

DESIGN STRATEGIES BASED ON 'AMBIENTAL CHARACTERISTICS' – CONCEZIO PETRUCCI'S PLANS OF 1930 AND 1932

Property owners in Bari opposed Veccia's plan, as did Luigi Piccinato and his Roman group of urbanists, the *Gruppo Urbanisti Romani* (GUR). Both therefore called for an intervention by the national *Consiglio superiore per le antichità e belle arti* (Cucciolla 2006: 103-106). The Consiglio established a national committee with members Giovannoni and Alberto Calza Bini (the director of the recently founded Istituto Nazionale di Urbanistica) to develop authoritative urban guidelines for redesigning the center of Bari. In the summer of 1930, Giovannoni's student Concezio Petrucci (1902-46) was given the task of elaborating a definitive plan, to be based on the principle of a meticulous and picturesque style of urban renewal (Di Bari 1968: 31-40). Born in Apulia, Petrucci had graduated from the Scuola Superiore di Architettura in Rome in 1926 and in 1931 was installed as director of the Urban Planning Office of Bari. He left this position after a short time to become a lecturer at the University of Florence. Pietro Maria Favia (1895-1972), another former student of Giovannoni and a native of the city of Bari, became his replacement in 1932 (Mangone 2003: 323).

Petrucci suggested the broadening of four existing roads, all of them leading to the cathedral; its spire would then become the visual focus for each street (Fig. 1). He attached considerable importance to the media representation of this new concept. In line with the plans for the *Quartiere del rinascimento* in Rome and in particular for the renewal of the Via dei Coronari (Giovannoni 1913:

449-472), Petrucci published a ground plan of the historic city which marked the major as well as minor monuments for conservation and the new vistas to be created (Làera/Riccardi 1988: 269). These new perspectives were visualized by suggestive vignettes in the tradition of Camillo Sitte's idea of the picturesque prospect, as already adopted by architects such as Karl Henrici (1842-1927) (cf. Piccinato 1992; cf. Sonne 2003) or Marcello Piacentini (cf. 1917).

Figure 1: Concezio Petrucci: Redevelopment plan for Bari, 1931

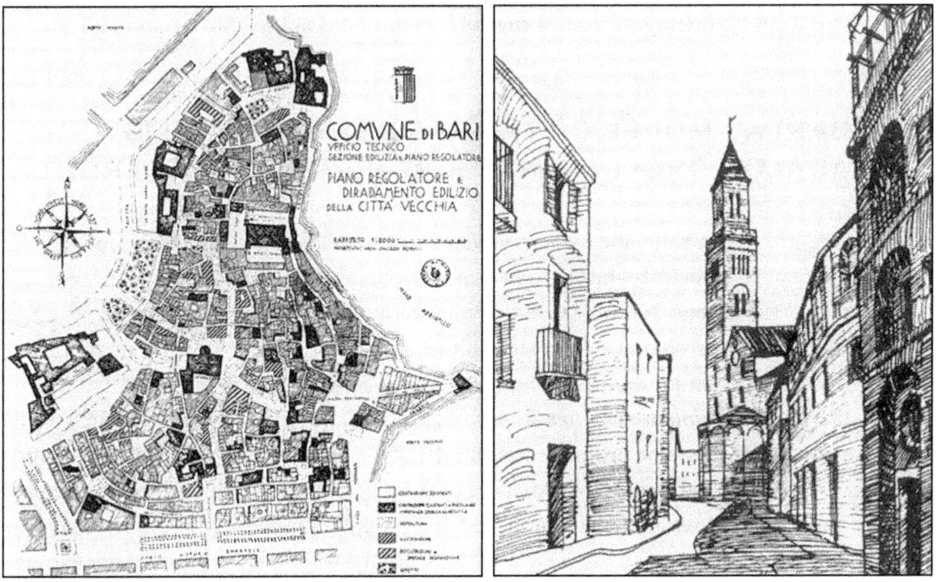

Cucciolla 2006: 114

In contrast to Sitte (1843-1903), whose aim had been to establish guidelines for town extensions by distilling urban design prototypes – such as the architecturally closed square or the grouping of squares according to their functions (cf. 2003) – Giovannoni and Petrucci sought principles for the modernization of historic city cores based on the characteristics of urban tissue which had grown over the centuries (cf. Fraticelli 1982; cf. Giovannoni 1997). The historical courses of streets and the proportions of lots as well as three-dimensional building masses were taken up and used as the basis for the further growth and development of this texture. 'Ambiental characteristics' were meant to provide materials and parameters for design strategies as well as a means by which to strengthen local identity. Thus continuity did not only refer to abstract and timeless design principles but also to the materiality, history, and memory of a specific site.

In the case of Bari, these considerations immediately showed their conceptual and practical limitations in confrontation with the *borgo murattiano*, which borders directly on the headland of Bari and the old town. Continuity in terms of tradition ideally builds on the idea of an uninterrupted thread, on the passing of concepts and methods from one generation to the next. Given the historical reality of the *borgo murattiano*, this kind of transmission had to take the form of a renewal rather than a continuous development. With regard to the regime's efforts to achieve a spiritual and cultural unification of the nation, it is possible to assume that a strengthening of local forms and identity did not result from this effort.

BARI AS MODEL OF THE FASCIST METROPOLIS – ARALDO CROLLALANZA'S MONUMENTAL SEAFRONT

According to Crollalanza, the townscape of Bari should not primarily represent its own specific identity, but instead a more general idea of a Fascist "metropoli sul mare" (Mangone 2003: 324) capable of communicating to visitors a larger message about the character and strength of Italian cities. For this the municipality began to construct the imposing Lungomare Nazario Sauro – against the will of the local *Soprintendenza per le Antichità e le Belle Arti*, which had rejected this plan in 1927. A new promenade connecting the eastern and the western seafronts was also built around the headland and the historic city center. In this way a new image of Bari was created, composed of a monumental seafront dominated by the public buildings of the regime and the old city wall. These developments overshadow the vernacular architecture of the *borgo murattiano* and the historic center (Colonna/Lastilla 1987: 21; Fig. 2). Although officially approved in November 1931, Petucci's plan for the cautious modernization of the old city core was never implemented (Làera/Riccardi 1988: 269) because it clearly did not meet Crollalanza's conception of a Fascist metropolis.

Nevertheless, in February 1932 Vella ordered Petrucci to create a general master plan which would include the *borgo murattiano* as well as the urban hinterland (Colonna/Lastilla 1987: 21). Based on the teachings of his professor, the Roman town planner Marcello Piacentini, Petrucci proposed shifting the railway and extending the Via Cavour towards the south in order to create new inner-city building opportunities as well as green parkways. In deliberate contrast to the tissue of the *borgo murattiano*, Petrucci's vision aimed at variation with lots and squares, an approach Piacentini had absorbed from the work of Joseph Stübben (1845-1936). Both of these urbanists called for functionally and formally-defined extension plans that would create hierarchical systems of spaces and buildings dependent on the character of each quarter (cf. Beese 2015: 80-97). Piacentini himself had adopted the idea of a relocated modern civic center in his plan for Rome of 1925, and was soon joined by his student Luigi Piccinato (1899-1983), who in 1929 founded the aforementioned Gruppo Urbanisti Romani (Zucconi 1989: 151).

Together with his GUR colleagues, the young and ambitious Piccinato sought to extend the sphere of architectural influence into urban planning. Stimulated by examples such as the German Settlement Association of the Ruhr Coal District (Siedlungsverband Ruhrkohlenbezirk, SVR) and the competition for a new town plan for Milan (both discussed at the IFHTP conference), the GUR presented its first regional plan for the Roman hinterland at the Town Planning Exhibition, which was an important element of the 1929 conference in Rome (Fraticelli 1982: 435-436). The declared aim of the GUR plan was to maintain a separation of functions through the active steering of industrial zones to the outskirts of Rome, and to prevent building activities between the borders of the city and the surrounding settlements. A regional transport system sensitive to the functions of the surrounding villages and their relation to the capital was designed (Zevi/Occhipinti 2016). All of these elements are easily identifiable in Petrucci's regional plan for Bari. Not surprisingly, local resistance to shifting the railway, especially on the part of local property owners, prohibited the realization of Petrucci's plan.

Figure 2: Alberto Calza Bini, Grande albergo delle nazioni, Lungomare Nazario Sauro, Bari 1931-1934

La Gazzetta del Mezzogiorno online, 2018 June 29

CONTINUITY AFTER WORLD WAR II – THE ENGAGEMENT OF PIACENTINI AND CALZA BINI IN 1949

It was not until the end of the 1940s that urban extension concepts for Bari once again came under discussion. Concezio Petrucci had passed away in the meantime and could no longer be consulted. Pietro Maria Favia, since 1932 the appointed head of the Municipal Town Planning Office and the architect responsible for the construction of the Lungomare Nazario Sauro (Colonna/Lastilla 1987: 21-22), did not favor an open competition for a new town plan. As a former student of the Scuola Superiore di Architettura in Rome and corresponding member of the Istituto Nazionale di Urbanistica (INU), Favia counted on the expertise of the traditional urban planning élite; he therefore assigned the role of external consultants to Piacentini in 1949, together with Alberto Calza Bini and his son Giorgio (Di Bari 2000: 57). In his capacity as president of the INA-case popolari, Alberto Calza Bini had already erected the Albergo delle Nazioni at Lungomare Nazario Sauro. As a member of the national committee of 1931, he had played a role in establishing the urbanistic criteria underlying the Petrucci plan.

In this way, an attempt was made to maintain continuity in terms of both planning concepts and individuals. As Paolo Nicoloso has recently pointed out, Piacentini had faced considerable opposition between 1945 and 1948 due to the antifascist purge of the immediate postwar years. Thanks to his contacts in existing political circles, however – and especially to State Undersecretary and later cabinet minister Giulio Andreotti (1919-2013) – he was able to return to the scene and to resume work on projects such as the EUR Quarter and the Via della Conciliazione in Rome. The parliamentary election of 1948, which resulted in victory for the Democrazia Cristiana (DC) party and a change in official policy concerning the Fascist past, marked an especially important turning point for Piacentini's projects and his university career. His architectural studio – which had reopened at Tor di Nona in 1947, in association with Giorgio Calza Bini – was now awarded entire new commissions, such as the planning of Bari or the rearrangement of Piazza del Duomo in Ferrara in 1952 (cf. Nicoloso 2018; Beese 2015: 479-492).

In line with an international policy of decentralization, Piacentini and the Calza Binis opted for a regional plan based on a figure of 500,000 inhabitants. Further growth of the city was to be prevented by the creation of independent satellite towns. With regard to the city center, the authors referred to the Petrucci plan of 1932, which was still in force. To facilitate the traffic flow they proposed implementing one-way roads as an alternative to broadening streets such as the Via Cavour, which would otherwise run the risk of losing their urban character. Piacentini and Calza Bini are credited with realizing that if such broadening were carried out, "the most beautiful street in Bari would end up as an ordinary peripheral road" (1952 March 14: 17).[1] Like Petrucci, the authors of the regional plan attempted to convince the national railway company as well as local property owners to relocate the station and tracks to the south. This effort also failed to bring the desired change, however, as it neglected to take into account the growing number of buildings that were being erected south of the station. These could no longer be eliminated and had to be connected to the civic center. Rather than extending the Via Cavour into a classical boulevard as Piacentini suggested, it instead had to be elevated to cross the railway tracks (Beese 2015: 420f.).

Figure 3: Marcello Piacentini: Four skyscrapers defining the overbridge of Corso Cavour, Bari ca 1951

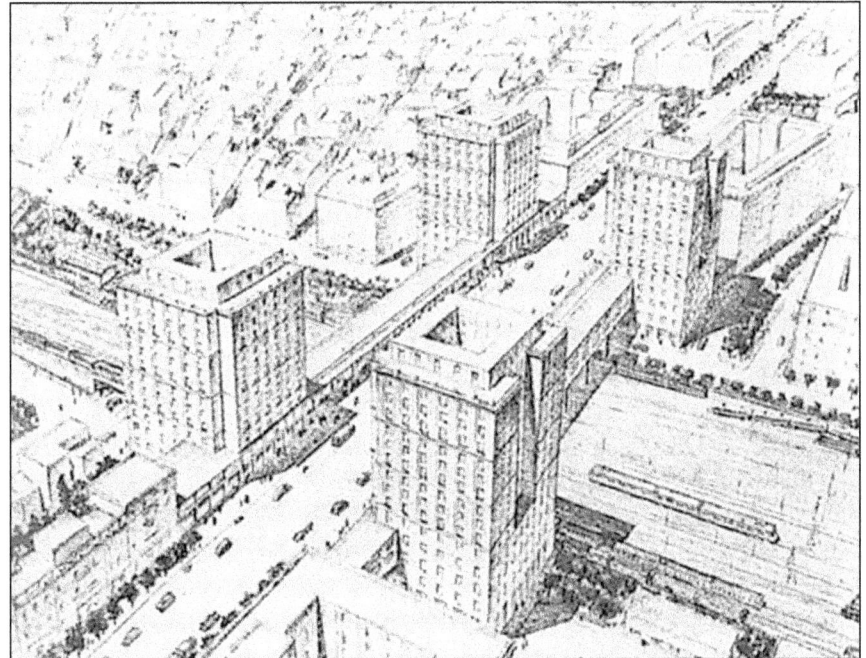

Di Bari 2000: 93

---

1 "Temiamo assai che col suo prolungamento di così ampia sezione, la strada più bella di Bari finirebbe col diventare un comune vialone della periferia."

FROM PICTURESQUE DESIGN PRINCIPLES TO TIME-TESTED ARCHETYPES – PIACENTINI'S PLAN FOR THE VIA CAVOUR AND THE PIAZZA DEL FERRARESE

To avoid the impression of "leaving the city and entering a much less inviting periphery" (Piacentini/Calza Bini 1952 March 14: 17),[2] Piacentini proposed building architecturally closed bridges that would shield the view of the tracks below. These proposed bridges were meant to be lined with shops, arcades and planters, in the manner of the Ponte Vecchio in Florence or the Rialto Bridge in Venice. The second section of the Via Cavour should "take up and preserve the first section's ornamentation" (ibid).[3] As the archival documents show, Piacentini tried to transfer the concept of high-rise buildings to the context of Bari. Such buildings had already been used to even out height differences in the case of the Torre Invernizzi in Genoa (Beese 2015: 422-424). Connected by porticoes, these bridge towers designed for Bari were to create the illusion of a classical urban boulevard (Fig. 3). Once realized, this vision of the Via Cavour would have fit into the overall pattern of the *borgo murattiano* and its extension to the south. In apparent contrast to this concept, the bridge was instead realized in the form of an elevated motorway, a common feature of the car-friendly American metropolis.

Already during the 1930s, the junction of the Corso Cavour, the Corso Vittorio Emanuele and the newly established Lungomare Imperatore Augusto had become an important traffic hub. In order to create a visual axis from the Corso Vittorio Emanuele to the old port, the Municipal Building Office had planned to demolish the market hall, the fish market and the Margherita Theatre in 1939. The traffic moving along the Corso Cavour and the seafront should remain separated and pass to either side of the Piazza del Ferrarese, which was to become the link between the old and the new town. Piacentini had always been a staunch opponent of open spaces and therefore tried to implement an architecturally framed square. Sketches show the idea of a roundabout which would have blocked the Via Cavour towards the north (Beese 2015: 425). In order to imitate the masses of the market buildings, Piacentini proposed the construction of three rectangular structures connected by

---

2   "Oltrepassare nelle attuali condizioni la frattura ferroviaria è per i cittadini Baresi come l'andare 'fuori porta' in altre città; è andare verso una periferia meno appetibile e avulsa della vita elegante del centro."

3   "Più semplice quello di Via Manzoni, più solenne quello del Corso Cavour, come si conviene ad una così importante arteria cittadina, che dovrà in tutto il suo prolungamento riprendere e mantenere il decoro del suo primo tratto."

continuous porticos, which would visually close the northern side of the roundabout (Fig. 4). A second and much quieter square would be created behind this.

It is clear that Piacentini was making use of design strategies derived from Camillo Sitte and his idea of architecturally closed-off squares and the grouping of squares according to their functions. Prominent examples of this concept include the downtown of Bergamo and the Piazza della Vittoria in Brescia, built by Piacentini in 1911 and 1932 respectively (Beese 2015: 364-379, 433-454). While Piacentini tried to take advantage of the historic footprint offered by the ancient buildings in Bari, the architectural language was changed considerably. Instead of the two-storied market halls, the new commercial buildings had more than six floors and extended the *borgo murattiano* into the historic city. Following the tradition of picturesque town planning, Piacentini tried to integrate an existing church into the new building development. This approach led to the degradation of the historic fabric rather than to its valuation. The idea of picturesque design principles, once so innovative, had now fossilized into rigid and abstract formulas. It is no coincidence that Piacentini's plans for the Piazza del Ferrarese resemble the design of Le Havre, which was entirely rebuilt by the classicist Auguste Perret (1874-1954) after 1946. Instead of taking into account the 'ambiental characteristics' of the specific site, Piacentini sought to apply patterns that lost their significance once taken out of their context.

Figure 4: Marcello Piacentini: Bird's eye view of Piazza del Ferrarese, Bari ca 1951

Fondo Marcello Piacentini, busta 247-54, Biblioteca di scienze tecnologiche, Università degli studi di Firenze

CONTINUITY, IDENTITY, PERMANENCE – THE ARCHITECTS' DIFFERENT INTERPRETATIONS OF TRADITION

Coming back to the different classifications of tradition, it becomes obvious that Piacentini supported the idea of tradition as permanence, where Giovannoni did not. Like his modernist colleagues, Piacentini aimed at the distillation of town planning archetypes bearing an eternal Italian spirit, beyond all boundaries of time or space. Artificially applied to specific urban situations having their own local building history, these archetypes became what Piacentini himself had criticized with regard to modernist architecture – namely, academic and abstract. One reason for Piacentini's standardization of the principles espoused by Sitte might be found in his will to create a homogeneous national language, not only in architecture but also in urban planning; a language that was able to express a specific Italian modernity distinct from the International Style. While such an approach seems reasonable in the case of new towns such as Sabaudia, the concept appears inappropriate and ill-suited to historic city centers and their individuality.

Ironically, Pietro Maria Favia, once an important promoter and designer of the representative and monolithic seafront project Lungomare Nazario Sauro, openly criticized Piacentini's plans in 1954, saying that "the proposal presented is not very considerate of the adjacent part of the old city [...] and does not include many reflections on, or sensitivity to, the great monuments, the vernacular architecture and the ambience of the old town." (Di Bari 1968: 52).[4] Favia's renewed interest in spontaneous and popular architecture at the end of the 1940s coincided with the idea of neorealism in general. In contrast to the architectural rhetoric of Fascist culture, looking at marginalized forms of expression should reveal the human and therefore non-Fascist identity of the true Italian people (cf. Casciato 2000: 25-53). With that a new chapter of tradition as identity was opened.

---

4   "La progettazione presentata sia poco riguardosa della contigua parte della Città vecchia [...] e scarsa di riflessi e di sensibilità nei riguardo dei superbi monumenti e delle architettura minori e di ambiente della Città vecchia."

REFERENCES

Di Bari, Domenico (1968): Bari: Vicende urbanistiche del centro storico (1867-1967) (Quaderni dell'istituto di architettura ed urbanistica), Bari: Dedalo Libri.
Di Bari, Domenico (2000): La città fuori legge: Bari; Progetto e attuazione del Prg Piacentini – Calza Bini, 1954-1976, Bari: Ecumenica Editrice.
Casciato, Maristella (2000): "Neorealism in Italian Architecture." In: Sarah W. Goldhagen/ Maristella Casciato (eds.), Anxious Modernisms: Experimentation in Postwar Architectural Culture, Cambridge/Massachusets: MIT Press.
Colonna, Angela/Lastilla, Michele (eds.) (1987): Storia e cultura di una città: Edifici pubblici a Bari 1900-1950, Bari: Regione Puglia – Assessorato cultura.
Cucciolla, Arturo (2006): Vecchie città – città nuove: Concezio Petrucci, 1926-1946, Bari: Edizioni Dedalo 2006.
Fraticelli, Vanna (1982): Roma, 1914-1929: La città e gli architetti tra la guerra e il fascismo, (collana di architettura 22), Rome: Officina Ed.
Giovannoni, Gustavo (1913): "Vecchie città ed edilizia nuova." In: Nuova antologia XLVII/ 995, pp. 449-472.
Giovannoni, Gustavo/Zucconi, Guido (eds.) (1997): Dal capitello alla città (di fronte e attraverso), Milan: Jaca Book.
Làera, Rosa Angela/Riccardi, Carmela (1988): "Pianificazione urbana e territoriale nella politica di regime di Araldo Di Crollalanza (Bari)." In: Giulio Ernesti (ed.), La costruzione dell'utopia: Architetti e urbanisti nell'Italia fascista; Casa, città, territorio, Rome: Edizioni Lavoro, pp. 265-279.
Mangone, Fabio (2003): "La costruzione della 'Grande Bari' negli anni del fascismo, tra ricerca di identità e omologazione." In: Vittorio Franchetti Pardo (ed.), L'architettura nelle città italiane del XX secolo: Dagli anni venti agli anni ottanta, Milan: Jaca Book, pp. 316-325.
Nicoloso, Paolo (2018): Marcello Piacentini: Architettura e potere; Una biografia, Udine: Gaspari.
Petrignani, Marcello/Porsia, Franco (1982): Bari (le città nella storia d'Italia), Rome: Laterza.
Piacentini, Marcello (1917): Per la restaurazione del centro di Bologna, Rome: Bodoni.
Piacentini, Marcello (1929): "Che cosa ci ha insegnato il congresso degli urbanisti." In: Il giornale d'Italia September 24, p. 3.
Piacentini, Marcello (1929a): Le due relazioni generali (di inizio e di chiusura) svolte al congresso internazionale dell'abitazione e dei Piani regolatori: Sistemazione delle città a carattere storico per adattarle alle esigenze della vita moderna, Rome: Selecta S.A.I.

Piacentini, Marcello/Calza-Bini, Alberto (1952, March 14): Relazione al Piano regolatore della città di Bari. Fondo Marcello Piacentini, busta 246. Biblioteca di scienze tecnologiche, Università degli studi di Firenze (FPF).

Piccinato, Giorgio (1992), "Sitte e le parole dell'urbanistica italiana". In: Guido Zucconi/Armand Brulhart (eds.), Camillo Sitte e i suoi interpreti, Milan: Franco Angeli, pp. 116-127.

Riboldazzi, Renzo (2009): "Roma 1929". In: Renzo Riboldazzi, Un'altra modernità: L'Ifhtp e la cultura urbanistica tra le due guerre, 1923-1939, Rome: Gangemi, pp. 109-124,

Sitte, Camillo (2003[1889]): "Der Städtebau nach seinen künstlerischen Grundsätzen." In: Klaus Semsroth/Michael Mönninger/Christiane Crasemann Collins (eds.), Camillo Sitte Gesamtausgabe, Wien: Böhlau.

Sonne, Wolfgang (2003): "'The entire city shall be planned as a Work of Art:' Städtebau als Kunst im frühen modernen Urbanismus, 1890–1920." In: Zeitschrift für Kunstgeschichte 66/2, pp. 207–236.

La Sorsa, Saverio (1934): Il duce e la Puglia, 3.1/Bari, Molfetta: Scuola Tipografica per Sordomuti nell'Istituto provinciale Apicella.

Wagner, Philip (2018): "Zwischen grenzübergreifender Standardisierung und nationalem Lobbying: Der internationale Kongress für Wohnungswesen und Städtebau in Rom 1929." In: Christine Beese/Ralph-Miklas Dobler (eds.): L'Urbanistica a Roma durante il ventennio fascista (Quaderni della Bibliotheca Hertziana 1), Rome: Campisano Editore, pp. 153-170.

Zevi, Sergio Fabio/Occhipinti, Giuseppe (eds.) (2016): Idee e piani per il territorio romano: Un contributo dell'Archivio Luigi Piccinato, Rome: Gangemi Editore.

Zucconi, Guido (1989): La città contesa: dagli ingegneri sanitari agli urbanisti, 1855-1942, Milan: Jaca Book.

Bergamo as a *Case Study*

Sandro Scarrocchia

Bergamo played a central role in 20th century Italian architecture having offered a specific contribution to the definition of the historic centre as "a single monument" or "ensemble". However, in order to make the city's particular orographic features a historical fact, artistic and architectural action was needed, which took the recognition of monumentality to a new environmental scale and for which the city's culture must thank Marcello Piacentini, Luigi and Sandro Angelini, Giovanni Astengo and Luigi Dodi.

This paper aims to: first, outline the relevance of Bergamo for the theory and history of monument conservation and restoration in particular and for the history of 20th century architecture in general, second, acknowledge that the continuity of its urban development, as well as its framework and management, constitute a recognizable civic tradition and a heritage and finally explore the possibility for this tradition to take charge of the more recent changes and trends characterizing urban development, especially that of medium-sized towns that form the load-bearing infrastructure of the historic, economic, social and cultural areas of Italy.

We are dealing with the fabric that Carlo Cattaneo (1801-69) referred to as that of the "100 cities" [of Italy, editor's note] and which he claimed was the beginning of the Nation (cf. Cattaneo 1931 [1858]). It is not just by chance that the artistic guides of the series "Italia Artistica" of the early 20th century, edited by the best art historians of the time, were inspired by the very principles of Cattaneo and that the edition dedicated to Bergamo, edited by Pietro Pesenti, already provided a canvas for thought on the matter, being amongst one of the first cities to reveal the continuity of development: "The current design of the [Upper] town still reminds us close up of how it was in olden days, even though in several areas an innovative, and not always laudable spirit has altered or destroyed the historic characteristics of the town", but the new Centro Piacentiniano [editor's note: built by Marcello Piacentini (1881-1960)] offers "an architectonic spectacle that is sober enough to avoid any unpleasant contrast with the exquisitely picturesque setting of the high town" (Pesenti 1927: 34, 136-7).[1]

The case of Bergamo has a dual exemplariness due to an urbanistic policy and an avant-garde practice of architecture and restoration both in the first half of the 20th century and in the post-war period, although they obviously had different characteristics and outlooks in the first and second half of the century. However, my reconstruction will depart from the accredited perspective, which confines the exemplariness of the city's history to the first half of the 20th century (cf. Irace 1997; Scalvini/Calza/Finardi 1987). Apart from the chapter on urban history between the two wars, I would, therefore, like to draw attention to the matter of the post-World War II period, which I consider to be equally emblematic and of importance for European culture.[2] Bergamo played a key role in the Italian architecture of the 20th century for particular reasons, the first being the specific contribution that it offered to the definition of the historic center as a "single monument" or *ensemble*, as part of the movement that produced the Carta di Gubbio (1960) and the foundation of ANCSA (National Association for Historical-Artistic Urban Cores, *Associazione Nazionale Centri Storico-Artistici*) (1960-61). Secondly, it is important for the strategic role that it has been acknowledged to have played for urban development during the 1960s, as the "pattern for [further] urban development", that is an organic urban expansion (cf. Scarrocchia 2017).

Bergamo was facilitated in achieving this result by its orographic features, characterised by an old settlement on the hills and by the building development in the lower town (cf. Angelini, L. 1962). Yet, in order to transform the orographic features into a historical fact and an element for conservation and design, a cultural, artistic and architectural action was required which took the recognition of monumentality to a new environmental scale. In this sense, a way of thinking, a professional standpoint, a civil posture, which we could briefly define as a specific "tradition" or *genius loci*, allowed this further cultural and disciplinary step forward to be taken. But even this latter environmental data belonging to the second half of the 20th century should not be taken for granted, it is the fruit of personal commitment and passion for the city. The two protagonists linking the first part of

---

1   "La conformazione attuale della città [Alta] ricorda ancora da vicino quello che essa era anticamente, sebbene in vari punti uno spirito innovatore non sempre lodevole abbia alterato o distrutte le memorabili caratteristiche cittadine"; "uno spettacolo architettonico abbastanza sobrio per evitare ogni contrasto sgradevole con la scena squisitamente pittoresca dell'altura".

2   The reconstruction by Spagnolo (2001, 2002, 2003) moves in this direction.

this event to the second not only belong to two generations, but, significantly, are also father and son: Luigi and Sandro Angelini (1884-1969; 1915-2001). They are the ones who will guarantee a continuity; it is their action, although with different training and following different artistic and professional trends, that will guarantee the tradition and its local traits, but with a relevance that goes far beyond the local dimension.

Figure 1: Luigi Angelini, Plan for the Restoration of the Upper Town, detail, 1942

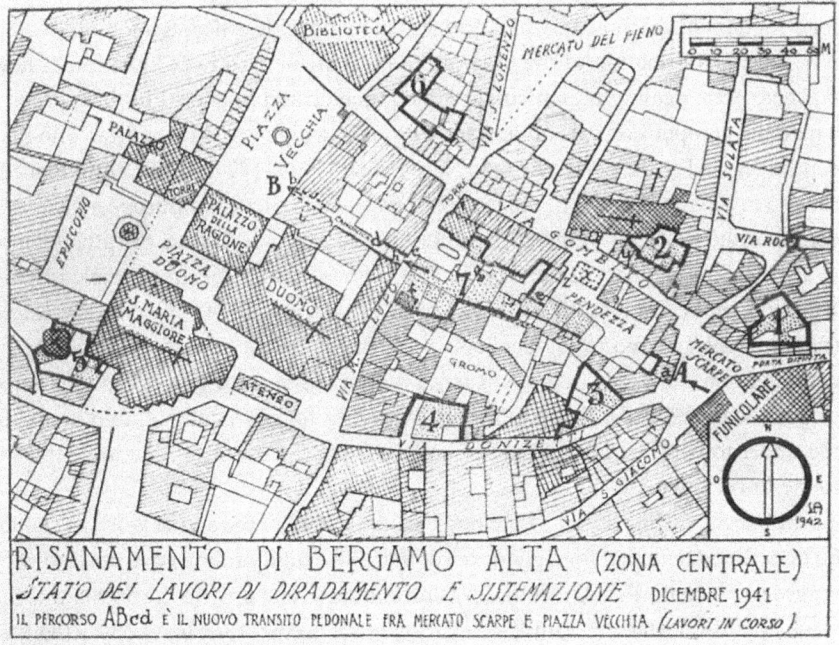

Angelini, 1963

The idea of the historical center as part of a city that has reached a level of historicity to be preserved and protected with precise strategies of rehabilitation and restoration, was in an embryonic stage for a long time, especially with regard to the French and German theoretical tradition. In Italy, the idea was formalized as a principle in 1931 by Gustavo Giovannoni (1873-1947) with his theory for the "thinning out of historic building fabric" (*diradamento*) (cf. Pane/Sette 2018; Pane 2007, 2017; Belli 2002; Ventura 1995). Apart from the Selicotto district in Siena and in the Plan for Old Bari, as the manuals tell us, the principle was applied for the first time on a large scale in Bergamo with the Plan for the Restoration of the

Upper Town by Luigi Angelini in 1935 (Fig. 1), which was welcomed by the same Giovannoni as a manifestation of his theory (cf. Giovannoni 1943; Angelini, L. 1963). However, this plan, but above all the incisive action undertaken for the redevelopment and redefining of the Upper Town, is still struggling to be recognized as a contemporary fact, the fruit of contemporary architectural culture (cf. Bonfantini 2008, 2015). Angelini's Plan highlights three points: the surgical nature of the redevelopment processes, the clever insertion of recognizable modern features and the detailed definition of the conservation measures such as the shop signs (Scarrocchia 1986, 1987).

At that time, the city had already been involved in another very important plan for a modern development, which had attracted the widescale attention of specialists: the transformation of the area of the old Fair in the lower town into a new business area, dealing in particular with commerce and finance. For this purpose, a national competition was organized (1906-07), which was won by Marcello Piacentini and led to the creation of the New Centre (1912-1927). The Centro Piacentiniano in Bergamo is one of the few examples of an Italian and European business center of the first half of the 20th century. In Aldo Rossi's terms of "architecture of the city", it is a part of the city. In Piacentini's terms, it is an example of City Building, as he claimed in his teaching at the Faculty of Architecture in Rome (Papini 1929; Lupano 1995; Iacobone 2010; Beese 2016). The reasons behind Piacentini's new centre of Bergamo cannot be limited to the city's exceptional orographic features or the fact that the area was free for development, thus enabling the upper town to be left untouched and allowing the business area to be moved to the lower town.

In Bergamo, Piacentini's "method" can be traced in the actual work. It should be underlined here that for a good part of the 20th century referring to method with regard to Piacentini's architecture was meaningless and only in the 1990s was his work appraised, starting with Paolo Portoghesi's prediction when he was the first to speak of the "irresistible rise of Piacentini".[3] His method, therefore, is connected with "on site" updating: urban references and the theories of Camillo Sitte (1843-1903), Charles Buls (1837-1914) and Joseph Stübben (1845-1936) on a theoretical level are, in fact, accompanied by a knowledge of American Civic Design that he experienced first-hand initially at Expo in Chicago and then at Expo in San Francisco, where his design of the Italian citadel announced that principle of urban unity and a variety of building forms which was then implemented in Bergamo. In the background, or perhaps it is better to say in the foreground, as constant

---

3   Apart from the fundamental Lupano (1995), see now also Nicoloso (2018) and on the "method" Beese (2016), as well as Scarrocchia (2013: chap. "Architettours").

references to classic modernity, or if we prefer to a classic modern, there were the beloved Viennese, in our case especially Joseph Maria Olbrich (1867-1908) in relation to the Palace of Justice (Fig. 2).

Figure 2: The Centro Piecentiniano in the 1950s

Museo delle storie di Bergamo, Archivio fotografico Sestini, Raccolta Domenico Lucchetti

This is where the exemplariness of the early 20th century Bergamo lies. And all of this, Piacentini in the lower town and Angelini in the upper town, belongs to the history of architecture, the history of town planning and the theory and history of restoration on an urban scale. In which other Italian city, and perhaps not only Italian cities, was the conservation of the historical center and the building of the modern city able to find such an emblematic realization, anticipating the thought of Le Corbusier (1887-1965) and of Hans Sedlmayr (1896-1984)? However, in order for this unified context of old and modern, high and low to become a cultural legacy, concrete acts of recognition were and remain necessary from people willing to continue the work and, therefore, to build a tradition.

Perhaps it was the presence of these two elements, a financial district, a *city*, in the lower town built ex novo and a revitalized and restored historic center in the Upper Town, and indeed the fact that the city had remained untouched after the

World War II, that led Bergamo to become the venue for the 7th CIAM in 1949, the second International Congress of Modern Architecture of the post-war period (Sacchi 2001). Even if the focus of the discussion concerned the *grid* and the urban schemes for comparing the different situations of growth and urban planning, what remains in the collective memory of this Congress are the astonished looks of Alvar Aalto (1898-1976) and of Le Corbusier in the alleyways of the Upper Town, a trace of which remains in the famous drawing of the latter with the caption: "When I enter a friend's house, I leave my umbrella outside the door; visitors to old Bergamo can do the same with their car",[4] which was to become an edict for the banning of vehicles from old towns.

The profile of Bergamo in the history of architecture and restoration finishes here, in other words with the acknowledgement of the extremely important role to be allotted to this city as part of the reconstruction of the architectural events of the city and the conservation of the old urban fabric.

Yet, to consider the Upper Town as an "ensemble" the Venetian walls sketched by Le Corbusier are not sufficient. The acknowledgement came later and derived from Sandro Angelini's plan for the historic center of Bergamo, which began in 1962 and was concluded in 1975. This change is part of a wider renewal of the Italian culture, with an anthropological and social importance, which enjoyed the positive effects of artistic, literary, musical and theatrical research, in other words the cultural research undertaken in those years. However, it should be noted that while in international culture, Bologna with its Social Housing Program for the historic center represented a well-known case study (Scarrocchia 2013, 2015), the case of Bergamo has, unfortunately, remained in the shadows. Nonetheless, the city demonstrates and maintains a regulatory and pedagogical value on two levels that are still surprising and of international relevance: a) in fact, it considers the historic fabric, "all" the historic fabric as a "monumental whole" (*ensemble*) (cf. Angelini 1982; Scarrocchia 2017); b) as a fundamental instrument of the plan, it provides for the cataloguing of all the historic buildings as monuments, according to a historical-artistic and conservative approach extended to all the historic and environmental phenomena regardless of their value as a memory or their artistic relevance (Scarrocchia 2011). To these two a third element must be added: the value represented by the building of the center as a pattern or model and the consequent historic fabric for prefiguring and planning an organic urban development of the contemporary city (fig. 3).

---

4   "Quand j'entre chez un ami, je laisse mon parapluie à la porte; les visiteurs de la vieille Bergame peuvent bien laisser leurs roues à la porte."

Figure 3: Giovanni Astengo and Luigi Dodi, General urban development plan of Bergamo 1969, example of structural development as "overturning of the historic city on the new one"

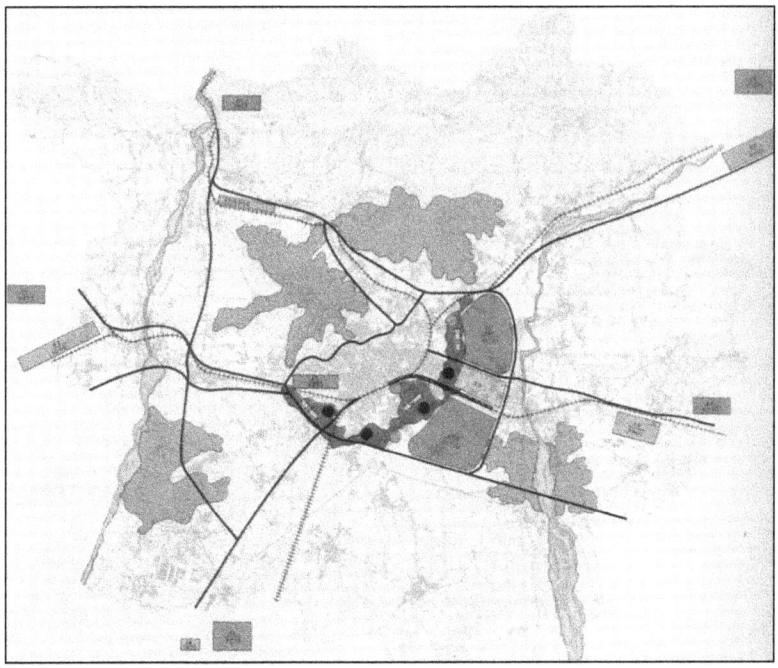

Bergamo: gli studi per il nuovo P.R.G., 1965-1969, Comune di Bergamo, 1970

The principle of analogic urban development, in other words the employment of the historic fabric as a pattern for the new development project belongs to the Urban Planning scheme of Giovanni Astengo (1915-90) and Luigi Dodi (1900-83; 1969-72), which skillfully guided the development of Bergamo up until the 1980s (Astengo 1970).[5] It is thanks to Astengo that the Upper Town and the Lower Town were brought back into a sole concept of urban planning, in an attempt to extend the praiseworthy relationship between the historic fabric and the new settlement to the whole of the municipal area, amplifying the concept of historic center to the outlying districts and integrating the marginal developments into an organic framework. Like Piacentini's plans for the new center of the Lower Town, and Luigi Angelini's for the restoration of the Upper Town before the war, Sandro Angelini's conservative plan of restoration for the Upper Town and the Districts

---

5   For the Astengo plan, Mazzoleni (1983) continues to be exemplary.

and the land use plan of Astengo/Dodi in the post-war period and at the beginning of the economic boom, also represent paradigmatic chapters in the history of Italian town planning in the 20th century. They led to the belief that it was possible for the architectural plan and culture to characterize the development of the organic city, in which the new was widely compatible with the old, respecting first and foremost the logic of the settlement, and even adopting it as the pattern of reference in an inclusive social horizon. This is still evident and verifiable today in the fine conservation of the characteristics of the Upper Town and the historic districts on one side and, on the other, in the high urban quality of the new districts of expansion, in other words in the suburbs, which do not represent an exception in the national panorama, but are certainly one of the most significant examples (Fig. 4).

Figure 4: Example of Sandro Angelini's Index of historic buildings from the Comune di Bergamo (1978)

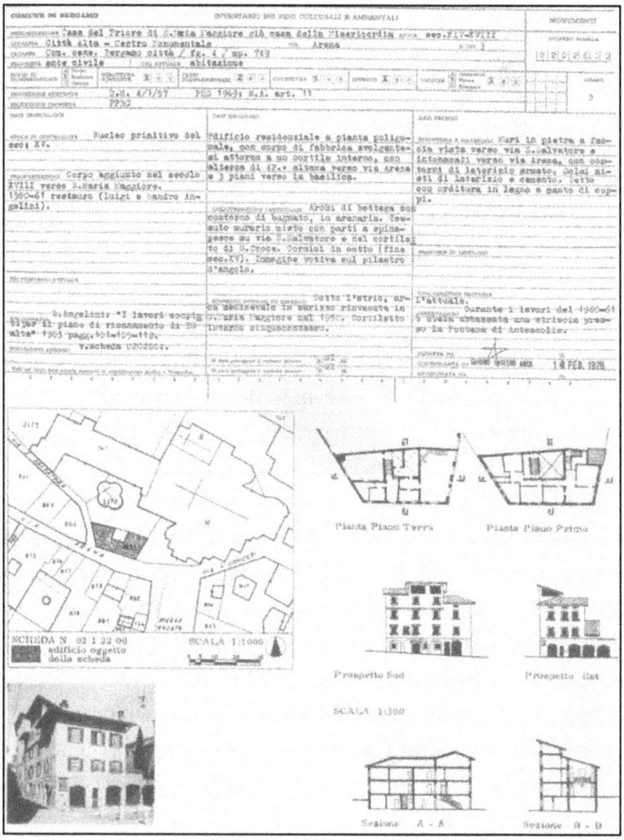

Bergamo, Archivio Angelini

Therefore, the exemplariness of the case of Bergamo not only concerns the period between the two wars, but also the period following the World War II. In this second period, the centrality of the new architecture and of the new city below, as theorized and implemented by Piacentini, is upturned by the centrality of the conservation of the old city above, considered not as a city-museum according to Sandro Angelini, but rather as the barycenter and principle of the territorial development according to Giovanni Astengo.

There are multiple factors for the decline of the exemplariness of the case, but in general even the crisis of Bergamo as a model must be seen against the general reduction in power and resources of the local council, both as town planner and investor or investment coordinator which characterizes instead both the period between the two wars and the period after the World War II, certainly in a different way and with different political and social inspirations. The idea of attributing monumental value to all architectural buildings of the past reached a crisis at the end of the 20th century, at the same time as the decline in importance of the index of historic buildings and of the idea itself of urban planning as the guiding principle of urban development being a common asset in the hands of the local council as the decision-maker of last instance. This led to the re-emergence of old ideologies, such as the hierarchical and selective idea of the monument and to the appearance of new phenomena such as the transformation of historic centers into theme parks or exclusive areas for the rich. The controversy raised by Sandro Angelini in the last period of his life moved in this direction, that is against reducing the Upper Town to a "town of little squares", in other words of increased, but poorly qualified tourism.

Some other aspects in the case of Bergamo that mark the "local council's" loss of hold over the territory and, therefore, an eclipse in the management of quality urban development involve the lower town and urban expansion in general. Firstly, there was the difficulty in tackling the problem of the industrial buildings that fell into disuse and the failure to recover the heritage that they represented. Historically, they constituted a strong fabric set in the outskirts between the city and the countryside and they could have represented the structure for a new organic development.

Secondly, the barrier of the railway was not "overcome", even though it had been the subject of a competition organized immediately after the war,[6] and there was the difficulty linked to the recovery of the land occupied by the railway, which

---

6   The Competition for the Railway flyover of 1947 was won by Sandro Angelini and Pino Pizzigoni (cf. Spagnolo 2001).

represents a strategic area for any future plan for metropolitan integration (Pizzigoni 2017).

Finally, the confirmation of a centripetal model yet again to the detriment of a metropolitan vision, lies in the new Parking alla Fara car park located in front of the Venetian Walls, which were recently declared to be a Unesco world heritage site, and alongside the row of terraced houses built by Pino Pizzigoni (1901-67) between 1949 and 1953,[7] which represent one of the few, but also one of the most important contemporary architectural works within a historic center.

However, the fact that the Centro Piacentiniano still represents a focus point of the administrative policy today so that the city as a whole returns to concentrating on itself, as occurred one century ago, has been demonstrated by the recent competition which concentrates on renovating the public areas in this part of the city. Nonetheless, the city still awaits the involvement of artists or talented sculptors who can provide a suitable representation of Sandro Angelini's dream, to place a seal on the whole matter as a symbol and provide illuminating inspiration for the civil re-appropriation of the consciousness of urban tradition represented by art. On 2nd July 1999, Sandro Angelini sent his last proposal to the councilor for culture, regarding the placing of sculptures along the promenade called Sentierone:

We could install realistic and gently ironic bronze figures representing, for example, pensioners in animated conversation under the trees or someone reading a newspaper near the news stand or a mother with child drinking at the water fountain or a little boy playing with his pets or a tourist taking a photograph of the monument to Donizetti. A recent trip to Spain enabled me to complete these guidelines. Having seen in front of a building designed by Gaudì in Leon the bronze figure of the architect sitting on a bench facing the building and drawing, I had the idea of installing a figure of the architect Marcello Piacentini looking at a drawing of his new center possibly in the company of Luigi Angelini who was the manager of the works and designer of some of the buildings. The figure could be placed under the trees in front of Balzer. (Simoncini 2015: 119-120)[8]

---

7   The car park in question is in total contradiction with the choice of the Secchi Plan of the 1990s which insisted greatly on the east-west axis of the territorial development as the core of the metropolitan city (cf. Secchi 1994; Scarrocchia 2018).

8   "Si potrebbero collocare figure in bronzo realistiche di garbata ironia, come, per esempio, pensionati in animato colloquio sotto le piante o lettore di giornale presso l'edicola o mamma con bambina che beve alla vedovella o bambino che gioca con animali domestici o turista che fotografa il monumento a Donizetti. Un viaggio in Spagna in questi giorni mi ha dato l'occasione di completare indicazioni. Avendo visto di fronte

Three days later, he announced a proposal made by three students, who he had helped prepare a thesis on the Upper Town, which involved installing a bronze cast of the famous cartoon by Gian Battista Galizzi (1882-1963) of 1911 depicting his father on a study trip by bicycle armed with all his drawing materials, to be set up in the center of the Piazzetta Angelini, in the aim of, "creating a visual attraction with its own representative function: in fact, it is not only the key architectural emergencies that condition the way an urban location is experienced, but also the minor elements" (ibid: 119-120).[9]

These two monuments are reminiscent of the one to the writer Peter Altenberg (1859-1919) at the Café Central in Vienna, to the choreographer Piotr Cezary Skrzynecki (1930-97) in the Vis à Vis pub in the Market Square in Krakow, to the writer Fernando Pessoa (1888-1935)in the "A Brasilia" bar in Lisbon and, as Sandro Angelini himself recalled, the one to Antoni Gaudi (1852-1926) in Leon in front of Casa Botines. If these monuments should ever be made, they would represent a passing of the baton, of the city's acceptance of a legacy, reviving the city's consideration of itself as being worthy of a tradition.

REFERENCES

Angelini, Luigi (1962): Lo sviluppo urbanistico di Bergamo nei secoli: La progressiva configurazione della forma urbis, Bergamo: Bolis.

Angelini, Luigi (1963): I lavori compiuti per il Piano di risanamento di Bergamo Alta, 1936-1943, 1950-1960, Bergamo: Stamperia Conti.

Angelini, Sandro (1982): Bergamo: Città Alta; Una vicenda urbana (Edizione del Comune di Bergamo), Bergamo: Poligrafiche Bolis.

Astengo, Giovanni (1970): "Relazione". In: Bergamo: Gli studi per il nuovo P.R.G., 1965-1969, Edizione a cura della rivista Urbanistica, Torino, Bergamo: Comune di Bergamo, pp. 103-107.

---

a un palazzo progettato da Gaudì a Leon la figura in bronzo dell'architetto che disegna seduto su una panchina e rivolto al palazzo mi è venuto in mente di mettere la figura dell'architetto Marcello Piacentini che guarda un disegno del suo nuovo centro eventualmente con Luigi Angelini che fu direttore dei lavori e progettista di alcuni degli edifici. La collocazione potrebbe essere sempre sotto le piante all'altezza del Balzer."

9 [...] "creare un polo visuale con una propria funzione rappresentativa: non sono infatti solo le emergenze architettoniche dei riferimenti che condizionano il modo di vivere un luogo urbano, ma anche gli elementi minori".

Beese, Christine (2016): Marcello Piacentini: Moderner Städtebau in Italien, Berlin: Reimer.

Belli, Attilio (1996): Immagini e concetti nel piano: Inizi dell'urbanistica in Italia, Milano: Etaslibri.

Bonfantini, Bertrando (2008): Bergamo: Piani, 1880-2000, Santarcangelo di Romagna (RN): Maggioli, pp. 166-171 Bonfantini, Bertrando (2015): "Bergamo, 1926-1960: Il piano di Luigi Angelini per Bergamo Alta, snodo per il progetto dei centri storici." In: Albrecht Benno/Anna Magrin (eds.): Esportare il Centro storico, Milano: Guaraldi, pp.162-169.

Cattaneo, Carlo (1931 [1858]): La Città considerata come principio ideale delle istorie italiane, a cura e con introduzione e note di G. A. Belloni, Firenze: Vallecchi. [In: Crepuscolo 42, 44, 50, 52/XI, 1858, pp. 657- 659, 689-693, 785-790, 817-821].

Giovannoni, Gustavo (1943): "Una teoria ben applicata: Il risanamento di Bergamo." (Prefazione a Luigi Angelini: Il Piano di risanamento di Bergamo Alta: Le opere realizzate ed in corso) In: Urbanistica XII/3, pp. 4-12.

Iacobone, Damiano (2010): "Marcello Piacentini et alii a Bergamo Bassa." In: Marina Docci/Maria Grazia Turco (eds.): L'architettura dell'"altra modernità": Atti del XXVI Congresso di Storia dell'architettura, Roma 11-13 aprile 2007, Roma: Gangemi, pp. 246–255.

Irace, Fulvio (1987): "Le due città: Picentini e Angelini." In: Giorgio Rumi/Gianni Mezzanotte/Alberto Cova (eds.): Bergamo e il suo territorio, Milano: Cariplo, pp.161-198.

Lupano, Mario (1995): Marcello Piacentini, Roma-Bari: Laterza.

Mazzoleni, Chiara (ed.) (1983): Teoria del Piano: Giovanni Astengo e il Piano di Bergamo; un caso paradigmatico, Milano: Franco Angeli.

Nicoloso, Paolo (2018): Marcello Piacentini: Architettura e potere; Una biografia, Udine: Gaspari.

Pane, Andrea (2007): "Il vecchio e il nuovo nelle città italiane: Gustavo Giovannoni e l'architettura moderna." In: Alberto Ferlenga/Eugenio Vassallo/Francesca Schellino (eds.): Antico e Nuovo: Architetture e architettura, Atti del Convegno, Venezia, 31 marzo–3 aprile 2004, Padova: Il Poligrafo, pp. 215–231.

Pane, Andrea (2017): "Diradamento e risanamento delle 'vecchie città'. L'opera di Piccinato tra continuità e rottura con Giovannoni da Padova a Napoli." In: Gemma Belli/Andrea Maglio (eds.): Luigi Piccinato, 1899-1983: Architetto e urbanista, Roma: Aracne, pp. 53-78.

Pane Andrea/Sette Maria Pia (2018): "Città, ambiente, paesaggio: tra vecchio e nuovo." In: Gustavo Giovannoni tra storia e progetto, Roma: Quasar, pp. 117-154.

Papini, Roberto (1929): Bergamo rinnovata, Bergamo: Istituto Italiano d'Arti Grafiche.

Pesenti, Pietro (1927 [1911]): Bergamo. Coll. di Monografie Illustrate, serie 1ª, Italia Artistica, diretta da Corrado Ricci. Bergamo: Istituto Italiano d'Arti Grafiche.

Pizzigoni, Attilio (2017): La città ostile: Realtà dell'architettura urbana nelle sue contraddizioni storiche, Milan: Christian Marinotti.

Sacchi, Nestorio (2001): "Il Cinquantesimo anniversario del VII Congresso Internazionale di Architettura Moderna – C.I.A.M. Bergamo (1949-1999)." In: Atti dell'Ateneo di Scienza, Lettere ed Arti di Bergamo", LXII, pp. 25-36.

Scalvini Maria Luisa/Calza Gian Piero/Finardi Paola (1987): Bergamo (coll. Le città nella storia d'Italia), Roma-Bari: Laterza.

Scarrocchia, Sandro (1986, 1987): "Bergamo Alta di Luigi Angelini." In: Restauro & Città 3-4, pp. 254-259; 5/6, pp. 207-212.

Scarrocchia, Sandro (2011): "Urbanistica e conservazione a Bergamo: l'inventario dei Beni culturali e ambiantali." In: Ark (Suppl. de "L'Eco di Bergamo"), 7, pp. 40-43.

Scarrocchia, Sandro (2013 [1999]): Albert Speer e Marcello Piacentini: L' architettura del totalitarismo negli anni Trenta, Milan: Skira.

Scarrocchia, Sandro (2013): " 'Bologna rossa' e la Civiltà dell'Arte." In: Vismara, Gisella (ed.): Giovanni Maria Accame: Un pensiero plurale, Milano: Silvana, pp. 79-88.

Scarrocchia, Sandro (2015): "Denkmalpflege und Avantgarde: Das 'Rote Bologna' und der soziale Gesichtspunkt bei der Politik der Altstadtsanierung." In: Michel Falser/Wilfried Lipp (eds.): Eine Zukunft für unsere Vergangenheit: Zum 40. Jubiläum des Europäischen Denkmalschutzjahres (1975-2015), (coll. Icomos, Monumenta III), Berlino: Hendirik Bäßler, pp. 322-331.

Scarrocchia, Sandro (2017): "Il piano di Bergamo Alta tra 'Carta di Gubbio', 'Carta di Venezia' e 'Anno Europeo del Patrimonio Architettonico' (1962-1975)." In: ASUP (Annali di Storia dell'Urbanistica e del Paesaggio), 5, pp. 150-163.

Scarrocchia, Sandro (2018): "A Bergamo: parcheggio alla Fara e città ostile." In: 'Ananke, 85, pp. 142-146.

Secchi, Bernardo (1994): Tre piani: La Spezia, Ascoli, Bergamo, Cristina Bianchetti (ed.), Milano: Franco Angeli.

Simoncini, Carlo (2015): "Quell'uom di multiforme ingegno": Vita di Sandro Angelini, Bergamo: Lubrina.

Spagnolo, Roberto (2001): "L'architettura a Bergamo tra tradizione e nuovi linguaggi." In: Maria Cristina Rodeschini Galati (ed.): Arte a Bergamo, 1945-1959, Bergamo: Lubrina, pp. 116-137.

Spagnolo, Roberto (2002): "Verso un'architettura della città." In: Maria Cristina Rodeschini Galati (ed.): Arte a Bergamo, 1960-1969, Bergamo: Lubrina, pp. 99-104.

Spagnolo, Roberto (2003): "Architettura a Bergamo negli anni '70: teoria e pratica." In: Maria Cristina Rodeschini Galati (ed.): Arte a Bergamo, 1970-1981, Bergamo: Lubrina, pp. 91-95.

Ventura, Francesco (1995): "Attualità e problemi dell'urbanistica giovannoniana." In: Giovannoni, Gustavo: Vecchie città ed edilizia nuova, ristampa a cura di F. Ventura, Milano: Cittàstudi, pp. 13-39.

Zucconi, Guido (2002): "Gustavo Giovannoni: Vecchie città ed edilizia nuova, 1931; Un manuale mancato." In: Paola: Di Biagi (ed.): I classici dell'urbanistica moderna, Roma: Donzelli, pp. 57-70.

Restoration and Invention

Planning the Past I
Giulio Ulisse Arata: Urban Renewal in Emilia Romagna

Elena Pozzi [EP], *Marco Pretelli* [MP], *Leila Signorelli* [LS]

During the 1920s, while the foundations of contemporary architectural thinking were being laid in America and Europe, Italy was still a field strongly linked to 19th-century culture.

In Bologna, Giulio Ulisse Arata proposed the restoration and construction of new buildings for the medieval district between Via Marchesana and Via Piave, that would not fail to give "a physiognomy inspired by the formal characteristics of the surroundings" in an alleged medieval-14th-century style. These were also the years of his best-known project for the reconfiguration of the Dantean area, in the heart of the city of Ravenna.

Starting from an analysis and comparison of these two case studies, our paper reflects upon the dynamics, both ideological and operational, that in the 1920s guided the transformation of some fragments of cities in the province of Emilia-Romagna, in order to examine the reasons underlying the logic of medieval re-writing, that is to say the redefinition of existing buildings in a medieval style, and to study the relationships that exist between the new – or rather, the 'fake old' – and the consolidated historical substratum.

THE NEW AND THE OLD IN THE DEBATE AFTER THE FIRST WORLD WAR

The architect Giulio Ulisse Arata (1881-1962) contributed to the debate taking place during the 1920s about the relationship between the old and the new city, by developing a design approach that may initially appear to be of a contrasting nature. In reality, upon careful analysis by the authors, his ideas seem to be in accordance with his professional and cultural context.

Arata's personality is multifaceted and complex. Born in Piacenza at the end of the 19th century, he attended the school of decorative arts Gazzola Institute (1895-1899, Fondazione Istituto Gazzola – Scuola d'arte); then, after two years in Naples, where he completed his military service and began working as a decorator, he moved to Milan. There he cultivated his professional experience and frequented the Brera Academy (Accademia di Belle Arti di Brera). These were the years during which the presidency of the Academy was held by Camillo Boito (1897-1914), about whom Arata held ambivalent views. Arata acknowledged Boito's cultural abilities as a teacher, especially for the themes dealt with here, namely the perception of traditional and in particular medieval architecture as an irreplaceable point of reference for the new national architecture, as well as the deep interest in restoration. Despite this, in disagreement with others in the Academy's sphere, he accused Boito of indifference to progress and to the contemporary art movement (cf. Mangone 1993: 25-38).

After completing his academic studies in Rome in 1906, Arata established himself – still at a very young age – in the Italian architectural scene. His projects for the Berri-Meregalli houses (Milan, Mozart street, 1910-1912) and Felisari (Milan, Settembrini street, 1910) contributed decisively to his fame, which had already began spreading in Naples thanks to his project for Mannajuolo Palace (Filangeri street, 1907-1908). His architecture partook of the neo-eclectic tendency of the period, which was shared by his contemporaries Aldo Andreani (1887-1971), Gaetano Moretti (1860-1938) or Piero Portaluppi (1888-1967). Their activity followed European Art Nouveau, a movement which, although already in decline, had supported their own interpretation of modernism. The latter consisted in the search for an architectural language capable of freeing itself from the constraints of the typological and formal tradition, from which, however, it inevitably took its inspiration. The design process was defined in the framework of a cultural environment that was still bound to the legacy of the historical conception of the late 19th century, which acted as a filter through which the world could be observed and built. The dialectic between history and myth that moved artistic and cultural production was most closely related to the eclectic style of the 19th century, among the most famous exponents of which is Cesare Bazzani (1873-1939). Early critical reception of Arata affirmed him as a modern architect, and as one of the young architects "prepared for the current architectural language" (Melani 1910:

627)¹ that "builds according to the needs that modern life imposes, and at the same time draws its motives from picturesque, medieval and Byzantine architecture" (Buffoni 1913).² Within a few years, however, his career (already) started a phase of decline in terms of the same critical reception (cf. Mangone 1993: 15).

The period after the World War I, and the socio-economic consequences related to it, marked a point of no return for Western culture and for Italian architectural history as well: it was the end of utopias and the beginning of uncertainties about the future of any national style. In this context the Modern Movement found new perspectives: it directed the architectural debate towards the transformation of a compositional logic by refusing every reference to the past. Thus, a handful of years after his debut, Arata was ousted from the national scene (his name almost disappeared from the press) and relegated to the position of an "architect of tradition" (Pagano 1934: 4). Giuseppe Pagano (1896-1945) speaks of the drama of the generation born in the early 1880s, unable to be masters for new generations, because of the 19th-century education and the cultural fracture caused by the spread of the Modern Movement.

Arata's progressive detachment from the debate coincided with his changed way of approaching the restoration of architectural heritage. In this context, he was involved as a 'ghost-architect' in numerous projects commissioned by members of the middle and political class of Emilia-Romagna.

THE 'COMPANY FOR BUILDING RENEWAL'³ PROJECT FOR A DISTRICT BETWEEN THE STREETS DÈ TOSCHI, MARCHESANA, PIAVE AND DE' MUSEI IN BOLOGNA, 1925

Between the end of the 19th and the first decade of the 20th century, Bologna, like many other Italian and European cities, experienced a period of socio-economic and cultural change that left a profound mark on the shape of the city. The widening of roads, the construction of new buildings, and projects to clear away the urban fabric around monuments, in particular those considered – in that period –

---

1   "[…] preparati al linguaggio architettonico attuale". The critic Alfredo Melani recognized Arata's ability to reinvent tradition without copying it, underlining that he understood the lesson of European Art Nouveau.

2   "[…] costruisce secondo le necessità che la vita moderna impone, e che trae nel tempo stesso i suoi motivi dall'architettura pittoresca, medioevale e bizantina".

3   "Società Anonima per il Rinnovo edilizio".

to be the most relevant in terms of historic and artistic value, are just some of the operations provided for in the 1889 Town Planning and Extension Plan (*Piano regolatore e di ampliamento*) (cf. Penzo 2009). Its implementation, although not entirely completed, took place over the course of more than thirty years. The main actors of these operations were frequently engineers and architects who experimented with the use of new building materials (such as reinforced concrete), typically disguised behind a formal repertoire belonging to the tradition of 19th-century stylistic eclecticism.

The activity of Alfonso Rubbiani (Bologna, 1848-1913), the best-known author of neo-medieval-inspired restorations in Bologna, found a broad consensus for this kind of approach in the historical city, although it was not without controversy (cf. Monari 2013).

He carried out dozens of projects, together with numerous collaborators gathered in the Arts and Crafts workshop Aemilia Ars (cf. Bernardini, Davanzo Poli, Ghetti Baldi 2001), a company of artists who produced everyday objects and furnishings with a floral taste, and in the Committee for Historical and Artistic Bologna (cf. Comitato per Bologna Storica e Artistica: 999), an association of architects and engineers dedicated to the protection and conservation of historical architectural heritage; both were groups inspired by the experience of England's William Morris (1834-96). Rubbiani's work aimed at re-composing the medieval facades of the monuments – in his opinion the original ones – in keeping with contemporary practices. However, his work was also characterized by the desire to combine this goal with that of Aemilia Ars, which was to produce applied art, furnishings and decorative systems with an Art Nouveau taste and with the allegorical ethical content of medieval imagery. Moreover, Rubbiani not only worked on the most famous local monuments, such as the Basilica of San Francesco in Bologna, but extended his interests to minor buildings as well. His attention focused on simple medieval houses and embraced both the environmental surroundings of the monument and the documental monuments of the medieval period themselves; the heritage had to be preserved and restored in order for it to pass on its historical-ethical values. His project presented to the municipality is exemplary of this view. It was an alternative to the 1909 executive Urban Implementation Plan (Piano attuativo) of the 1889 Town Planning and Extension Plan mentioned above (cf. Penzo 2009), which proposed the demolition of some medieval buildings (between the streets Rizzoli and Caprarie) to build three modern multi-story structures for office and residential use. Rubbiani aimed to protect the medieval buildings but his attempt was unsuccessful. He suggested conserving the district and modifying it at only a few selected points, increasing the width of the road only where it was strictly necessary, and in this way anticipating the thinning theory (Teoria dell'ambientamento or *ambientismo*) formulated by the well-known theorist in the field of architectural restoration, Gustavo Giovannoni (1873-1947), as the latter also states (cf. Giovannoni 1913: 59-63).

When Arata was called to Bologna by the Fascist *podestà* Leandro Arpinati (1892-1945), the architect worked in an urban context strongly characterized by a medieval image. This is due to the multiplicity of buildings brought back to their initial medieval appearance, according to a taste that, still in the 1920s, found, anachronistically, broad consensus in Bologna. This is the reason why Arata's compositional approach, which derived from the education of neo-eclectic Art Nouveau culture, and which validated the formal contents of ancient architecture instead of the historical-documental ones, paradoxically found coherent application in Bologna.

In his project to transform the Palazzo Ghisilieri into the local Casa del Fascio (1922), Arata chose to propose ancient forms and decorations. This was due to a more aesthetic rather than ethical logic, and in this way he completed the work undertaken in the 15th-century portion of the palace in 1915 by Rubbiani's most famous student, Guido Zucchini (1882-1957).[4] For the ornamental terracotta framing the window openings, he initially tried to

avoid imitating the frontal leaves [designing new consoles, with] schematic lines, without decorations [...] in the belief that he would pay homage to the puritanism of the concepts mentioned above. But, [he says]: such stumps, alternated between the old and graceful finely decorated consoles, seemed to me so clearly disharmonious and made such a contrast with the authentic ones that, at the cost of any excommunication, I immediately replaced them with copies traced back to the specimens that the sixteenth century had handed down to us. (Arata 1942: XXXVII)[5]

---

4 On Guido Zucchini, see Giulia Favaretto and Chiara Mariotti's essay in this volume: "Planning the Past: Rimini and Forlì in the Twenties; The Replanning of Two Squares in Romagna".

5 [...] "evitare l'imitazione delle foglie frontali [progettando nuove mensole, dalla] linea schematica, senza decorazioni [...] credendo così di rendere omaggio al puritanismo dei concetti innanzi accennati. Ma, [afferma]: simili monconi, alternati tra le vecchie e aggraziate mensole finemente decorate, mi parvero di una così evidente disarmonia e facevano un tale contrasto con quelle autentiche che, a costo di qualsiasi scomunica, li sostituii immediatamente con copie ricalcate sugli esemplari che ci aveva tramandato il Cinquecento."

This adherence to the neo-medieval tradition took place exclusively on an aesthetic level. Twenty years later, in fact, Arata would affirm that among the rare occasions in which "the architect [...] can boast of having given back to the buildings their original primitive purity", we can count Rubbiani [with his restoration of the Palazzo Ghisilieri]. Even though he was "cautious and prudent in his additions and parsimonious in his renovations, [he let himself] be carried away by the imprudence of even a disciplined imagination" (Arata 1942a: XLIX).[6] It is equally essential to stress the political value of his choices of intervention. In fact, the podestà himself, in presenting the intervention, programmatically declared: "our Casa must be like a loggia of the fourteenth-century knights and like the palaces of the communal age" [emphasis by the authors] (Arpinati 1922: 5).[7] Arpinati's ideological aspiration to preserve and exalt the memory of the medieval period

Figure 1: Bologna, Medieval District. On the right and on the left buildings 'restored' by Arata along Marchesana street

Photograph: Elena Pozzi

---

6 "l'architetto [...] può vantarsi di aver restituito, agli edifici la loro casta e originaria purezza primitiva", si può annoverare Rubbiani, benché, pur essendo stato "guardingo e prudente nelle aggiunte e parsimonioso nei rifacimenti, [...] si sia lasciato trascinare dall'imprudenza di una pur disciplinata fantasia."

7 [...] "la nostra Casa deve essere come una loggia dei cavalieri trecenteschi e come i palazzi dell'età comunale."

(cf. Penzo 2009: 149-162) could be interpreted as a political strategy to mark an alternative position to the previous Socialist government, which had instead favored initiatives aimed at the renewal and modernization of the city.

In continuity with this approach, the podestà approved two modifications to the above-mentioned Town Planning and Extension Plan (1923 and 1929), the first of which modified the intention of demolishing the district between the streets Dè Toschi, Marchesana (Fig. 1), Piave (now Clavature) and Dè Musei, proposing instead the restoration of the buildings. Giulio Ulisse Arata was commissioned for the project, and proposed to "save from modernist effrontery an entire old-district, where traces of old architecture emerged almost everywhere on the facades that had been damaged by time and some of which bore a mark that left no doubt" (Arata 1942a: XXVIII).[8]

Figure 2: Bologna, Medieval District. On the right: 2.1) Medieval district in Piave street; on the left: 2.2) Interior space of the pedestrian gallery

Photograph: Elena Pozzi

Arata projected some selective demolitions in order to open pedestrian galleries (Fig. 2) that would connect Marchesana and Toschi streets, and Toschi and De' Musei streets, thus evoking the modern type of building that was established in the post-unification years, but which was interpreted as an extension of a

---

8 [...] "salvare dall'improntitudine modernista, tutto un vecchio quartiere dove tracce di vecchie architetture affioravano un po' dappertutto sulle facciate guaste dal tempo e di cui alcune recavano un'impronta che non lasciava dubbi."

'medieval' porch – though built ex-novo. Other demolitions were planned in order to create a small square along the current Clavature street, at the corner of De' Musei street, from which opens a view of the church of Santa Maria della Vita, while facilitating passage. On the formal level, the external and internal fronts (along the galleries) are regularized through a series of openings with a regular rhythm that evoke, albeit with ornaments in a simplified shape, the forms of medieval architecture: pointed-arch openings, and single or double-lancet windows.

The particularity of the Bolognese project is therefore the richness of details, which recalls the production of Aemilia Ars. The dialectics between the neo-medieval tradition, as a methodological term of reference for restoration, and the Stile liberty [Italian Art Nouveau analogy], as a formal solution for decorative furnishing elements – which had already found a successful synthesis in Rubbiani's work – here mediates with Arata's background.

As if to demonstrate the scientific correctness of the intervention, Arata strictly fixed the date of the execution of the intervention, evoking a tradition belonging to the Middle Ages. With this choice, Arata demonstrated that he embraced the methodological theories of Giovannoni, to whom he referred as his master. Giovannoni's contribution can also be found in the choices made regarding the construction of the new parts of the complex, such as the gallery. In fact, Arata affirmed:

when, out of necessity, I was forced to raise new buildings alongside those of undoubted archaeological value, I did not fail to give the new buildings a physiognomy inspired by the formal characteristics of the environment, without for this reason [...] having unimaginatively repeated old formalisms, or falsified the creative function of new ones. (1942a: XXVIII)[9]

The project remained anonymous until 1942, when Arata announced the authorship of the intervention in the publication Costruzioni e progetti (cf. Arata 1942b); it has not yet been possible to establish with documentary support the reasons for the anonymity. Certainly, it must be considered that at the time, the debate about the possibility of 'modernization' of the ancient centers suffered from strong political interference; it is also true that the possibility of mediation between 'old and

---

9 [...] "quando, per necessità, fui costretto ad elevare nuovi edifici accanto a quelli di indubbio valore archeologico, non ho mancato di dare alle nuove costruzioni una fisionomia ispirata alle caratteristiche formali d'ambiente, senza per questo [...] aver pedestramente ripetuto vecchi formalismi, o contraffatto la funzione creativa di nuovi."

new' did not find a solution in the national debate, and it had become more difficult to take part in it especially for those who, like Arata, did not adhere to a specific stylistic or cultural trend. Moreover, at the local level, the controversy regarding the possible demolition and reconstruction of 'modern' structures between Rizzoli and Caprarie streets had not been resolved.

PROJECT FOR 'DANTEAN AREA'[10] [RAVENNA, 1927]

The paper now deals with another city in Emilia-Romagna in which Giulio Ulisse Arata left a profound mark, namely Ravenna. Ravenna acts not only as a touchstone, but also as a confirmation of the thesis that is maintained in this paper's main argument, namely that the young Fascist regime, especially in the beginning, used the Middle Ages in this region to convey its own imagery; a Middle Ages from which it drew its semantic and symbolic repertoire.

In Ravenna, the founding reason for the interventions here considered was an urban renewal initiative triggered by the celebrations associated with the personality of Dante Alighieri, the most important Italian medieval poet, considered the father of the Italian language. In fact, 1921 was the 6th centenary of Dante's death, and the city, with which the poet had a profound relationship and in which he is buried, was preparing to celebrate this anniversary. It was in Ravenna, the city that granted him asylum, that Dante completed his seminal work, the Divine Comedy (Divina commedia). The building site identified as the 'Dantean area' was developed with the intention of consecrating a district of the historical city and transforming it into a zone for the contemplation of the poet: inside the 'Dantean area', the plan was to enlarge the surface area of Marini, Ricci and Guidone streets, prohibiting transit along Da Polenta and Dante streets and thus imposing a real "zone of silence" around the tomb.

The 'Dantean area' so defined was the theatre and the epicenter of the interest of Corrado Ricci (1858-1934), the young director of the Italian Superintendency for Cultural Heritage (*Soprintendenza per le Antichità e Belle Arti*; 1906-19), established here in Ravenna in 1897.

In the framework of celebrating historical characters, the church of San Francesco underwent important changes that were aimed at bringing it back to its 'Dantean' conformation, that is to say to a medieval conformation. All of the Baroque elements were eliminated: the main portal was removed and a mullioned window

---

10 "Zona dantesca".

was constructed in place of the central window; a proposal to elevate the bell tower was also prepared. Though the refurbishment of the church was not designed by Arata, the project remains particularly significant for understanding the climate in which he worked. Furthermore, it is crucial for detecting the compositional logic that defines the Palazzo della Provincia (Fig. 3, 4), through which the church establishes a close relationship to the public space of Byron square (today Piazza San Francesco). The use of that medieval repertoire stands out on the palace, so Arata wrote accordingly in 1942:

Even in my post-war reconstructions I tried to maintain their structure in a traditional atmosphere. In devising them, I have always had the utmost respect for the monuments to which my buildings have, by the necessity of chance, stood adjacent. So in Ravenna, with the building where the Rector's Office of the Province is located, I wanted to create a backdrop to the old Church of San Francesco, to which it is attached. (Bolzani 2008: 39)[11]

Figure 3: Ravenna, Provincia palace. On the left: 3.1 The building from S. Francesco square (1928); on the right: 3.2-3.3 Some medieval-inspired details (2007)

Bolzani 2008: 110, 145

---

11 [...] "anche nelle mie ricostruzioni del dopoguerra ho cercato di mantenere la loro struttura in un'atmosfera tradizionale: nell'idearle ho sempre avuto il massimo rispetto per i monumenti ai quali i miei edifici sono andati per necessità di cose ad accostarsi. Così a Ravenna dove ha sede il Rettorato della Provincia, ho inteso creare una 'quinta' alla vetusta chiesa di San Francesco cui è affiancato."

It is easy to read in these words an interpretation of Giovannoni's thinning theory (*diradamento*).

The Palazzo della Provincia has the peculiarity of having two main public facades, the one on Byron square and the one on the square that in the 1930s would become Littoria square. The junction between the two spaces is marked by the balcony – arengo – grafted on the corner. The facade on Byron square has a stepped silhouette. From the corner of the arengo, a terraced tripartite loggia lowers towards the church, slightly offset, defining a salient point on the path that interlaces the building and the garden. The craftsmanship of the details reveals a link with the medieval repertoire that is far from being casual; indeed, as for medieval architecture, it is not so much that the materials used were precious in themselves, but that the workmanship and its refined use were. An example of this is the elaborate tripartite band that runs along the facade – a detail that undoubtedly derived from Arata's Bolognese work experience – as well as the polychromic marble that defines the foyer and the council room.

After long preparations, the Dante celebrations were held in September 1936, the year in which the Palazzo della Provincia underwent a modification that ex-

Figure 4: Ravenna, Provincia palace. On the left: 4.1 The south facade before 1936; on the right: 4.2 the same facade modified with the marble incrustation

Bolzani 2008: 131, 143

pressed symbolically Arata's decision to leave the medieval repertoire and transition to the so-called Stile Littorio, that is to say the style inspired by the Roman imperial tradition and developed during the regime. On the bricks of the facade on Littoria square (today Piazza dei Caduti per la libertà), slabs of white limestone were superimposed on the ground floor to alter it and the oculi were modified to turn the architecture towards more rational lines; the "modernized front" marks the end of the medieval repertoire, hidden under the marble incrustation.

If the use of the medieval paradigm and the sudden distance from it is demonstrated by the case of the Palazzo della Provincia, then Arata's subsequent intervention at the Casa di Oriani, with its metaphysical expressiveness, clearly confirmed his change of register. The architect rose to fame and importance at a time when medieval revivalism enjoyed favour, even among the representatives of more progressive architectural movements such as Expressionism. During the Fascist regime, this enthusiasm for the Middle Ages and for restoration was corrupted by its use in the (political) reinterpretation of urban space – a process in which Arata took part. This is particularly clearly visible in Emilia Romagna during this short but significant period of time.

CONCLUSION

Arata was fascinated by medieval residential architecture as a compositional reference for his new architecture. His curiosity was directed towards minor architecture, which for him embodied a set of precepts for interpreting the world and space, and which he developed through his projects. If in Arata's opinion a new architectural movement could be developed in relation to tradition (cf. 1942b), then the projects analyzed in this paper – especially the ones in Ravenna – were an opportunity to experiment and introduce a new way of doing architecture. Arata's projects tried to mediate between new architecture and existing cultural heritage in opposition to the rationalist movement that was presumably unable to represent tradition and the nation. In his 1942 text, *Ricostruzioni e restauri* (cf. 1942a), in fact, Arata dedicated a chapter to the theory of restoration, in which he simultaneously declared that "restoration is also, and above all, critical thinking" (1942a: XI).[12]

REFERENCES

Arata, Giulio Ulisse (1942a): Ricostruzioni e restauri, Milano: Hoepli.
Arata, Giulio Ulisse (1942b): Costruzioni e progetti, Milano: Hoepli.
Arpinati, Leandro (1922): "La Casa del Fascio." In: L'assalto, December 23.

---

12   "il restauro è anche, e soprattutto, un fatto critico".

Bernardini, Carla/Davanzo Poli, Doretta/Ghetti Baldi, Orsola (2001): Aemilia Ars: Arts & Craft a Bologna, 1898-1903, Bologna: A+G edizioni.

Bolzani, Paolo (2008): Arata e Ravenna: Opere e progetti nella città di Corrado Ricci, Ravenna: Longo Editore.

Buffoni, D. (1913): "Architettura pittorica." In: La Perseveranza August 3.

Comitato per Bologna Storica e Artistica (1999): Centenario del Comitato per Bologna Storica e Artistica, Bologna: Pàtron.

Giovannoni, Gustavo (1913): "Il 'diradamento' edilizio dei vecchi centri: Il quartiere della Rinascenza in Roma." In: Nuova Antologia 250, Roma, pp. 53-76.

Mangone, Fabio (1993): Giulio Ulisse Arata: Opera completa, Napoli: Electa.

Melani, Alfredo (1910): Architettura italiana antica e moderna, Milano.

Monari, Paola (2013): Giornate di studio su Alfonso Rubbiani, Bologna: BUP.

Pagano, Giuseppe (1934): "Il concorso per il Palazzo del Littorio." In: Casabella 32, October 1934, p. 4.

Penzo, Pier Paola (2009): L'urbanistica incompiuta: Bologna dall'età liberale al fascismo, 1889-1929, Bologna: CLUEB.

Planning the Past II

Rimini and Forlì in the 1920s: The Replanning of Two Squares in Romagna

Giulia Favaretto [GF], *Chiara Mariotti* [CM]

In the 1920s, the bases of contemporary architecture were being laid in America and in central Europe. Nevertheless, architectural interventions were still closely linked to 19th-century culture.

In the Italian region of Emilia-Romagna, this phenomenon can be observed in different historical squares: here, restoration works rediscovered, recovered or reinvented the stylistic features of an idealized past. As a matter of fact, squares were an ideal place to bring about and convey new political and moral contents by using that past, whose supposed meaning proved extremely useful for political propaganda and tourism. In Rimini, the destruction caused by the earthquake of 1916 presented a chance to recover the 'medieval' appearance of the Town Hall buildings surrounding Piazza Cavour; in Forlì, the Fascist regime redeveloped the Piazza Saffi in a 'traditional' way, reviving a glorious past through the restoration work.

Starting from the analysis and comparison of these case studies, this article considers the ideological and pragmatic dynamics that led, between the two World Wars, to the partial transformation of these two city centers in Romagna, and investigates the reasons behind this rewriting of the past as well as the relation between the new buildings and their historical context.

INTRODUCTION

The revival of and particular attention to the formal elements of tradition is a cultural phenomenon common to different geographical areas; it can actually be observed all across Europe, and it concerns architecture as well as other neighboring research fields.

In Italy, in the 1920s, "the value of history as a design tool" aimed to "reaffirm the close link between national monuments and national style" (Zucconi 1997: 23).[1] The idea, already supported in the Romantic era, started being actually implemented after the unification of Italy in 1861 and thrived for decades, with emblematic episodes in the 1920s, when, next to the contemporary architectural style, Italy showed a certain attitude to falsification or invention in restoration, as a strategy to help cities reconnect with the most important periods in their historical past.

The physical appearance of several Italian cities was thus changed through nostalgic restorations; the idea was to convey specific political and moral contents using the harmonious and austere proportions and forms of the past, which would strengthen or even build a local identity. Squares were the scenery for the city's main events and the focal point for social, economic and political life, thus they were the preferred places where theoretical assumptions and practices with regard to restoration had always been tested.

This process can also be observed in Romagna. Rimini and Forlì represent two interesting examples of city centers which saw, between the two World Wars, the buildings surrounding the two squares, called Piazza Cavour and Piazza Saffi respectively, being restored following a similar strategy. This paper starts with a critical-descriptive presentation of these two cases, then goes on to investigate why and how common urban and architectural spaces were changed, without omitting the physical and formal relation between old and new buildings. [GF, CM]

RIMINI: THE 20TH-CENTURY CONSTRUCTION OF THE 'MEDIEVAL' IDENTITY OF THE TOWN HALL BUILDINGS ON THE PIAZZA CAVOUR

At the very center of the medieval city of Rimini, the Town Hall buildings on the Piazza Cavour were directly affected by the neo-medievalism – that is, the tendency to recover the world and the myths of the Middle Ages – that would mark the facades of different monumental buildings, not only in Italy. In the 1920s, the city saw the radical transformation of a whole urban setting, thus becoming one of the cases in which the Middle Ages played an instrumental as well as an ideological function.

---

1 "valore della storia come complemento della progettazione"; "riaffermare la consequenzialità tra monumenti nazionali e stile nazionale".

The focus was, not surprisingly, the historical Piazza della Fontana, one of the most representative and bustling spots in the city. At the beginning of the 12th century it became the pounding heart of economic, trade, civic and religious life, outshining the previous main square, the Roman Forum (today's Piazza Tre Martiri). On the northern side of the Piazza della Fontana, together with some of the most interesting "urban artifacts" (Rossi 2002 [1966]: 21)[2] of the multi-layered architectural heritage of Rimini, were the Town Hall buildings that appear today as three distinct architectural units: the Palazzo del Podestà on the far left, the Palazzo dell'Arengo in the center and Palazzo Garampi on the far right. Other main historical buildings in and near the Piazza Cavour are the remains of Saint Columba's Cathedral (1015), the Castel Sismondo (1446), the Pescheria or historic fish market (1747), and the Galli Theatre (1857).

The current appearance of the Town Hall buildings is in fact the result of a bold renovation in the medieval style which occurred after the 1916 earthquake, an event that "for all the bad things it brought about, had at least one merit: that the old and sturdy building finally got rid of [...] its patches, camouflage structures and additions of the 16th and 17th centuries" ("I palazzi comunali" 1921).[3] The earthquake delivered the long-awaited chance to replan a building that, in the eyes of Rimini's citizens, was just an "attempt at a very noble and beautiful palace, as it featured only a series of rooms and not the courtyards, loggias and other spaces that noble palaces usually have" (Adimari 1616: 34).[4] It should though be noted that the palace, described in the 17th century by historian Raffaele Adimari, does not correspond to any of the three above-mentioned buildings, referring rather to a pre-existing building whose appearance was the result of the 16th-century urban renovation that changed the structure of the square and its north side. In the 20th century, that very complex of buildings took center stage and became the object of a cultural debate on the restoration of monuments. The debate saw, in Rimini, the participation of local as well as more famous and authoritative professionals at the regional and national level, like Corrado Ricci (1858-1934). He was the former Director General of the High Council for Antiquities and Fine Arts and

---

2   "fatti urbani": Aldo Rossi (Milan 1931-1997) intended "The Architecture of the City" as a concentration of "urban artifacts". He defined urban artifacts as primary elements whose existence has contributed to the morphological and cultural evolution of the city.

3   [...] "fra le tante sue malefatte fece questo di buono, che scrollò di dosso al vecchio e robusto palazzo [...] i rappezzi, i mascheramenti e le aggiunte dei secoli XVI e XVII".

4   [...] "principio d'un nobilissimo et bel palazzo, per essere una tirata sola di stancie senza haver i suoi membri, cortili, logge, et altre cose, che convengono alle fabbriche nobili di Palazzi."

Superintendent of Monuments in Ravenna; the medieval appearance of today's Emilia-Romagna is due mainly to his work (Muzzarelli 2007: 10-22; Zucconi 2007: 36-38).

Figure 1: Rimini, Town Hall buildings. From the top: 1.1 The buildings before restoration (prior to 1916); 1.2 The buildings in the first restoration project drafted by the Commission (1917); 1.3 The buildings in the second restoration project drafted by the Commission (1917); 1.4 The buildings in the second restoration project drafted by the architect Gaspare Rastelli (1919)

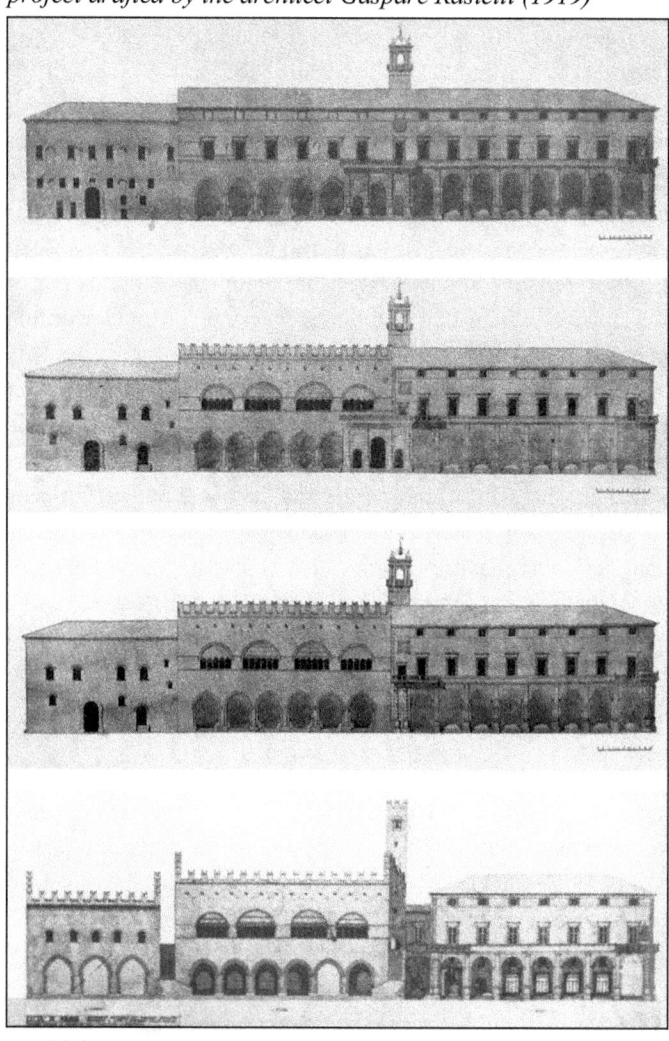

Turchini 2010: 171, 192

Actually, however, the story needs to be retraced more deeply. The earthquake of the early 20th century revealed the original features of the Town Hall buildings, thus enabling scholars to reconstruct their origins and transformations (Turchini 2010: 113-166). In 1204 that side of the square featured only the *palatium comunis* or Arengo, a crenelated building following the usual pattern: porticos on the ground floor (five Gothic arches), one large room for the General Council of the People on the first floor, and a clock tower. The *palatium novum* or Palazzo del Podestà was built much later, in 1334, next to the first palace; it had ancillary functions and featured smaller, lower and more sober porticos. The structure of the Town Hall buildings changed again in 1528, as Rimini went through a phase of political instability connected to its disputed status between the Papacy and the Empire; in that year the city fell once more under the rule of the Papal State, which reorganized this urban area for aesthetic, functional and prestige reasons (ibid: 143-166). In works that continued until the second decade of the 17th century, the square took on a new shape, expanding up to the decumanus, and the architecture surrounding it gained a new structure and language (ibid: 160-161).[5] A third building was erected next to the *palatium comunis*, thereby increasing the built area on that side of the square; more importantly, the building unified parts of the piazza's urban facade. The result was a single palace with a long portico, where the five early-Gothic arches of the Arengo are still visible – almost the only medieval feature to survive – next to eight new round arches, connected by a portal with three framing arches and embossed half-columns. Since then, the appearance of the square – which would be called Piazza Cavour only in 1862, thus after the unification of Italy – has remained more or less the same, consisting of the Palazzo del Podestà and the new Palazzo del Comune. The latter, after having absorbed the Arengo, was damaged by the earthquake of 1672 (ibid: 151) but was rebuilt exactly as it had been by the architect Francesco Garampi, to whom it owes its name today. The Palazzo Garampi is the palace described by Raffaele Adimari in the 17th century (Fig. 1.1/Fig. 2.1).

This is the point at which the story of the Town Hall buildings becomes interesting once again. For the city of Rimini, hit by the 1916 earthquake and bombed during the World War I, restoration took on a broader meaning: it was not only a material reconstruction but also an ideological one, a quest for identity and for a sense of belonging. The choice of a mode in which to rebuild necessarily fell on

---

5 This transformation caused the demolition of the entire block of San Silvestro that closed, at the time, the square on the side of the main road (the ancient decuman). The works were allegedly directed by Filippo Terzi.

the Middle Ages, an era to be retrieved through the historical remains that had emerged (Turchini 2010: 167-180) and, if need be, reinvented as a tribute to and symbol of the ideals of unity and independence of the age of communes (11th-14th century). Stratigraphic data, as well as information on materials and on the preservation strategy applied to the Town Hall buildings, are obtainable from the reports associated with the projects as planned (G. Zucchini, 1917) and later implemented (G. Rastelli, 1919).

This ideological significance explains the ongoing public attention to the whole restoration matter, a solution for which seemed hard to find. A Commission made up of the engineers Guido Zucchini, Francesco Boriani and Professor Vittorio Guaccimanni was appointed by the municipality to study the structures that had come to light with the earthquakes and to put forward a restoration proposal. The resulting project, designed in 1917, did not achieve the desired consensus. After a 'philological' analysis of the surviving structures, a new restoration project was presented. Although deliberately aimed at reviving the Arengo (Zucchini 1917: 18), this second proposal did not fully satisfy those who so urgently wanted to "undress the beautiful medieval façade of everything that the centuries had added to it"; for economic and structural reasons, the Commission therefore decided to preserve some post-medieval elements that did not seem to "disturb the harmony of the façade" (ibid: 16-17).[6] Restoration documents from this phase show great attention to the most characteristic features of the original building (Fig. 1.2/Fig.1.3), such as the crenelated parapet, the multi-lancet windows on the first floor, and the portico, all of which were restored; more complex operations, such as revealing the embossed arches and restoring the central balcony were instead carefully avoided. The idea of "separating the two buildings completely" was set aside, because it would have meant forcing "fantastic solutions entrusted to problematic picturesque effects" (ibid: 18).[7]

Nevertheless, the final reconstruction was much influenced by a sequence of interlinked events. In 1916 the earthquake hit the city hard, causing the plastering of the Church of Sant'Agostino to collapse and revealing a 14th-century pictorial cycle in which Dante Alighieri's face could be recognized (Tosi Brandi 2013: 281-284). The newly discovered frescoes created a direct link between Rimini and Ravenna, where Dante had been born about six hundred years earlier in 1321. In 1908, Ravenna had tried to recreate a true 'Dante area' within the city. The mind

---

6 "svestire la bella facciata medievale di tutto ciò che i secoli le aggiunsero"; "disturbare l'armonia della facciata".

7 "suddividere del tutto i due palazzi"; "soluzioni fantastiche affidate solamente a problematici effetti pittoreschi".

behind the whole idea was a priest and Dante scholar, Don Mesini, who decided to appeal to the Catholic faith of the people of Ravenna by starting a powerful transformation of the area in a clearly medieval style, which was implemented by Corrado Ricci (Muzzarelli 2007: 17-19; Benini 2007: 201-226). In 1917, the Commission in Rimini submitted the first restoration project of the Town Hall buildings, which was found not bold enough even for Zucchini, who had always been loyal to the position held by the influential restorer Alfonso Rubbiani (1848-1913) from Bologna (Bordone 2007: 290).[8] Last but not least, in 1918, the Ministry of Education allocated substantial funding to celebrate the sixth centenary (or 600th anniversary) of the death of Dante, the embodiment of all civic and patriotic virtues (Tosi Brandi 2013: 282; Turchini 2010: 201). The publication "Rimini nel VI centenario dantesco" ("I palazzi comunali" 1921) devotes much attention to the description of Town Hall buildings. The discovery of the frescoes propelled the city of Rimini into the circuit of events organised to celebrate Dante, together with Ravenna, Florence and Rome. It was time to achieve much more.

This is when Rimini-born architect Gaspare Rastelli, the primary author of the new medieval Rimini, took center stage. Already known for having independently drawn up a restoration proposal for the Town Hall buildings, in 1918 he was officially appointed by the municipality to carry out a new project, thus bypassing the Commission (Turchini 2010: 187-193). Rastelli conceived a first version of the project but soon abandoned it:

the forced coexistence of the two buildings was so easily recognizable that it resulted in a non-harmonic contrast to me [...] I could not give up [...] I had to separate them [...]. The case was a remarkably interesting one. (Ibid: 193)[9]

This is how a second version of the project took shape, which would later lead to the actual version we see today (Fig. 1.4). At its very heart was the idea that local identity could be strengthened or even produced by physically separating the two

---

8   Alfonso Rubbiani (Bologna 1848-1913) was one of the main protagonists of the Italian restoration as well as one of the major proponents of the practice of staging and reinventing the past. Rubbiani directed the restoration work on the main buildings in Bologna, following the medieval revival.

9   [...] "tanto l'avvicinamento forzato, che il compenetrarsi delle due differenti architetture, riuscivano per me un contrasto poco armonizzante [...] non potevo rassegnarmi [...] bisognava separali [...]. Il caso si prestava mirabilmente" (cf. Rastelli, Gaspare (1919): Relazione al progetto definitivo di restauro e sistemazione dei palazzi comunali di Rimini).

(or three) buildings and by formally representing a real and imagined version of the Middle Ages, composed of towers, merlons and lancets. Hailed as "brilliant" ("I palazzi comunali" 1921), the project immediately gained the favor of Rimini's citizens. Monument conservation offices, among them the Superintendence, requested changes – to the connection between the two buildings, and to the external staircase – and demanded the reinstatement of the ancient Arengo room, which should have looked, according to Rastelli in the abovementioned project statement, "much bigger and somehow perfected" (Turchini 2010: 193-197).[10] The restoration work was also stopped several times: its progress was even interrupted at the Palazzo del Podestà in 1924 due to what was considered the arbitrary, unfounded and unhistorical nature of the interventions, but was soon resumed without significant revisions (ibid: 179-180).

Figure 2: Rimini, Town Hall buildings. 2.1 The buildings before restoration (prior to 1916); 2.2 The buildings during the restoration work (1920)

Turchini 2010: 118; Conti/Pasini 1982: 162

Shortly thereafter, the rebirth of the Town Hall buildings was complete. Benito Mussolini inaugurated the square on September 21, 1924. The northern side of the Piazza Cavour had been replanned in medieval style, a perfect urban stage set composed of the three buildings described at the beginning of this article: the Palazzo dell'Arengo and the Palazzo del Podestà were presented, as stated in the commemorative epigraph, in their "pristine forms",[11] and the Palazzo Garampi was detached and distinguished as a clear 16th-century addition (Fig. 2.2). [CM]

---

10 "ampliata, ed in certo qual modo, perfezionata" (cf. Rastelli, Gaspare (1919): Relazione al progetto definitivo di restauro e sistemazione dei palazzi comunali di Rimini).
11 "pristine forme" (cf. Memorial epigraph walled up on site).

FORLÌ: NOSTALGIA, REPRODUCTION, INVENTION; PIAZZA SAFFI DURING THE YEARS OF THE FASCIST REGIME

The main city in the province where Benito Mussolini was born, Forlì, fully represents the urban and architectural change that occurred in the years of the Fascist regime. As a matter of fact, the desire to "modernize the Romagna area" ("Le opere del Regime fascista a Forlì" 1929: 3)[12] led to the total redefinition of the city in the period between the two World Wars.

As one of the centers of Mussolini's attention, the entire town of Forlì underwent major renovation during the regime, although some areas proved more suitable than others to embody the construction policy objectives of the National Fascist Party (PNF). After the demolition of the town walls, the urban development plan approved in 1923 (Tramonti 1999a: 57-61) immediately highlighted the main architectural and urban planning problems, tasks and challenges of the time: "The renovation of the old neighbourhoods […], an expansion plan that was supposed to get rid of old barriers, but above all the construction of public works" (ibid: 61).[13]

In this scenario, particular attention was given to the town's key areas: the Piazza Aurelio Saffi, in the old city center, and the Piazzale della Vittoria, a strategic point of intersection with the axis of the Via Emilia. A further urban hub had to be added to the changing urban structure, however: a new railway station (planned by engineer Ezio Bianchi, Director of the Technical Division of the Italian State Railways in Bologna) (Tramonti 1999b: 115-116), which would connect the country to "Mussolini's town" (Fregna 1972: 27),[14] became the starting point of a wide road that was lined with public buildings and guided visitors and citizens all the way to the Piazzale della Vittoria and eventually to the city center.

If several buildings in Forlì seem able to combine "the alleged Mediterranean classicism with the most advanced instances of the European rationalist movement" (Tramonti 1999a: 66),[15] the renovation of the Piazza Saffi is marked by a clear imbalance in favor of 'tradition'. Here, work carried out on existing buildings on the southern side of the square served the production of a prestigious past.

---

12 "svecchiare la Romagna".
13 […] "la sistemazione dei vecchi quartieri […], il piano di ampliamento oltre le vecchie barriere, ma soprattutto la costruzione di opere pubbliche".
14 "città del Duce".
15 "il presunto classicismo mediterraneo con le istanze più avanzate del movimento razionalista europeo".

While the urban development plan was being analyzed and adjusted (Prati/Tramonti 1999: 99-109), the Palazzo del Podestà was further transformed. Built in the 15th century, the building featured a facade with a series of single and double-lancet windows, and pointed arches (Buscaroli 1938: 33-34). However, some changes can already be registered at the end of the 19th century:

> The three pointed arches [...] overlooking the square are decorated with terracotta friezes; the windows of the main floor have been remade and aligned on the axis of the three arches, while originally pointing in the direction of the three double-lancet windows that still exist. (Calzini/Mazzatinti 2011 [1893]: 8)[16]

Announced at the beginning of the 20th century, the restoration of the building offered the opportunity to redesign its facade. Work started despite disagreement on the former historical appearance of this architecture, which was uncertain due to a lack of documentation (Canali 1999a: 110). The alignment of the openings in accordance with the original scheme was a key design problem and, at the same time, the alleged stylistic features of a long-vanished past were proposed. It was indeed in the 1920s that "stringcourses were added; single-lancet windows on the first floor were reopened, terminating in a semi-circular instead of a rectilinear profile as they were before; double-lancelet windows on the second floor were stylistically unified" (ibid: 111).[17]

Figure 3.1: Forlì, Palazzo Albertini and Palazzo del Podestà before restoration; 3.2 Palazzo Albertini, restoration project; 3.3 Palazzo del Podestà, restoration project

Prati/Tramonti 1999: 112, 143

---

16 [...] "i tre archi [...] che guardano la piazza, sono a sesto acuto, adorni di fregi in terra cotta; le finestre del piano nobile sono state rifatte e impostate su l'asse dei tre archi, mentre in origine erano nella direzione delle tre bifore superiori che ancora esistono".

17 [...] "furono aggiunte le cornici marcapiano; vennero riaperte le monofore, con terminazione semicircolare invece che rettilinee come si mostravano fino ad allora, del primo piano; furono stilisticamente omologate le bifore del secondo piano."

The local Superintendence then suggested adding a balcony inspired by coeval examples, and proposed two possible solutions for the crown of the building: the Municipality of Forlì preferred a crenelated parapet, while Corrado Ricci and Gustavo Giovannoni[18] supported the choice of a pitched roof. Once the idea of crenellation was discarded, the second option prevailed: the aim was that of "reproducing a Tuscan 'Renaissance style' roofing for the buildings on the southern side of the square, in order to create visual continuity with the neighboring Palazzina Albertini in a 'Bramante style'" (ibid: 111)[19] (Fig. 3.1/Fig. 3.3).

The double intent of "giving back to the city some of the prestigious features of the 'age of Melozzo'"[20] and of "creating a worthy backdrop for the square itself" (Canali 1999b: 141)[21] affected not only the Palazzo del Podestà, but also neighboring buildings. In this connection, the aforementioned Palazzo Albertini testifies to the desire of the municipal government to "continue 'decorating' other building complexes" (ibid: 141).[22] Hanging between the time of Melozzo and that of Palmezzano,[23] the building dates back to the period between the 15th and 16th centuries (Buscaroli 1938: 37). It was purchased by the PNF and would host the Forlì headquarters of the Fascist party (cf. Secretary of Forlì Federation of Italian Fasci of Combat, 1942). This was why it had to be renovated, although the restoration served as a pretext for redesigning the facade of the building. At the beginning of the 20th century, the complex was,

> made up of two different buildings, supported by two and three Tuscan-order arches respectively. The first building, the one that is supported by three arches and that borders the Palazzo del Podestà, has great artistic value. [...] In the arches, the friezes and terracotta

---

18 Gustavo Giovannoni (Rome 1873-1947) was an academic and architect who was highly influential in Italy during the period between the two World Wars (cf. Enciclopedia Treccani, Giovannoni, Gustavo, ad vocem; Zucconi, Guido (ed.) (1997): Gustavo Giovannoni. Dal capitello alla città, Milano: Jaca Book).
19 [...] "'rinascimentalizzare' alla toscana, le coperture del lato meridionale della Piazza, così in continuità visiva con la vicina, 'bramantesca', Palazzina Albertini".
20 Melozzo da Forlì (Forlì 1438-1494) was a painter whose education was influenced by Piero della Francesca's theories (cf. Enciclopedia Treccani, Melozzo da Forlì, ad vocem).
21 "restituire alla città alcuni episodi aulici dell''età di Melozzo'"; "rappresentare un degno fondale alla Piazza stessa".
22 "procedere al 'decoro' anche degli altri complessi".
23 Marco Palmezzano (Forlì 1459?-1539) was a painter and a student of Melozzo (cf. Enciclopedia Treccani, Palmezzano, Marco, ad vocem).

medallions are missing, as are the decorations on the main floor, and we can see traces of the pilaster strips and Corinthian capitals. The top floor is crowned by a loggia. (Casadei 1928: 19-20)[24]

However, if "this original part of the Palace is the one above the first three arches, the part that rises above the other two arches is the modern one": The 20th-century restoration project was aimed at "reviving" the building "as the glorious Renaissance architects planned and created it" (ibid: 20-21).[25] The architect Ariodante Bazzero from Milan was therefore appointed to produce the first drawings of the interiors, and superintendent Luigi Corsini drafted the project that extended the focus to the facade (ibid: 21).

Especially, the intervention on the facade of the Palazzo Littorio (cf. Plan of Piazza Saffi [without date]) – also called Casa del Fascio (Casadei 1928: 21), that is, the headquarters of the local branch of the PNF – was an attempt to emulate an alleged past, not only in the portion marked off by the three arches next to the Palazzo del Podestà, but also in the more recent part of the complex (Fig. 3.1/Fig. 3.2). The new building, the result of a 20th-century re-reading aimed at celebrating a prestigious past, could be admired from the center of the square. And it can still be admired today: restoration has contributed to giving this urban landscape the invented appearance from another era.

Lastly, the southern side of the Piazza Saffi ends with the Palazzo del Credito Romagnolo (formerly Palazzo Mangelli and Talenti Framonti) (ibid: 22). The local bank Credito Romagnolo purchased the building in 1913 (ibid: 22) and adapted it to the changing needs of the institution. The renovation project thus included a new roof over the court which was not visible from the square. The solution designed by engineer Gian Luigi Reggiani was approved by the Municipal Building Commission, but on one condition: the restoration project must also restyle the facade. After the construction of the new main portal, the main problem was the

---

24 [...] "formato da due diverse costruzioni, sostenute rispettivamente da due e da tre archi, di ordine toscano. La prima di esse, cioè quella sostenuta da tre archi e confina col Palazzo del Podestà, ha un pregio artistico notevolissimo. [...] Negli archi mancano i fregi e i medaglioni in terra cotta; mancano anche le decorazioni del piano nobile, nel quale veggonsi le traccie delle lesene e dei capitelli d'ordine corinzio. L'ultimo piano, come coronamento, è formato da una loggia".

25 "questa parte originale del Palazzo sovrasta i tre primi archi; quella che si eleva sugli altri due è di costruzione moderna"; "rivivere"; "come lo volle ideato e creato l'aureo Rinascimento".

corner between Via Volturno and the Piazza Saffi. Cesare Bazzani,[26] a technician from Rome, then suggested a solution that would later be accepted. Once the existing building was demolished, the new strategic corner met the need to define a majestic entrance to the square, even though such a building configuration had never existed before. After various vicissitudes and the death of Bazzani, Gustavo Giovannoni would complete the work (Canali 1999b: 141-144) (Fig. 4.1/Fig. 4.2).

Figure 4: Forlì, the Palazzo del Credito Romagnolo. 4.1 The building before restoration; 4.2 The building in the restoration project

Archivio di Stato di Terni, Fondo Cesare Bazzani (u. 093, n. 1732-1733)

In a way, the approach adopted for the southern side of the Piazza Saffi is in line with the solutions adopted for the other sides of the city square in the years of the Fascist regime: the Palazzo Comunale was "embellished" based on alleged "fragments from the 'golden age' of the city" (Canali 1999c: 140),[27] while the Palazzo delle Poste e dei Telegrafi, the Uffici Statali and the Chiesa del Suffragio confirmed the 'traditionalist' orientation supported by Bazzani (Prati/Tramonti 1999: 154-157, 160-162, 191-193; Nicoloso 2008: 151-153). Finally, the religious complex of San Mercuriale was renewed by Gustavo Giovannoni (Prati/Tramonti 1999: 227-229) in order to create new views and architectural volumes capable of reproducing, albeit through falsification, the atmosphere of long past centuries. [GF]

---

26 Cesare Bazzani (Rome 1873-1939) studied at the Regia Scuola d'Applicazione per gli Ingegneri in Rome. Bazzani was an extremely prolific academic whose work as an architect further increased during the Fascist period (cf. Enciclopedia Treccani, Bazzani, Cesare, ad vocem).

27 "abbellimento"; "lacerti dell''epoca d'oro' della città".

CONCLUSION

In the 1920s, the restoration of historic buildings involved practices strongly linked to the recovery of the past: revival seemed to be the most effective option for interventions in existing architecture, and restoration became a means for evoking the glories of the past. Rimini and Forlì are two cities in Emilia-Romagna that document this scenario well.

The first question to be considered is now why. In Rimini, "retrieving the medieval appearance is the direct result of a will to celebrate the old communal liberties" (Turchini 2010: 199)[28] capable of strengthening the identity of the city. In Forlì, the creation of continuity between past and present was aimed at "strengthening the power of the new Fascist leadership" with the goal of "exploiting for the Party's purposes the sense of belonging that the historical-artistic heritage [...] created" (Muzzarelli 2007: 22).[29] This is how the use of revival became a leitmotif in the two cities that deliberately chose to implement it in the very heart of their city centers.

The second question worthy of attention is what they meant to retrieve with these restoration campaigns. In Rimini, the Middle Ages were considered a "reference era", to the extent that the city did not hesitate "to demolish anything covering or masking the city's medieval appearance" (ibid: 23).[30] In this regard, Rubbiani set a precedent and Guido Zucchini, or even more so Gaspare Rastelli, applied that lesson in Rimini. In Forlì, "where the historical-artistic component was very weak, the reference to the old 'heroic' times of the city" (Balzani 2007: 59)[31] became fundamental. On this basis, the "enhancement of the artistic, architectural and literary remains of the history of Forlì between the 15th century (the 'age of Melozzo' [...]) and the first decades of the 16th century (the 'age of Palmezzano'

---

28 "il recupero dell'aspetto medievale si collega alle antiche libertà comunali".
29 "il senso di un rafforzamento del potere dei nuovi signori fascisti"; "usare a fini propri il senso di appartenenza che il patrimonio storico-artistico [...] era in grado di stimolare".
30 "come periodo di riferimento"; "intervenire con l'accetta su tutto quello che copriva, anzi mascherava il volto medievale".
31 [...] "dove la componente storico-artistica risultava assai debole, il richiamo alle fasi 'eroiche' della città in tempi remoti."

[...])" (Canali 1999d: 36)[32] became the established practice for the restoration of existing buildings.

The common denominator in both cities was Corrado Ricci, who not only supported the transformation of the two city centers, but also confirmed the above-mentioned tendencies: if in Rimini, the Middle Ages should be privileged, in the main square in Forlì it was the period between the era of Melozzo and Palmezzano that took center stage.

Finally, the link with tourism should not to be forgotten. A planned past was also useful for attracting visitors. In this regard, if the sixth centenary of Dante's death "was certainly a driver for tourism" (Muzzarelli 2007: 17),[33] it did not only concern Ravenna: in Rimini, the rediscovery of Dante's face in the 14th-century fresco in the Church of Sant'Agostino helped the city to enter the circuit of events planned to celebrate the poet. This whole process had a much wider span, leading, for example, to the transformation of the Romagna Castle of Gradara into the stage setting for Dante's tragedy of Paolo and Francesca. At the same time, in Forlì, the material reproduction of the city's prestigious past created the ideal backdrop for exhibitions on the topic; the one dedicated to Melozzo in 1938 (cf. Gnudi/Becherucci 1938) was thus an instrument of cultural aggrandizement, deeply rooted in tradition and, also, in tourist propaganda.

Events and exhibitions therefore produced a new 'historical' consumer good, one whose attractiveness was also due to the reproduction of history which was heavily present in the restoration work on these two squares in Emilia-Romagna. [GF, CM]

REFERENCES

Adimari, Raffaele (1616): Sito riminese, II, Brescia: Per Giò. Battista & Ant. Bozzòli (www.archive.org/details/sitoriminese00adim) [2018/05/28].

Balzani, Roberto (2001): La Romagna, Bologna: Il Mulino.

Balzani, Roberto (2007): "Quando le parole sono pietre: Toponomastica urbana, politica e memoria culturale nella Romagna fin de siècle". In: Muzzarelli Maria Giuseppina (ed.), Neomedievalismi: Recuperi, evocazioni, invenzioni nelle città dell'Emilia-Romagna, Bologna: Clueb, pp. 39-60.

---

32 "valorizzazione delle testimonianze artistiche, architettoniche e letterarie della Storia forlivese compresa tra il Quattrocento (l''età di Melozzo' [...]) e i primi decenni del Cinquecento (l''età di Palmezzano' [...])".

33 "fu certamente un volano per il turismo".

Benini, Maria Giulia (2007): "Celebrazione, evocazione, invenzione nella zona dantesca a Ravenna". In: Muzzarelli Maria Giuseppina (ed.), Neomedievalismi: Recuperi, evocazioni, invenzioni nelle città dell'Emilia-Romagna, Bologna: Clueb, pp. 201-226.

Bordone, Renato (2007): "Postfazione". In: Maria Giuseppina Muzzarelli (ed.), Neomedievalismi: Recuperi, evocazioni, invenzioni nelle città dell'Emilia-Romagna, Bologna: Clueb, pp. 287-296.

Buscaroli, Rezio (1938): Forlì, Predappio, Rocca delle Caminate, Fornò, Pieve Quinta, Pieve Acquedotto, Bergamo: Istituto Italiano d'Arti Grafiche.

Calzini, Egidio/Mazzatinti, Giuseppe (2011 [1893]): Guida di Forlì, Sala Bolognese: Arnaldo Forni.

Canali, Ferruccio (1999a): "Restauri al Palazzo del Podestà, 1921-1942". In: Luciana Prati/Ulisse Tramonti (eds.), La città progettata: Forlì, Predappio, Castrocaro; Urbanistica e architettura fra le due guerre, Forlì: Comune di Forlì, pp. 110-112.

Canali, Ferruccio (1999b): "La sistemazione del lato meridionale di Piazza Saffi: Il Palazzo Albertini,1929, e il Palazzo del Credito Romagnolo, 1927-1932". In: Luciana Prati/Ulisse Tramonti (eds.), La città progettata: Forlì, Predappio, Castrocaro; Urbanistica e architettura fra le due guerre, Forlì: Comune di Forlì, pp. 141-144.

Canali, Ferruccio (1999c): "I restauri del Palazzo del Comune (ovvero 'del Governo') in Piazza Saffi, 1928-1929". In: Luciana Prati/Ulisse Tramonti (eds.), La città progettata: Forlì, Predappio, Castrocaro; Urbanistica e architettura fra le due guerre, Forlì: Comune di Forlì, p. 140.

Canali, Ferruccio (1999d): "Le 'città del Duce' e la cultura architettonica nazionale: Una difficile sintesi tra la modernità urbana e il restauro della 'città di Melozzo'". In: Luciana Prati/Ulisse Tramonti (eds.), La città progettata: Forlì, Predappio, Castrocaro. Urbanistica e architettura fra le due guerre, Forlì: Comune di Forlì, pp. 29-55.

Casadei, Ettore (1928): La città di Forlì e i suoi dintorni: Guida storico-artistica della città di Forlì, Forlimpopoli, Bertinoro, Meldola, Predappio Nuova, Castrocaro e Terra del Sole, Forlì: Società Tipografica Forlivese.

Castelnuovo, Enrico/Sergi, Giuseppe (2004): "Il Medioevo al passato e al presente", IV. In: Enrico Castelnuovo/Giuseppe Sergi (eds.), Arti e storia nel Medioevo, Torino: Einaudi.

Conti, Giorgio/Pasini, Pier Giorgio (1982): Rimini: Città come storia, Rimini: Litografia Giusti.

Fregna, Roberto (1972): "Forlì città del duce: Dal 1° dopoguerra alla crisi del '29". In: Parametro 14, pp. 26-47, 75-76.

Gnudi, Cesare/Becherucci, Luisa (eds.) (1938): Mostra di Melozzo e del Quattrocento romagnolo, Catalogo della mostra, Forlì, Palazzo dei Musei, giugno-ottobre 1938, Bologna: Il Resto del Carlino.

Gobbi, Grazia/Sica, Paolo (1982): Rimini, Roma: Edizioni Laterza.

"I palazzi comunali" (1921): In: Il Gazzettino Azzurro, 24 July 1921.

"Le opere del Regime fascista a Forlì" (1929): In: Il Popolo di Romagna, 24 March 1929, p. 3.

Muzzarelli, Maria Giuseppina (2007): "Introduzione". In: Maria Giuseppina Muzzarelli (ed.), Neomedievalismi: Recuperi, evocazioni, invenzioni nelle città dell'Emilia-Romagna, Bologna: Clueb, pp. 7-23.

Nicoloso, Paolo (2008): Mussolini architetto: Propaganda e paesaggio urbano nell'Italia fascista, Torino: Einaudi.

Plan of Piazza Saffi [without date]. Provincia di Forlì, Carteggio (b. 1668, f. 13). Archivio di Stato di Forlì-Cesena (office of Forlì).

Prati, Luciana/Tramonti, Ulisse (eds.) (1999): La città progettata: Forlì, Predappio, Castrocaro; Urbanistica e architettura fra le due guerre, Forlì: Comune di Forlì.

Rossi, Aldo (2002 [1966]): L'architettura della città, Torino: Città Studi Edizioni.

Secretary of Forlì Federation of Italian Fasci of Combat [institution's name translated by the authors] (1942, January 10). Letter to the Head of Technical Services Unit for the National Fascist Party. Partito Nazionale Fascista, Direttorio nazionale, Servizi, Seconda serie a (b. 452, f. "Forlì"). Archivio Centrale dello Stato, Roma.

Tonini, Luigi (1975): Rimini dopo il mille, Rimini: Bruno Ghigi Editore.

Tosi Brandi, Elisa (2013): "Neomedievalismi italiani: Bologna e la Romagna". In: Arciniega García Luis (ed.), Memoria y Significado: Uso y recepción de los vestigios del pasado, Cuadernos Ars Longa 3, València: Universitat de València, Departament d'Historia de l'Art, pp. 273-286.

Tramonti, Ulisse (1999a): "Forlì, architettura e urbanistica per una nuova 'imago urbis'". In: Prati Luciana/Tramonti Ulisse (eds.), La città progettata: Forlì, Predappio, Castrocaro. Urbanistica e architettura fra le due guerre, Forlì: Comune di Forlì, pp. 57-71.

Tramonti, Ulisse (1999b): "Stazione ferroviaria, 1924-1925". In: Prati Luciana/Tramonti Ulisse (eds.), La città progettata: Forlì, Predappio, Castrocaro. Urbanistica e architettura fra le due guerre, Forlì: Comune di Forlì, pp. 115-116.

Turchini, Angelo (1992): Rimini medievale: Contributi per la storia della città, Rimini: Bruno Ghigi Editore.

Turchini, Angelo (2010): "I palazzi comunali". In: Turchini Angelo, I luoghi della memoria: Le cattedrali e i palazzi comunali di Rimini, Cesena: Il Ponte Vecchio, pp. 111-255.

Zucchini, Guido (1917): Il palazzo comunale di Rimini: Progetto di restauro della Commissione nominata dal Municipio, Bologna: Cooperativa Tipografica Azzoguidi.

Zucconi, Guido (ed.) (1997): Gustavo Giovannoni: Dal capitello alla città, Milano: Jaca Book.

Zucconi, Guido (1997): L'invenzione del passato: Camillo Boito e l'architettura neomedievale, Venezia: Marsilio.

Zucconi, Guido (2007): "Il Medioevo degli architetti italiani, tra scienza e arte (1860-1940)". In: Maria Giuseppina Muzzarelli (ed.), Neomedievalismi: Recuperi, evocazioni, invenzioni nelle città dell'Emilia-Romagna, Bologna: Clueb, pp. 25-38.

Architectural and Urban Transformations in Romagna during the Fascist Era between Tradition and Modernity
The Cases of Predappio, Forlì and Imola

Micaela Antonucci, Sofia Nannini

This essay focuses on the urban and architectural transformations that took place in the region of Romagna during the Fascist regime, with specific reference to the cases of Predappio, Forlì and Imola. Being the region where Benito Mussolini was born, Romagna was a centre of the Fascist propaganda that used monuments and urban renovations as political representations, with the double aim of defining a local architectural identity and creating a tight link – both physical and symbolic – with the city of Rome.

Fascism's use of art and architecture as a major means of propaganda in Italy between the two World Wars has already been noted and widely researched by scholars (among others, see: Doordan 1983; Cresti 1986; Ciucci 1989; Painter 2005; Gentile 2007; Nicoloso 2008, 2012; Hökerberg 2018). A prime example of this practice is the region of Romagna, birthplace of Benito Mussolini, where the regime's propaganda aimed at highlighting the connections between this territory and the *Duce*, thus creating a direct link to Rome. This topic has been the subject of many recent studies (Prati/Tramonti 1999; Dogliani 2006; Serenelli 2013, Tramonti 2015b; Proli 2017). One of the most recent takes a sociosemiotic approach, analysing the Fascist architectural projects in Forlì – one of the region's major cities – as a case study in what it calls "environmental propaganda", which "spreads cultural artifacts and enacts political rituals about the built environment" (Nanni/Bellentani 2018: 379). In addition to Forlì, the cities of Predappio and Imola also represent important case studies in the connection between propaganda and architecture in Romagna during the Fascist era, and they too have been analysed recently in new investigations and archival research, some of which is currently underway.¹ In this paper, some of this research is presented and its current results are analysed.

From the early days of his meteoric political rise, Benito Mussolini took a keen interest in the fate and development of his childhood village of Dovia di Predappio, and in the province of Forlì within which it lay. His motives were undoubtedly in part sentimental, but he also recognized propaganda opportunities. These places should embody the core myths of the *Duce*: his turbulent youth, his first forays into politics, and the popular and rural background which he used to present himself as a "man of the people". This was all the more reason to reclaim the city of Forlì from its peripheral geography, and transform it into *The City of the Duce*. This change also had to be clearly visible in the heart of the city, and was reflected in an assortment of buildings and monuments erected to remind everyone of the rise to power of its famous son.

Fascist propaganda was based on a vision of Italy that was fragmented into several centres, each characterised by its own identity; these identities might be real and tangible or built through a process of cultural reconstruction, the aim of which was to find the mythical foundations and the traditions of each municipality. To this end, a new cultural policy was carried out in the region of Romagna, one that overlaid its specific traditions with a genealogy that could connect the local identities to the regime and strengthen the bond with the capital city of Rome (cf. Cassani Simonetti 2015: 21-25). One of the key symbols of this policy is a ceramic decoration, a roundel, preserved at the Istituto statale d'arte per la ceramica (National Art Institute for Ceramic) in Faenza, made in 1939 by the sculptor Domenico Rambelli (1886-1972) and his students. It can be considered a model representation of "the vulgate of a standard cultural regionalism as revisited by Fascism" (Balzani 2001: 146; the image is reproduced in: Cassani Simonetti 2015:

---

[1] A study of the architecture of Imola between the two World Wars is currently underway, with special attention to the work of the architect Adriano Marabini (see the biographical information provided below); an exhibition and a monograph, edited by Micaela Antonucci and Luigi Bartolomei with support from Sofia Nannini, are due in 2020. The case of Predappio has recently been analysed in the context of the restoration of the Casa del Fascio (Delizia/Di Francesco/Di Resta/Pretelli 2015). The primary source on the work of Cesare Valle in Predappio and Forlì is the exhibition catalogue *Cesare Valle. Un'altra modernità: architetture in Romagna* (Tramonti 2015b). The results of the recent research on Cesare Valle are going to be published in the forthcoming volume *Cesare Valle: architettura, ingegneria, urbanistica*, edited by Micaela Antonucci and Cesare Valle Jr. (currently in preparation).

22). The roundel depicts the territory of Romagna not only through its local histories and traditions, but also by linking the so-called pioneers of the regime to their cities: in addition to the traditional representations of Faenza as the "city of ceramics" or Rimini as the "city of the Malatesta family", Lugo appears as the hometown of the aviator Francesco Baracca (1888-1918), Casola Valsenio as the birthplace of the poet Alfredo Oriani (1852-1909) and Predappio as the epicentre of Mussolini's mythical image.

Despite the proximity to large northern cities, not least Milan, where modern architecture was firmly established thanks in part to the patronage of the ruling class and the leading local economic circles, the province of Forlì proved largely impermeable to modern influences during the twenty years of the Fascist era (the *Ventennio*), except in some isolated cases: these include the designs of Cesare Valle, which reconcile monumentality and rationalism; and Giuseppe Vaccaro's Colonia Marina "Sandro Mussolini" in Cesenatico, part of the extensive network of "holiday camps" that flourished on the Adriatic coast during the Fascist era (Vaccaro 1939; Cao 1994; Massaretti 2005). The close link with Rome – which the writer Margherita Sarfatti (1880-1961) condensed into the iconic title of her book *Flight of the Eagle from Predappio to Rome* (Marga 1927) – made this territory into a sort of architectural colony of the capital city, permeated by the grand monumentality of the architecture of the regime.

The presence of buildings related to the regime's programme of architectural propaganda left lasting traces in the image of several towns in Romagna that underwent important urban changes, especially during the third decade of the 20th century. Different professionals worked on these projects, the aim of which differed from place to place: sometimes it was commemorative, as in the case of Lugo, where the Bolognese architect Giuseppe Vaccaro (1896-1970) was entrusted with the renovation of aviator Francesco Baracca's native town (cf. Vaccaro 1934); or in the case of Casola Valsenio, where Giulio Ulisse Arata (1881-1962) designed the house and mausoleum of the poet Alfredo Oriani, whose work had been idealised by Fascist rhetoric (Baloni 1988). Encouraging tourism within the province of Forlì was one of Mussolini's main goals, and with this in mind he promoted important projects in many cities, such as the rebuilding of the resort town of Castrocaro, a spa popular since the end of 19th century (cf. Prati/Tramonti 1999: 83-96; Gori/Tramonti 2005), and the architectural and infrastructural development of the seaside resort of Cesenatico on the Adriatic coast (cf. Orioli 2008).

Among these geographies, this essay will deal with three particular cases: the renovation of the city centre of Imola, located in the province of Bologna but culturally closer to the provinces of Ravenna and Forlì; and the cases of Predappio and Forlì, the two cities most directly connected to Mussolini, where architecture can be considered a built celebration of the *Duce* and his regime.

THE RENOVATION OF SMALL CITIES BETWEEN TRADITION AND MODERNITY: THE DEBATE SURROUNDING THE NEW CENTRE OF IMOLA AND ITS CASA DEL FASCIO IN THE 1930s

Despite its small dimensions, the town of Imola was also included within the dense network of Mussolini's geographies of propaganda, as the Duce traveled around the peninsula dedicating the countless architectural products of the regime (Nicoloso 2008: 13). In 1936 Mussolini opened the newly-built *Casa del Fascio* in Imola (Fig. 1) and gave a passionate speech in the main square,[2] in front of the monument to the fallen soldiers of the Great War designed by the Roman engineer Giovanni Battista Milani (1876-1940).[3] What Mussolini saw during his visit was a town in transition. In fact, since the beginning of the 1930s the centre of Imola had been the scene of two major building projects, located next to each other along the Via Emilia, that characterise its urban shape to this day: the controversial *Nuovo Centro Cittadino* (1932-1938) by Milani, and an iconic *Casa del Fascio* (1933-1936) by the local architect Adriano Marabini (1897-1975).

The Nuovo Centro Cittadino (New City Centre) was at the centre of a political and architectural debate that began in 1929 and revolved around the need for a wider and covered public space for the inhabitants. At first, the engineer Remigio Mirri (1867-1946) – who was active in Imola and the surrounding area and whose education had been strongly influenced by the works of Giuseppe Mengoni (1829-1877) (cf. Buscaroli 1932; Bolognesi 1997) – was entrusted with the project, which resulted in a *galleria* arcade connecting the Via Emilia with the square behind and replacing the old market hall and some residential constructions. Mirri's proposal (cf. 1930, 1930–1931) – the drawings of which are now collected at the

---

[2] See also the video report: Istituto Nazionale Luce 1936 (see the *Archival references* of this paper for details).

[3] This monument, from which decorative references to the Fascist regime were removed after the World War II, was at the centre of several debates in the 1960s and 1970s, and in 2011 was moved from Imola's main square (*Piazza Matteotti*) to a garden at the edge of the city centre.

Municipal Library of Imola[4] – was named after Principe Umberto, and its forms and decorations mirrored, on a smaller scale, the Galleria Vittorio Emanuele II in Milan. Imola's *galleria* also included an underground theatre, which the Municipality insisted upon against the designer's wishes (cf. Mirri 1932: 11). Yet Mirri's project would become a political case and would end in failure: in 1932, despite his complaints (cf. Mirri 1932), three years' worth of work was recycled as the draft material for an architectural competition brief. The competition was in fact a way to cover up the reassignment of the works to Giovanni Battista Milani, at that time engineer and architect to the wealthy family of Imola's mayor (*podestà*), Annibale Ginnasi. Officially, the arcade by Mirri was called into question on the grounds of cost (see Ginnasi's letter to Mirri in: ibid: 32). As Mirri's historicist dreams were pushed aside, Milani entered the competition and won it; his design as realised included the required underground theatre (now closed), a glass brick covered *passage*, shops at the ground level, and apartments as well as classrooms for a school on the upper floors (cf. Milani 1932). Evidently, the influence of 19th-century eclectic architecture that inspired Remigio Mirri could no longer play a role in urban public spaces: the architectural language of the *Nuovo Centro Cittadino*, with reinforced concrete structural frame and its sober brick finishing, was going to be the model and the necessary basis of comparison for the new Casa del Fascio immediately adjacent, in which the built monumentality of the regime would be expressed at its best.

The Casa del Fascio of Imola was the result of a call for tenders launched in 1933 and won by the architect Adriano Marabini together with his brother Giuseppe (1895-1977). Born in Imola and educated in Bologna, Adriano Marabini had been very active between the two towns since the 1920s. During the Fascist regime, he worked on many private and public commissions, also collaborating with the Municipality of Imola and frequently working together with his brother, who was an engineer. He continued his professional career after the World War II, collaborating with architects such as Giuseppe Vaccaro, and opened architectural design offices in Imola, Bologna and Macerata (cf. Gresleri/Massaretti 2001: 43).

The area for the new *Casa del Fascio* surrounded a plot owned by the Cassa di Risparmio (Savings Bank). It was connected to the Nuovo Centro Cittadino and faced the Via Emilia and the square behind (drawing 15.64 in: Milani 1932).

---

4   Biblioteca Comunale di Imola. Disegni Ufficio Tecnico (see the *Archival sources* section of this paper for details).

Marabini's proposal, dubbed "A.M XI",[5] is characterised by a tall tower, that marks the corner between the streets Via Emilia and the Via XX Settembre. The verticality of this element is enhanced by three undivided windows as well as by the masonry facing of the structure; on the facades, the stone cladding of the portico and the decorative use of bricks at the upper levels create a figurative and physical connection to the contiguous project by Milani. Two giant cylindrical pillars mark the entry gate under the tower, forming a revised and modern triumphal arch that emphasises the monumentality of the whole building. Their shafts are decorated with bas-reliefs depicting the idealised, muscular figures of Fascist citizens, both women and men, performing their working and fighting duties. Above the gate, one can still read the words of Mussolini, taken from the Duce's speech in Rome on May 9, 1936, engraved in the stone.

Figure 1: View from the via Emilia in Imola on the Casa del Fascio with the tower (1933–1936) and the Nuovo Centro Cittadino behind (1932–1938)

Photograph: Sofia Nannini

---

5   Notes on the projects and reproductions of the original drawings by Adriano Marabini can be found in: *Archivio Adriano Marabini*, Fondazione Cassa di Risparmio di Imola (Imola, BO) and in the Historical Archives of the University of Bologna, Architectural Collections, *Fondo Adriano Marabini*. The collection owned by the Fondazione Cassa di Risparmio of Imola is now under study and a monograph on Marabini's work, edited by Micaela Antonucci and Luigi Bartolomei, is due in 2020.

Indeed, the architecture of the Nuovo Centro Cittadino and then the Casa del Fascio as finally realised were worlds away from the first historicist ideas of the disappointed engineer Mirri: in a town where almost no modern architecture had yet been built – Piero Bottoni's modernist renovation of the Villa Muggia on the hills of Imola was not finished until 1938 (cf. Bolognesi 2016) – two of the very first examples of modernity in construction were the projects by Milani and Marabini. These buildings mirrored the specific role played by architecture under the Fascist regime, namely as a bearer of political symbolism: as such it had to be simultaneously monumental and sober, Roman and local, rhetorical and functional. Its primary role was to radically change the political outlook of each town and to connect them to the image of Rome and its *romanità* (cf. Arthurs 2012).

ARCHITECTURE, PROPAGANDA, MODERNITY. FORLÌ, PREDAPPIO AND THE WORK OF CESARE VALLE

The majority of the regime's economic resources and attention was devoted to the city of Forlì, both with respect to the restoration of historical monuments and the construction of new buildings and quartiers (cf. Tramonti 1997; Prati/Tramonti 1999: 57-72; Antonucci 2014; Cassani Simonetti 2015; Nanni/Bellentani 2018).

The drive to transform Forlì happened at a time when the city was undergoing modernisation, a process pushed forward in part by the national regime but also by many powerful local figures. This small Romagna city, which in the 1920s had suddenly become very important in Italian politics because of its connection with Mussolini, saw a flow of substantial investment from Rome for the creation and development of industry and the construction of a new, grandiose centre. From 1929 onwards, huge urban transformation projects were carried out: the Fascist government promoted and financed the construction of over 300 new architectural and urban projects, and a new *piano regolatore* (urban development plan) for the construction of a city and its future development was approved; it was to be overseen by the architect Gustavo Giovannoni, who was called in from Rome (cf. Canali 1997). The new urban plan was mainly focused on two points: first, the modernisation of the historical centre; and second, the expansion of the city along a new south-eastern axis, which would pivot around an avenue named after Benito Mussolini (cf. Prati/Tramonti 1999; Canali 2010; Antonucci 2014). New public buildings were to be built along this avenue and many would be named after the members of Mussolini's family, thus emphasising his close personal connection with the construction of the "new Forlì". Like many of the new constructions in

Rome at this time, the buildings and urban spaces in Forlì referred to Classical architecture, using the rhetorical and monumental form of the so-called Littorio style (*Stile Littorio*). This style was named after the Roman *fasci littori* (bundles of wooden sticks tied together with leather straps, used as a symbol of Fascism), and it blended monumentality and classicism with rationalism in the search for a unified, national style to express the new vision of the State.

In order to carry out the large-scale modernisation of Forlì, architects and engineers were sent directly from Rome on the orders of Mussolini and his closest advisers: in addition to Giovannoni, they included Luigi Piccinato, Cesare Bazzani, Florestano Di Fausto and Cesare Valle, all of whom worked alongside local professionals who were highly visible in those years, such as Arnaldo Fuzzi, Saul Bravetti and Leonida Emilio Rossetti. The "great master" of Fascist architecture, Marcello Piacentini, never worked directly in Forlì but left that starring role to his friend and rival, Cesare Bazzani (cf. Canali 2001a; Tramonti 2015a); however, his ideas and suggestions made themselves felt there all the same, through his influence on both the commissions overseeing the architectural competitions and on the institutional clients. Moreover, many younger architects who had trained at his school worked in Romagna. One of these was the Roman engineer Cesare Valle (1902-2000). A student of Gustavo Giovannoni and then a collaborator of Marcello Piacentini, Valle was a versatile figure, able to develop a style that reconciled tradition and modernity, monumentality and rationalism; he was also one of the few professionals able to work in engineering, architecture and urban planning with equal skill. In the early 1930s, Valle was involved with various projects all over Italy and was awarded a series of prestigious national and international assignments commissioned directly by the Fascist regime. Among them is a series of architectural projects in Romagna and in particular in the two cities most directly connected to Mussolini: Forlì and Predappio (cf. Muntoni 2007; Canali 2011; Antonucci 2015; Tramonti 2015a).

According to his own testimony, Valle arrived in Forlì after having been recommended by Enrico Del Debbio, the architect charged with overseeing the construction of the Case del Balilla. This was the headquarters of the *Opera Nazionale Balilla* (ONB), the Italian Fascist youth organization which provided youth with military, physical, cultural and professional education, and which maintained local branches throughout Italy (cf. Santuccio 2005; Capomolla/Mulazzani/Vittorini 2008). Del Debbio brought Valle to the attention of Renato Ricci, the powerful president of the ONB, who decided to entrust him with the construction of the Forlì headquarters. On November 23, 1932, Ricci wrote to the regional Romagna Committee President of the ONB to inform him that Valle was charged by the Central Presidency in Rome with drawing up plans for the Casa del Balilla in Forlì (on this project, see: Prati/Tramonti 1999: 174-177; Antonucci 2015; Tramonti 2015b: 106-143; Canali 2016).⁶ Built in the years 1933-35, the Casa del Balilla received immediate and universal praise and was promoted by Fascist propaganda as a prime example of this new building type – as outlined by Valle himself:

The Casa del Balilla in Forlì has been recognised as pioneering in its facilities and in its perfect, functional efficiency; the foremost technical and architecture magazines have covered it in-depth, and the project was displayed in London at the invitation of the Royal Institute of British Architects. (Valle 1938: XX)

Figure 2: The Casa del Balilla in Forlì (1933–1935)

Photograph: Sofia Nannini

The building (Fig. 2) consisted of different stereometric blocks arranged in perfect spatial equilibrium. It was divided into two sections, each with a distinct purpose and its own separate entrance: one intended for sporting activities (with a gym, swimming pool, and fencing hall) with large windows illuminating the lower blocks and facing into the rectangular inner courtyard; and the other intended for cultural and official activities (with a theatre-cinema, library, offices, and a memorial dedicated to Arnaldo Mussolini), and distinguished by the dynamic contrast between the vertical thrust of the tower and the horizontal movement of the elegant curves of the main body, which housed the library. The complex was

---

6 Archivio Cesare Valle, Rome. CAR/22.

named after Benito Mussolini's younger brother and right-hand man, who had died in 1931; the Duce himself, with Ricci at his side, attended its inauguration on July 7, 1935, to emphasize the importance of this project to him and to the regime (cf. Popolo di Romagna 1935).

Aside from the Casa del Balilla in Forlì, Valle designed four other such *Case in Romagna*:[7] in Forlimpopoli (1933-36), Savignano sul Rubicone (1933-37), Mercato Saraceno (1936-40), and Predappio Nuova (1936-37) (cf. Architettura 1938). Compared to the building in Forlì, these were more modest, single-storey edifices, but Valle afforded each one a recognisable architectural twist. Thus in Forlimpopoli, the tower is asymmetrically skewed from the bottom, while in Savignano, the compact design of the main building is hollowed out unexpectedly in one corner, leaving only a giant pillar to identify the entrance. In Mercato Saraceno, the building blocks retreat and advance, creating a plastic game of forms; and in Predappio Nuova (New Predappio), Valle raised the low rectangular building onto a wide podium with steps leading up, rendering it more visible and giving it a hint of monumentality (Fig. 3). As had been the case in Forlì, the construction of this last *Casa* was entrusted to Valle by ONB President Renato Ricci, reflecting the importance of the project in the political and symbolic geography of the Fascist regime (cf. Architettura 1938: 149-152; Tramonti 2015b: 208-213). This building was in fact one of the main structures of Predappio Nuova, built a short distance from the Duce's birthplace of Dovia di Predappio.

Starting as early as 1922 and the March on Rome (the event organized by the National Fascist Party on October 28 of that year as an exhibition of paramilitary strength that facilitated Mussolini's rise to power), Predappio had become a pilgrimage destination for those who admired and supported Mussolini; indeed, the March gave rise to a thriving tourism industry in the formerly rural village – an industry which still continues today (cf. Serenelli 2012; Gundle 2013). The massive landslide that hit the village in 1923-24 provided a pretext for "moving" the village to a geologically safer location and for building a new and more modern city. There was thus a need both to give order to its development and to create a place that could glorify Mussolini and establish his myth. In 1925 the project was entrusted to the technical office of Forlì's *Genio Civile* (Statutory Corporation of Civil Engineers) and it was decided to locate the new town in Dovia, along the valley road. Its layout would be determined by two urban centres, both important places in Mussolini's life: the house in which he was born and the Palazzo Varano, where his mother Rosa Maltoni had worked as a teacher. The reconstruction of Predappio was accomplished over a period of only fifteen years, and expanded to

---

7   See the *Archival sources* section of this paper for details.

Figure 3: The Casa del Balilla in Predappio (1936–1937)

Archivio Cesare Valle, Roma

include further sites in the area related to Mussolini's life: particularly significant was the restoration of the Rocca della Carminate, Mussolini's residence in Romagna, and that of the Cemetery of San Cassiano in Pennino, where Rosa Maltoni was buried (cf. Prati/Tramonti 1999: 73-82; Tramonti/Lucchi 2010; Pozzi 2015a).

All of the main professionals involved in the reconstruction of Predappio came from Rome. The architect Florestano Di Fausto (1890-1965) was commissioned by Mussolini himself to design the new town in 1926, and conceived a project based on a settlement built in an eclectic style meant to recreate a "rural" environment (cf. Canali 2001b). The architect Cesare Bazzani (1873-1939) was the figure who, more than any other, brought Roman influence to Romagna, with an architectural style that tended to seek out the most acceptable compromise between 'modernism' and tradition (cf. Canali 2001a; Tramonti 2015a). Aside from Di Fausto's 'ruralism' and Bazzani's 'classicism', new trends in contemporary rationalist architecture also arrived in Predappio, thanks to young professionals such as the Forlivese architect Arnaldo Fuzzi (1893-1974), whose main project was the Casa del Fascio e dell'Ospitalità (Pozzi 2015b), and the engineer Cesare Valle with his Casa del Balilla.

Closing Valle's brief but intensive experience in Romagna was the construction of the Istituto Nazionale Fascista di Previdenza Sociale in Forlì (1932-37) and that of the Centro Sanatoriale "IX Maggio" in Vecchiazzano (1933-35). His most significant work in these years, however, was undoubtedly the Collegio Aeronautico della Gioventù Italiana del Littorio in Forlì (1936-41) (Fig. 4), which was dedicated to Mussolini's third son, Bruno. This building was constructed next to Valle's Casa del Balilla and engaged with it in a subtle dialogue. The "*Collegio*" was divided into functionally distinct sections, each with an independent entrance, and was defined by the external vision of a monumental yet simple and sober style, whilst the facades facing onto the inner courtyards consisted of large glass windows. The picturesque main entrance, marked by a colossal marble statue of Icarus by the sculptor Francesco Saverio Paolozzi, was arranged asymmetrically towards the empty corner (cf. Piacentini 1941; Prati/Tramonti 1999: 194-198; Antonucci 2015: 52-53; Tramonti 2015b: 162-199).

Figure 4: The Collegio Aeronautico della Gioventù Italiana del Littorio in Forlì (1936–1941)

Archivio Cesare Valle, Roma

From the documentation available at the Archivio Valle in Rome, we know that Valle rarely travelled to Romagna to oversee the works, but delegated both the construction and the administrative and bureaucratic issues to his assistants and to local technicians. The reasons for this are to be found not in any lack of importance that he gave to these assignments, but in the effort demanded by the work at the Governorate of Rome and in the great number of projects and undertakings for which he was responsible in these same years, both in Italy and abroad. Nevertheless, his work in Romagna was one of the fundamental points in his career: its positive reception earned him a place among the professionals entrusted with prestigious and challenging projects by the Fascist regime, both across Italy and in the so-called "Overseas Territories", the colonies of the regime.

CONCLUSION

This essay dealt with three case studies of urban renewal that occurred in Romagna during the Fascist regime, all of which employed architecture as a powerful means of propaganda in the service of different but complementary ends: the modernisation of small cities (Imola); the construction of Mussolini's mythology (Predappio); and the construction of a monumental capital city of the "Terra del Duce" (Forlì). In Imola, such transformations resulted in the construction of a modern and monumental urban centre embodied in the Nuovo Centro Cittadino by Giovanni Battista Milani and in the Casa del Fascio by Adriano Marabini, projects which oscillate between the local architectural practice and the Roman Stile Littorio. In Predappio and Forlì, the architectural and urban transformations carried an intense symbolic value, as a built celebration of the Duce and his power. Among the protagonists of this project, the Roman engineer Cesare Valle stands out as the one who introduced a monumental but non-rhetorical language into Romagna, a language contaminated by rationalist functionalism, in which technology and art naturally merged. Despite the differences among the cases discussed, these urban and architectural projects became a pivotal tool for the physical construction of Mussolini's mythology in this region.

This study was a collaborative effort; it should be noted, however, that the chapter on Imola was written by Sofia Nannini and the chapter on Cesare Valle by Micaela Antonucci, while the Introduction and Conclusions were written by both authors.

REFERENCES

Antonucci, Micaela (2014): "Architettura e regime: le opere realizzate da Fascismo in Romagna/Building construction under Fascism in Romagna." In: L'architettura, i regimi totalitari e la memoria del '900: Contributi alla nascita di una rotta culturale europea / Architecture, Totalitarian Regimes and Memory in the 20th Century: Contributions to the Birth of a European Cultural Route, Forlì: Casa Editrice Walden, pp. 75-84.
Antonucci, Micaela (2015): "Cesare Valle tra Roma e la Romagna (1924-1942). Ingegneria e architettura fra tradizione e modernità." In: Ulisse Tramonti (ed.), Cesare Valle: Un'altra modernità; Architettura in Romagna, Bononia: Bononia University Press, pp. 43-55.

Architettura (1938): "Tre case della Gioventù Italiana del Littorio in Romagna: Arch. Cesare Valle". In: Architettura: Rivista del Sindacato Nazionale Fascista Architetti, n. 3, March 1938, pp. 149-158.

Arthurs, Joshua (2012): Excavating Modernity: The Roman Past in Fascist Italy, Ithaca: Cornell University Press.

Balzani, Roberto (2001): La Romagna, Bologna: Il Mulino.

Baloni, Massimo (1988): Il fascismo e Alfredo Oriani: Il mito del precursore, Ravenna: Longo.

Bolognesi, Giorgio (1997): "Remigio Mirri: Ingegnere e architetto, 1867-1946." In: Pagine di vita e storia imolesi 6, pp. 207-222.

Bolognesi, Giorgio (ed.) (2016): Villa Muggia al Bel Poggio di Imola: Una storia incompiuta, Imola: Thèodolite.

Buscaroli, Rezio (1932): Un epigono del Mengoni: L'architetto Remigio Mirri, Bologna: Stabilimenti tipografici riuniti.

Canali, Ferruccio (1997): "Gustavo Giovannoni e il piano regolatore di Forlì, 1941: Il restauro urbano di «diradamento», la «nuova disciplina urbanistica» e la «legge urbanistica» del 1942." In: Studi Romagnoli XLVIII, pp. 587-630.

Canali, Ferruccio (2001a): "Architetti romani nella «città del Duce»: Cesare Bazzani a Forlì tra architettura del simbolismo, restauro novecentista, urbanistica della grande e della piccola dimensione". In: Ferruccio Canali/Virgilio Galati (eds.), Cesare Bazzani (1873-1939) e la Biblioteca Nazionale Centrale di Firenze, Firenze: Boneschi edizioni "Il Turismo", pp. 29-57.

Canali, Ferruccio (2001b): "Architetti romani nella «città del Duce»: Florestano Di Fausto a Predappio tra Storicismi 'd'avanguardia' e aulica ruralità: Urbanistica 'simbolista', ambientamento, restauro e gusto decò nella ricostruzione 'post-sismica' del 'paese di Mussolini'." In: Studi Romagnoli LII, pp. 1071-1024.

Canali, Ferruccio (2011): "Tra Avanguardia e Modernità architettonica: Un polimorfo 'allievo' lungo la via Emilia nella «Provincia del Duce» (1932-1943); Macchinismo navale futurista, purezza razionalista e moderno Monumentalismo imperiale nelle architetture romagnole di Cesare Valle". In: Anna Maria Guccini (ed.), La trasmissione del Sapere: Maestri e Allievi lungo la via Emilia, Comune di Fontanelice: Archivio Museo Giuseppe Mengoni, pp. 137-160.

Canali, Ferruccio (2016): "Nuovi sistemi costruttivi del cemento armato e dell'acciaio per il linguaggio architettonico del razionalismo a Forlì e a Riccione, 1933-1935: Monumenti del contemporaneo; Cesare Valle e il grande cantiere della casa dell'O.N.B.-G.I.L. a Forlì, 1933-1935; Renato Camus e l'abitazione tipica a struttura di acciaio' della 'V Triennale' di Milano rimontata

come 'Torre'900' a Riccione,1934." In: Studi Romagnoli, LXVII, pp. 461-500.
Cao, Umberto (ed.) (1994): Giuseppe Vaccaro: Colonia marina a Cesenatico, 1936-38, Roma: Clear.
Capomolla, Rinaldo/Mulazzani, Marco/Vittorini, Rosalia (2008): Case del Balilla: Architettura e fascismo, Milano: Electa.
Cassani Simonetti, Matteo (2015): "Centri e periferie nell'architettura in Romagna tra le due guerre e nell'opera di Cesare Valle." In: Ulisse Tramonti (ed.), Cesare Valle: Un'altra modernità: Architettura in Romagna, Bologna: Bononia University Press, pp. 21-42.
Ciucci, Giorgio (1989): Gli Architetti e il fascismo: Architettura e città, 1922-1944, Torino: Einaudi.
Cresti, Carlo (1986): Architettura e fascismo, Firenze: Vallecchi.
Delizia, Francesco/Di Francesco, Carla/Di Resta, Sara/Pretelli, Marco (eds.) (2015): La Casa del Fascio di Predappio nel panorama dell'architettura contemporanea, Bologna: Bononia University Press.
Doordan, Dennis P. (1983): Architecture and Politics in Fascist Italy, New York: Columbia University.
Dogliani, Patrizia (ed.) (2006): Romagna tra fascismo e antifascismo, 1919-1945, Bologna: Clueb.
Gentile, Emilio (2007): Fascismo di pietra, Roma-Bari: Laterza.
Gori, Mariacristina/Tramonti, Ulisse (2002): Castrocaro città delle acque, Castrocaro Terme: Vespignani.
Gresleri, Giuliano/Massaretti, Pier Giorgio (eds.) (2001): Norma e arbitrio: Architetti e ingegneri a Bologna, 1850-1950, Venezia: Marsilio.
Gundle, Stephen (2013): "The Aftermath of the Mussolini Cult: History, Nostalgia and Popular Culture." In: The Cult of the Duce: Mussolini and the Italians, ed. S. Gundle, C. Duggan, and G. Pieri, Manchester: Manchester University Press, pp. 241–256.
Hökerberg, Håkan (ed.) (2018): Architecture as Propaganda in Twentieth-Century Totalitarian Regimes: History and Heritage, Firenze: Polistampa.
Marga (Margherita Sarfatti) (1927): Il volo dell'aquila: Da Predappio a Roma, Firenze: Armando Rossini.
Massaretti, Pier Giorgio (2005): "La colonia 'Sandro Mussolini' dell'A.G.I.P. a Cesenatico." In: Walter Balducci (ed.), Architetture per le colonie di vacanza: Esperienze europee, Firenze: Alinea, pp. 87-90.
Mirri, Remigio (1932): Il centro d'Imola per la verità, Bologna: Poligrafica bodoniana.

Muntoni, Alessandra (2007): "Cesare Valle: architettura, urbanistica, istituzioni." In: Pippo Ciorra/Alessandro d'Onofrio/Luca Molinari (eds.), Studio Valle, 1957-2007: Cinquant'anni di architettura, Milano: Skira.

Nanni, Antonio/Bellentani, Federico (2018): "The Meaning Making of the Built Environment in the Fascist City: A Semiotic Approach." In: Sign and Society 6/2 (https://www.journals.uchicago.edu/doi/pdfplus/10.1086/696850 last access 14-04-2019).

Nicoloso, Paolo (2008): Mussolini architetto: Propaganda e paesaggio urbano nell'Italia fascista, Torino: Einaudi.

Orioli, Valentina (2008): Cesenatico: Turismo e città balneare tra Otto e Novecento, Firenze: Alinea.

Piacentini, Marcello (1941): "Collegio aeronautico Bruno Mussolini della Gioventù Italiana del Littorio a Forlì: Ingegnere Cesare Valle". In: Architettura: Rivista del Sindacato Nazionale Fascista Architetti, n. 12, December 1942, pp. 383-406.

Painter, Bordan (2005): "Architecture, propaganda and the Fascist revolution." In: Mussolini's Rome: Rebuilding the Eternal City, New York: Palgrave Macmillan.

Popolo di Romagna (1935): "Il Duce inaugura fra acclamazioni di popolo la Casa Balilla 'Arnaldo Mussolini'." In: Popolo di Romagna, 31 luglio 1935, p. 2.

Pozzi, Elena (2015a): "Un'architettura per «la Galilea di tutti noi»". In: Francesco Delizia/Carla Di Francesco/Sara Di Resta/Marco Pretelli (eds.): La Casa del Fascio di Predappio nel panorama dell'architettura contemporanea, Bologna: Bononia University Press, pp. 12-16.

Pozzi, Elena (2015b): "Dall'ambizione alla realtà: I limiti del costruire." In: Francesco Delizia/Carla Di Francesco/Sara Di Resta/Marco Pretelli (eds.): La Casa del Fascio di Predappio nel panorama dell'architettura contemporanea, Bologna: Bononia University Press, pp. 16-21.

Prati, Luciana/Tramonti Ulisse (eds.) (1999): La città progettata. Forlì, Predappio, Castrocaro: Urbanistica e architettura tra le due guerre, Forlì: Comune di Forlì.

Proli, Mario (2017): "Un 'grande set' per il culto del duce: Ipotesi di ricerca sulle trasformazioni urbane di Forlì durante il fascismo." Clionet: Per un senso del tempo e dei luoghi, 1 [16-10-2017]. (http://rivista.clionet.it/vol1/dossier/architetture_tra_le_due_guerre/proli-un-grande-set-per-il-culto-del-duce last access 27-05-2018).

Santuccio Salvatore (ed.) (2005): Le Case e il Foro: L'Architettura dell'ONB, Firenze: Alinea.

Serenelli, Sofia (2013): "A Town for the Cult of the Duce: Predappio as a Site of Pilgrimage". In: The Cult of the Duce: Mussolini and the Italians, eds. Stephen

Gundle/Christopher Duggan/Giuliana Pieri. Manchester: Manchester University Press, pp. 93-109.
Tramonti, Ulisse (1997): Itinerari d'architettura moderna: Forlì, Cesenatico, Predappio, Firenze: Alinea.
Tramonti, Ulisse (2005): Le radici del razionalismo in Romagna: Itinerari nel comprensorio forlivese, Forlì: Menabò.
Tramonti, Ulisse/Lucchi Alessandro (2010): Predappio e la valle del Rabbi: Storie del Novecento, Forlì: Edizioni In Magazine.
Tramonti, Ulisse (2015a): "Forlì. Una città per due Cesare". In: Ulisse Tramonti (ed.), Cesare Valle: Un'altra modernità; Architettura in Romagna, Bologna: Bononia University Press.
Tramonti, Ulisse (ed.) (2015b): Cesare Valle. Un'altra modernità: Architettura in Romagna, Bologna: Bononia University Press.
Vaccaro, Giuseppe (1934): "Progetto per la sistemazione del nuovo centro di Lugo". In: Architettura: Rivista del Sindacato Nazionale Fascista Architetti, January 1934, XII, fasc. I, pp. 1-7.
Vaccaro, Giuseppe (1939): "La colonia 'Sandro Mussolini' dell'AGIP a Cesenatico". In: Architettura: Rivista del Sindacato Nazionale Fascista Architetti, January 1939, XVII, fasc. 1, pp. 1-14.
Valle, Cesare (1938): "Notizie sulla operosità scientifica e sulla carriera didattica." Archivio Cesare Valle, Roma.

ARCHIVAL SOURCES

Biblioteca Comunale di Imola
Disegni Ufficio Tecnico (Segnatura 15): Milani, G. B. (1932). Centro cittadino [95 drawings of the project by G. B. Milani, partly signed by Studio Tecnico G. B. Milani, Via Balbo 31, Roma. Some drawings of the *Casa del Fascio* are included]; Disegni Ufficio Tecnico (Segnatura 22): Mirri, R. (1930). Prospetti Centro cittadino [5 drawings of the arcade's façade and plan]; Disegni Ufficio Tecnico (Segnatura 86): Mirri, R. (1931-1932). Centro cittadino [8 drawings of the arcade's façade].

Archivio Cesare Valle, Roma
Casa del Balilla "Arnaldo Mussolini" di Forlì (CV-PRO/036; CV-PRO-39); Casa Balilla di Forlimpopoli (CV-PRO/040); Casa Balilla di Savignano (CV-PRO/059); Casa del Balilla di Predappio (CV-PRO/064); Casa del Balilla, Mercato Saraceno (CV-PRO/063); Sede dell'Istituto Nazionale Fascista di Previdenza

Sociale (INFPS), Forlì (CV-CAR/032); Collegio aeronautico della GIL "Bruno Mussolini" di Forlì (CV-PRO/066); Centro sanatoriale di Vecchiazzano (CV-CAR/047).

Archivio Adriano Marabini, Fondazione Cassa di Risparmio di Imola
Casa del Fascio di Imola (AM 148.1-2; AM 149.1-2; AM 150.1-2; AM 151).

Istituto Nazionale Luce (1936)
La seconda giornata del Duce nell'Emilia. Visita di S. E. il Capo del Governo a Bologna: seconda giornata. Video report No. D065406.

Autarchy and Tradition in the Architecture during Italy's Fascist Period
Newly Founded Cities

Angela Pecorario Martucci

This paper aims to investigate how the autarchic policy of the Italian fascist regime has been translated into architecture. The foundation of new cities in fascist Italy, linked to the processes of industrial modernization, represents one of the most typical built expressions of this period. Therefore, a reading of the concept of self-sufficiency will be attempted from an architectural and urban point of view.

Changes in urban landscape reflect Italy's economic and political reorganization; In this paper, autarchy is interpreted not as a moral and political principle, but in its most immediate sense of economy, using only local materials as a concrete expression of national identity.

The Italian autarchic policy began between the end of 1935 and the first half of 1936 and was triggered by the international condemnation of Italy for its military attack on Ethiopia. The declaration of war by Mussolini on October 2, 1935 was followed by the immediate condemnation of the League of Nations that issued economic sanctions against Italy that included the embargo on arms and ammunition, prohibitions on the granting of loans and opening credits, and prohibitions on importing Italian goods and exporting to Italy items necessary for the war industry. These measures will be cleverly arranged by the regime during a short period of time between November 18 and July 4, 1936.

On March 23, 1936, there was a further turning point in autarchic politics. In fact, Mussolini exhibited the so-called local strategic plan for the new Italian economy (Piano Regolatore della *Nuova Economia Italiana*), defining a structured project for strengthening the nation. Ever since this date, autarchy stops being a defense strategy imposed by sanctions, and becomes a specific offensive plan based on emancipation from abroad in order to obtain economic and political independence.

Abandoning laissez-faire policy, Italy moves toward self-sufficiency, focusing as much as possible only on the domestic market and on the promotion of national resources. As Benito Mussolini affirmed in 1936, Italy should "achieve, as soon as possible, a maximum of autonomy in the nation's economic life. No nation in the world can realize on its own territory the ideal of economic autonomy in an absolute sense, that is one hundred percent [...]. But every nation tries to break free as much as possible from foreign servants." (Lojacono 1937: XVIII; Mussolini 1936).[1]

This kind of independence policy, in its totalitarian nature, also seeks its legitimazation in terms of building expression. The architecture, due to its representativeness, is suitable for becoming a further instrument of consensus and promotion of precise national values advanced by the regime, and more intensified in this new phase of "totalitarian acceleration" (Gentile 2007 [2005]: 27f).[2] Architects are asked to specify the new political turn through concrete examples.

Therefore, the industrial modernization courses, linked to the promotion and strengthening programs of the most lacking sectors of the Italian economy (fuels, cellulose, etc.), are accompanied by urban transformation episodes[3] that try to follow the independence turning point respecting, above all, the instructions on the quota system of materials.

The most typical expression of the autarchic spirit is the city in support of industry. The need to house the workforce for newly built factories led to the foundation of new cities. These are highly specialized cities of work, created in response to one precise function. For example, the newly founded air-base town of

---

[1] "Realizzare nel più breve termine possibile il massimo possibile di autonomia nella vita economica della Nazione. Nessuna nazione del mondo può realizzare sul proprio territorio l'ideale dell'autonomia economica, in senso assoluto, cioè al cento per cento [...]. Ma ogni Nazione cerca di liberarsi nella misura più larga possibile delle servitù straniere". The quote is taken from the speech held by Mussolini on March 23, 1936 before the second meeting of corporations, known as the town plan of the Italian economy. The speech is fully reported in: Lojacono, Luigi (1937): L'indipendenza economica italiana, Milano: Hoepli, pp. XVII-XXIV.

[2] "Accelerazione totalitaria".

[3] For an overall reading of urban transformations during the fascist period: Cf: Ruinas, Stanis (1939): Viaggio per le città di Mussolini, Milano: Bompiani.

Guidonia (1935) called "the city of air" by Mussolini.[4] ("Guidonia" 1938: 199); Carbonia and Arsia are cities of coal; Torviscosa is the city of cellulose.

So, the slogan "Italy will do itself", as the clear expression of the desire for emancipation from imports, translates into the search for a truly Italian aesthetics that pursues local and regional lines precisely in the construction of these new cities, which have arisen "with fascist speed [...] under the control of the new autarchic laws" (Caniglia 1940: 11).[5]

Changes in urban landscape reflect Italy's economic and political reorganization; autarchy is interpreted not as a moral and political principle, but in its most immediate economic sense as resorting to only local materials in a strong expression of identity. Additionally, having supplies in geographic proximity contributes to autarchy entirely because it saves on the fuel needed for the transport of products.

Therefore, the style, the forms, the urban image, and the choices about construction and materials adapt to this political protectionism and adopt the characteristics of an architecture that aims to be autarchic without losing its history, and in keeping with the local tradition. The aim of a national identity architecture is to use elements of the traditional lexicon in an instrumental way to strengthen the ideological message and promote, on urban scale, the new economic direction. The use of local materials (tuff, pozzolana, limestone, trachyte, marble, etc.) helps to reinforce the sense of independence and operates according to a logic of short local production chains.

The "contemporary call for an economy forced towards the resources of our country",[6] as the art critic Roberto Papini (1883-1957)[7] (Papini 1998 [1936]: 293) calls it, involves the use of local and indigenous materials, expressed in a powerful regionalism. It is no coincidence that in "Italy [...], the country of stones, from the

---

4   Mussolini's speech during the opening ceremony in 1937 is reported in the journal *Architettura* ("Guidonia" 1938).
5   "Con rapidità fascista [...] sotto l'imperio delle nuove leggi autarchiche". The quote belongs to Renato Caniglia, who has been a member of the Ministry for Popular Culture (the Ministry that dealt with the culture and organization of fascist propaganda). At first, he was editor of Lavoro Fascista and Cronache di Guerra, later in Corriere and Il Popolo di Roma.
6   "Il richiamo odierno all'economia obbligata delle risorse del nostro suolo".
7   Roberto Papini was a freelance journalist, art critic, official of the Ministry of Public Education; between 1930 and 1957 he published essays and articles about decorative arts, architecture and transformations of Italian cities in various magazines.

roughest tuff to the most sparkling marbles"[8] (ibid: 294), the "love for marble" is reborn, as architect and art critic Giuseppe Pagano (1896-1945)[9] (1938: 2) calls it, as marble is used in very typical Italian facades.

Autarchic dictates impose as many common and shared uses as possible. The economic restrictions weigh on the architectural examples substantially and by way of transposing autarchy on the figurative level, this translates into real demand especially for reinforced concrete and iron. Following administrative orders which had been disregarded, a ban in 1939 restricted the use of reinforced concrete, which was considered not nationalistic and anti-autarchic. Meanwhile, a real "iron psychosis"[10] arises (Pagano, 1939, p.35), as iron was forbidden even in furniture making, because it was considered essential for the war industry.

These aspects have a direct consequence on the architectural aesthetics that, in the attempt to adapt to the autarchic formula, leaves some solutions (such as the cantilevers), allowed by the reinforced concrete technique or, as Papini says, "the most sudden audaciousness of the empty spaces open wide, of the protruding and suspending of the filled ones, with amazing effects of improbable equilibrium"[11] (Papini 1998 [1936]: 293) in order to enhance the brickwork. Reinforced concrete reduces cracks, fills gaps, creates remarkable wall thickness, and is necessary in building brick curtains interrupted by marble or travertine blocks.

To save money, traditional elements of regional architecture are used. Where it is not possible to forgo reinforced concrete for technical reasons, a more rational estimate of the static stress allows for the reduction of necessary iron.

In cities built during this period of sanctions, an 'Italian identity' is represented, often taking on the features of a rustic style and tradition, so much that, in the competitions held in the national territory of newly founded cities, designers are explicitly asked to comply with the autarchic principles, thus constraining formal aspects of architecture.

---

8   "L'Italia è il paese delle pietre, dai più rozzi tufi ai più smaglianti marmi".
9   Giuseppe Pagano, a well-known rationalist, and critical and intellectual architect in the 1930s, became director of *Casabella* – one of the most prestigious architecture magazines, – which later will change names into *Casabella-Costruzioni* and then to *Costruzioni-Casabella*. The magazine was a sort of critical observatory on the evolution of modern architecture, in opposition to any form of academicism and traditionalism.
10 "Psicosi del ferro".
11 "Le più improvvise arditezze dello spalancarsi dei vuoti, dello sporgersi e sospendersi dei pieni, con effetti stupefacenti d'equilibri inverosimili".

Figure 1: Aprilia, the square as it was around 1936

Historical photograph from: Antonio Pennacchi, 2008, p. 19

In particular, after a series of competitions for new cities, for example, for the reclamation program of the Agro Pontino (*Bonifica Integrale*) undertaken by the fascist regime, the calls for bids on especially the cities of Aprilia (1936-1937) and Pomezia (1938-1939) dictate binding rules – also for what concerns the freedom of style – always following that all-encompassing program of self-sufficiency that combines spiritual, aesthetic and economic motivations. The text reads, in summary:

The constructive and architectural features of both public and private buildings – according to the Pomezia call for bids – must be inspired by sublime simplicity [...] reducing to very few cases the use of expensive structures and coatings in noble materials and avoiding the use of not sober decorative elements [...] as well as those used to mask [...] the use intended for the works [...]. There will be particularly appreciated all the solutions that, as far as possible, include the local regional historical-aesthetic characteristics in the current evolutionary movement of architecture, of course, always within the limits given by the aforementioned economic considerations. Construction types based on the use of local materials shall be adopted (tuff, flint, pumice, pozzolana). In view of the current circumstances, the use of metallic materials should be limited to the strict minimum: iron and reinforced concrete structures should be excluded if possible. (Nuti/Martinelli 1981: 125; National Soldier Charity [Italian acronym ONC][12], Historical archive of the Municipality of Pomezia).[13]

Italian identity, ruralism, simplicity and parsimony are present also in Aprilia, so that Concezio Petrucci (1902-46), the coordinator of 2PST (acronym identifying the group of architects to which Mosé Mario Tufaroli Luciano, Emanuele Filiberto Paolini and Riccardo Silenzi also belong), describes his winning project in a 1936 letter to Araldo di Crollalanza, the ONC President:

Figure 2: Pomezia, main square, 1939

Photograph: Stanis Ruinas, 1939

12 The National Soldier Charity was a moral and welfare organization active in Italy from 1917 to 1977. During fascism, the main tasks involved colonisation and reclamation of the Agro Pontino.
13 "Le caratteristiche costruttive e architettoniche degli edifici sia pubblici che privati dovranno essere ispirate a somma semplicità [...] restringendo a pochissimi casi l'adozione di strutture costose e di rivestimenti in materiali nobili e rifuggendo dall'impiego di partiti decorativi non sobri [...] come pure di quelli intesi a mascherare [...] l'uso cui le opere sono destinate [...]. Saranno particolarmente apprezzate soluzioni che, per quanto possibile, inseriscano le locali caratteristiche storico-estetiche regionali nell'attuale movimento di evoluzione dell'architettura, sempre - beninteso - nei limiti dati dalle suesposte considerazioni economiche. Saranno da adottare tipi costruttivi basati sull'impiego dei materiali locali (tufo, selce, pomice, pozzolana). Tenuto conto delle attuali contingenze l'uso dei materiali metallici dovrà essere limitato allo stretto indispensabile: possibilmente si escluderanno strutture in ferro e cemento armato."

We designed a typical fascist centre of peasants, where the rural population takes part in the collective and family life in cosy, intimate and human environments [...]. We have drawn, from our glorious construction systems and from our typical building materials, new forms and new architectural expressions fitting to our Latin spirit and the sensitivity of our field people; while our competitors, even today that the economic siege tightens all around us, cannot turn down imported materials and constructive systems that make us dependent abroad.[14] (Nuti/Martinelli 1981: 131; National Soldier Charity [ONC], Historical archive of the Municipality of Aprilia)

A moderate modernity, expressed through the use of vernacular elements and aimed at a refined Mediterranean style, using arcades, rounded arches, pergolas, pitched roofs, external stairs, brick walls and wooden gates, represents the figurative mark of those cities that we can define as autarchic both in chronology – as they were all inaugurated during the autarchic period – and in the aspiration to boost strategic and economic-industrial realities in the new reorganization of the national economy. The strengthening of the extractive, aeronautical and textile industry in Italian is accompanied by functional urban realizations that were initiated with the aim of showing to the public, the face of a new, competitive, dynamic and expanding Italy, promoting the emancipation from abroad. In fact, the cities of Arsia (Raša), Carbonia, Guidonia and Torviscosa, founded since 1935, can be defined autarchic because they are shaped under the economic and sober constraints, using local materials such as cut stones, marble, limestone, the hard trachyte, that in the buildings of Carbonia, "keeps alive a persistent nuragic [from the name of the ancient Sardinian culture] memory" (Giani 1940: 38).[15] The supply of sand, gravel and limestone is always obtained from quarries very close to the town. The stone is used for the walls, reducing the use of bricks to the internal

---

14 "Abbiamo progettato un tipico centro fascista di contadini, ove la popolazione rurale partecipi della vita collettiva e familiare in ambienti accoglienti, intimi ed umani [...]. Noi abbiamo tratto dai nostri gloriosi sistemi costruttivi e dai nostri tipici materiali di costruzione nuove forme e nuove espressioni architettoniche aderenti al nostro spirito latino ed alla sensibilità della nostra gente dei campi; mentre i nostri avversari, neanche oggi che l'assedio economico ci stringe tutt'intorno, sanno rinunciare a materiali d'importazione e a sistemi costruttivi che ci rendono tributati all'estero".

15 "Mantiene un tenace ricordo nuragico". The reference is linked to the Sardinian Native civilisation (1800 B.C. – Second century A.D.), whose name has been attributed to Nuraghe, impressive megalithic constructions built in polygonal boulders of trachyte. The quote is by Renato Giani, author of the regime's propaganda, and it is taken from his propaganda text about the city of Carbonia.

partitions only. In line with the requirements for the use of reinforced concrete and iron, the slabs are built with timbers – except for buildings destined to collective nature – extra-thin brickwork vaults are used as partial replacement of ceilings; the prominent cantilevers are almost completely abolished. In the representative buildings, the Apuan marble is used for floors and coatings, following the orders that support its use (cf. Giani 1940: 31-32). The buildings are based on a strict economy, excluding iron, expensive decorations and luxury materials. Instead, the architectural features of Guidonia are different because a rational language is used that is considered more suitable in expressing its nature as a city of research and experimentation linked to the aeronautical sector.

Figure 3: Workers' houses in Carbonia, 1940

Photograph: Renato Giani, 1940

In fact, in the coal cities of Arsia in Croatia and Carbonia in Sardinia the Italian feature was synonymous with rurality because it was considered more appropriate for a population of miners, while for a population of soldiers, scholars and technicians, it was judged more suitable exerting a language that rejects the rhetoric of local and rustic styles, because it was already regarded at the time as "frankly modern, even without the conventionalism of passing fashion: simple, refined, posh, yet despite the constraints of a severe economy." ("Guidonia" 1938: 200).[16]

---

16 "Francamente moderno, pur senza convenzionalismi di moda passeggera: sobrio, distinto, signorile, pur tra i vincoli di una severa economia".

This highlights how the principle of self-sufficiency really finds a form of direct implementation in these cities of work. These urban realizations are characterized by a frank and constructive 'honesty' in compliance with the more general program of autarchy, as the direct expression of national values. The technical and construction solutions are completely sustainable, especially for reducing the cost in foreign currency, even if we can attribute to these cities a lack of experimentalism. To conclude, the construction of these new cities, the sanctions find their clear equivalent in localism.

Figure 4: Guidonia, aerial photograph, 1940

Photograph: Marcello Gallian, 1940

REFERENCES

Caniglia, Renato (1940): Arsia, Torino: Arione.
Gentile, Emilio (2007 [2005]): Fascismo. Storia e interpretazione, Rome/Bari: GLF Ed. Laterza.
Giani, Renato (1940): Carbonia, Torino: Arione.
"Guidonia la città dell'aria" (1938). In: Architettura XVII, pp.193–238.
Mussolini, Benito (1936): Discorso del 23 marzo XIV in Campidoglio. In: Lojacono, Luigi (1937): L'indipendenza economica italiana, Milano: Hoepli, pp. XVII-XXIV.

Nuti, Lucia/Martinelli, Roberta (1981): Le città di strapaese: La politica di fondazione nel ventennio, Milano: Franco Angeli.

Pagano, Giuseppe (1938): "Variazioni sull'autarchia architettonica II". In: Casabella-Costruzioni 130, pp. 2-3.

Pagano, Giuseppe (1939): "Costruzioni metalliche: L'autarchia e l'architettura del ferro". In: Casabella-Costruzioni 144, pp. 34-35.

Papini, Roberto (1998 [1936]): "Il significato di un appello: Architettura e sanzioni". In: Cronache di architettura, 1914-1957: Antologia degli scritti di Roberto Papini, Firenze: Edifir, pp. 292-294.

Pennacchi, Antonio (2008): Fascio e martello: Viaggio per la città del duce, Bari: Laterza.

Ruinas, Stanis (1939): Viaggio per le città di Mussolini, Milano: Bompiani.

City Extensions

Urban Expansion in Venice, 1918-1939

Continuity of the Urban Form in the Internal Periphery of the Residential Area of Santa Marta

Alexander Fichte

Various residential areas were built in the internal periphery of Venice during the interwar period. In their physical urban form, they tried to connect with the historic city center while respecting the new sanitation rules. Despite being built during the same period, the residential areas differ in their characteristics. This paper will focus on the residential area of Santa Marta.

Residential areas in the internal periphery of Venice had to connect to the physical urban form of the city. Being surrounded by industry, the area of Santa Marta responds to this in various ways.

Over the centuries, Venice has developed a strong identity that has led to the continuous development of its physical urban form. The temporal continuity of the city image generated a prevalence of urban planning over architecture (cf. Bettini 1960: 53).[1] New building projects had to adapt to the existing city (cf. Concina 1989: 127).[2] On his trip to Venice in 1845, John Ruskin (1819-1900) was surprised to find modern gas lamps, as he would in any other European city (cf. 1845: 198). According to him, every new building project had to be modified and changed when faced with the strong Venetian identity (cf. Zucconi 2000: 60). Sixty years later in 1912, the identical reconstruction of the collapsed bell tower of St. Mark's Basilica was completed. It initiated an outpouring of reproductions, especially

---

1 "Caratteristico è la continuità temporale dell'immagine di questa città la quale porta a una prevalenza, per cosi dire, dell'urbanistica sull'architettura."
2 "Nel tessuto urbano di Venezia è indiscutibile il primato della continuità figurativa sull'autonomia di segno del singolo organismo edilizio e architettonico."

overseas, where some train stations, skyscrapers and universities were built with particular Venetian features. The image of Venice had become so strong that it was exported to other cities. However, the copies, being focused on few Venetian characteristics, always lacked the richness and diversity of the urban fabric of the real Venice (cf. Settis 2014: 60).

Figure 1: Urban districts built on the margins of the island between 1918 and 1939 (black), Santa Marta (framed)

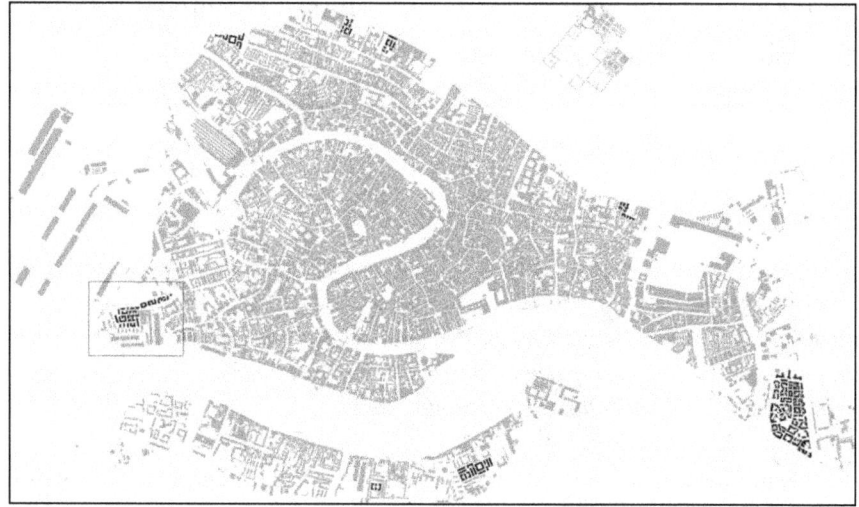

Alexander Fichte, 2017

According to the influential Italian architect Marcello Piacentini (1881-1960), the residential building is a complex art form full of compromises. It contains the doctrines of aesthetics, moral sociology, hygiene and security (cf. 1922: 60).[3] It was also Piacentini who pointed out that it was not possible to have a preconceived picturesque plan in advance. A place can only gather picturesque characteristics over time (cf. ibid: 60).[4] Regarding the social context, Gustavo Giovannoni (1873-1947) described the connection between old and new buildings as problematic

---

3 "L'edilizia generale è arte complessa è arte essenzialmente di sintesi, abbracciando essa molte altre dottrine: l'estetica, la morale, la sociologia, l'igiene, la sicurezza."

4 "Non si può concepire un piano pittoresco a priori. [...] L'ingenuità non può essere imposta: è un sentimento naturale e istitivo che trae tutta la sua forza dalla sua incoscienza."

because they respond to entirely different requirements (1931: 6).[5] Piacentini and Giovannoni witnessed the urban development of Italy in the interwar period that was connected to a European and North American planning tradition (cf. Bodenschatz 2009: 9). These points describe exactly the problems faced by the new residential areas, in this case Santa Marta, in the internal periphery of Venice. They tried to match the new residential areas to a picturesque image of the city, although the conditions imposed by society had changed dramatically.

URBAN FORM OF VENICE

One of the most consistent symbols of a city is its physical urban form. Even if it is continuously influenced by economic constraints and stylistic trends, the features of the urban culture of the past remain. City design can be motivated by ideological, political, economic or functional aspects. It is influenced by local conditions like geography, topography, demography and the climate. Local culture and everything linked to it also has an impact on the physical form of the city. In this paper, the physical urban form will be divided into three different urbanistic scales. The biggest scale is the *forma urbis*. The term describes the overall shape of all elements that the city consists of. The next scale is the urban structure of the city. It describes specific spatial sequences and connections. The last scale is the architecture of a city, which corresponds to building types and stylistic elements.

The physical form of Venice is the result of the location where it was built and the passing of time (cf. Romanelli 2005: 17).[6] A reference point for the urban development of Venice is the bird's-eye view by Jacopo de Barbari (1450-1516) that was made around 1500. It shows the island shaped like a dolphin isolated in the lagoon surrounded only by smaller islands and protected by different divinities. It

---

5   "Problema centrale quello dei rapporti tra l'edilizia vecchia e la nuova nelle sistemazionie delle città. Le città vecchie e le città nuove sono organismi che hanno tra loro essenzialissime differenze, che rispondono al diverso ordine di capacità, di esigenze varie; di ordinamenti e di mezzi, in cui a lor volta si riflettono i corrispondenti periodi della civiltà umana."

6   "La forma di Venezia e quindi prodotto del tempo e del luogo, oltre che di volontà d'arte; la linea sottile, impalpabile in cui s'unicsce l'artificiale e il naturale; il luogo senza luogo in cui le inquieditudini dell'occidente si confrontano con le certezze dell'oriente bizantino, in cui il tempo e la forma danno vita al più sfuggente enigmatica inimitabile dei miracoli dell'ingengno, la dove si agita indefinivamente, raddoppiata dai riflessi dell'acqua, la bilancia dei pesi e delle sostanze."

was used to transport a new self-image of the city and it defined the city's fishlike shape, the *forma urbis*, for centuries to come until today. Because of its highly detailed illustration, it can also be considered a quantitative representation of the city (cf. Concina 1998: 173).

The urban structure of Venice is shaped by its isolation in the lagoon. The high density of the built environment is a result of the limited building ground. The different parts of the city are linked by a vast network of channels that today is complemented by a pedestrian network as well. Using the same space, the two systems run parallel and sometimes even overlap (cf. Miozzi 1957: 43). The change between narrow streets (it. sing. *Calle*) and open urban spaces (it. sing. *Campo*), and the complexity of the linked connection systems are all spatial characteristics of Venice.

The architecture of the city shows different characteristics that are repeatedly utilized. Istrian marble is used for building decoration, but mostly to frame doors and windows. Wooden beams and brick walls are another regular feature (cf. Calabi 1993: 21). Almost every building shows signs of constant exposure to salt water. One of the reasons single buildings seem to follow the complexity and continuity of the physical urban form of the city (Cristinelli 1987: 20)[7] is that they are set on picturesque water reflections and are framed only by each other and the sky (cf. Howard 2002: 4). Among other things like the eastern influence on building style, the most significant and unique Venetian influence on all three scales of the urban form is the lagoon. Being a geomorphological intermediary state in between the mainland and the open sea, a lagoon usually vanishes with time. In the case of Venice, this special environment was kept and modified because it granted safety and wealth. Also, the Venetian perception of the lagoon changed from a defensive retreat to being considered an actual threat for the city. The lagoon is the most prominent feature of the city. Venice is limited because of it, but at the same time, the city did not lose its boundaries during the industrialization like other cities on the mainland (cf. Favilla 2002: 184).

---

7 "È noto che a Venezia, forse ancora più che in altre città, il singolo edificio è strettamente connesso al suo contesto. Tale constatazione è coglibile immediatamente nell'evidenza dell'immagine e si ritrova anche nell'intreccio o nella continuità delle fabbriche edilizie che insieme sembrano ritrovarsi nella logica più generale della fabbrica urbana."

INTERWAR PERIOD AND INTERNAL PERIPHERY

In the interwar period, the development of the lagoon city was determined by the need to respond to the industrial and demographic challenges. But the island alone could not provide enough space for further development. To remain capable of competing on a national and international level, the decision to build a new industrial zone on the mainland was made in 1917, including a linked port. In the following decades, the industrial port of Marghera grew, and with it the economic importance of the once subsidiary mainland. The settlements on the mainland and the city in the lagoon were considered to be two poles of one city. In order to centralize the urban development of the lagoon, the surrounding communities were inserted into the administration of Venice by a decision of the Ministerial Council in Rome in 1926 (cf. "Per la più grande Venezia" 1926: 234).[8] Thus the metropolitan region of Venice, called Greater Venice (*Grande Venezia*), was installed. The spacious urban expansion on the mainland answered most of the demands that were imposed on the city in the interwar period. The lagoon city was intended to be the administrative center with touristic potential, and its urban development focused on the continuity of its urban form. This urban development practice was institutionalized in the late 1930s. The special law N. 1901, published in 1937 was aimed at saving the unique urban environment of the lagoon and the monumental character of Venice. An urban master plan followed in 1939. This plan must be understood as a guideline for the future progress of the city's development. The main objective of the master plan was infrastructure modernization, while maintaining the unique identity of the city. Not only were new channels and new pedestrian connections built, but also new residences were planned in those areas where it was possible to build them. The plan consolidated the urban planning practice of the previous decades and determined the progress for years to come (cf. Bellavitis 1985: 238).

Enclosed within walls – or in the case of Venice, surrounded by the lagoon – the nature of such a historic city seems complete. An urban space can be defined by its limits. The margin is where the city ends and something else begins. This is essential because the city's cohesion and meaning is best experienced at the margin (cf. Settis 2014: 84). On the margins of Venice, the dense urban structure of the city meets the vast open space of the lagoon. The term 'internal periphery' describes the margins of Venice, which are away from the traditional urban center

---

8   "Venezia, per giungere a Marghera, che è parte del suo territorio ed alla cui sistemazione ha necessità di provvedere, deve traversare l'abitato di Mestre. Per queste ragioni i due centri costituiscono ormai un'unità di fatto."

in Rialto or San Marco, but still a part of the lagoon city. It is contrasted by the external periphery on the mainland in Marghera and Mestre. Residences were built on both peripheries in order to meet the needs of the population. Even if the residential areas of the internal periphery were much smaller, their creation was far more complex than the spacious residential areas on the mainland. Parts of the margins had to be reclaimed or created (it. pl. *Sacce*)[9] before the building activity could be initiated. Being attached to the physical form of Venice, they had to respond to the urban context. Another peculiarity is that on the internal periphery, mostly simple residences for the working class – so-called 'worker housings' – were built.

WORKER HOUSINGS AND CONTINUITIY

The law N. 251 (called *Legge Luzzatti*) was a suitable instrument to face the complex requirements for building worker housing in Italy. It was approved by the Italian Parliament in 1903 and emerged out of the government experience of its Venetian creator Luigi Luzzatti (1841-1927). Following article 22 of the law, the enterprises of the newly founded municipal agencies had to be linked to social principles instead of the rules of profit, and were part of the public administration. A following law that benefited the construction of worker housings was the T.U. N. 89 (it. precept *Testo Unico*). It was passed in 1908 and brought innovations to the already existing law N. 251. New standards for construction, sale, succession and sanitation were introduced and bank credits linked to worker housing projects were available more easily. These benefits were focused on a certain type of company founded following the *Legge Luzzatti* and excluded private venturers. At this point, it was also determined who was allowed to live in the newly built worker housings (cf. Di Sivo 1981: 29). In the law N. 1858, ratified in 1919, the character of worker housings was defined. In order to keep the above-mentioned advantages, buildings had to either remain property of the official agencies authorized by law or had to be built by companies providing residences for their members to rent or buy. Also, single apartments needed to include their own entrance from the stairway, a toilet and running water. Furthermore, buildings had to comply with the sanitation rules of the local administration (cf. ibid: 49).

In Venice, the autonomous institute of working-class housing (IACP or Istituto Autonomo Case Popolari) emerged out of the pre-existing communal agencies in

---

9   Further informations about the "sacce" and their development in Cosmai/Sorteni (2007).

1913. After the World War I, there was a visible shift in building practices regarding the aesthetic demands imposed onto worker housings. A pleasant environment was considered to have an educative effect on its residents and would contribute to making them better individuals (cf. Donatelli 1928: 21).[10] In Venice, according to the major Venetian architect Duilio Torres (1882-1969), such an environment was to be linked to the history and tradition of the city. The mere application of sanitation rules and stipulations of worker housing contracts would deny its peculiarity (cf. Torres 1924: 213).[11]

SANTA MARTA

Despite being built during the same period, the residential areas of the internal periphery, erected in the interwar period, differ in their characteristics. The residential areas of Madonna dell'Orto (1919-1921), Sant'Alvise (1929-1930), San Girolamo (1929-1930), and Celestia (1938-1939) completed the northern edge of the city. San Giacomo (1919-1921) and Campo di Marte (1919-1929) filled the blank spots left on the Giudecca island. Sant'Elena (1922-1927) and Santa Marta (1922-1935) completed the eastern and western points of the island.

In Santa Marta, local references to the urban form are displayed by all buildings, while respecting the new laws and standards. The residential area is located on the extreme western edge of Venice and houses over 3,400 people. Local industrialization of an old fishing island called Mendigola, was developed in order to make room for large-scale industry on the channel of the Giudecca at the end of the 19th century. Most of the newly created space that was facing the lagoon was used by industry, but around the remnants of the fishing village, further residential buildings were built. While the first new housing was added to the existing village, it later was completely replaced by construction that respected the new residential standards. The residential area is enclosed by industry. The big cotton factory, Fortuny, is located to the east. In the north it borders on the local gas

---

10 "Il soggiorno gradevole, comode disposizioni, qualche agio anche non necessario predispongono o coltivano il senso di pulizia e di ordine, elevano lo spirito, coltivano l'educazione, migliorano l'individuo."
11 "Il catapecchismo ha nulla a che fare col bello e col caratteristico, oggi l'igiene, e ne sia laude, si impone. [...] Il popolo si educa creandone piacevole l'ambiente dove vive e curandolo incessantemente. Il popolo Veneziano vive per gran parte in catapecchie insalubri o in case-caserme dove la individualità scompare, l'amore per la famiglia e per la casa si annulla."

supplier, while the south and west is bordered by the storage facilities of the harbor that are connected to the railway. All industrial structures are separated by walls.

Figure 2: Calle Ca'Matta that recalls the rii terà

Photograph: Jannike Fichte, 2017

Following the common goal to create healthy residences, the city administration cooperated with the IACP, the state railway residential cooperative and the surrounding industry. The central and northern parts were realized by the IACP. They got land and financial support by the local cotton factory. The southern and western parts were built by the state railway residential cooperative. Originally it had only one access to the east, where it was connected to the existing city by a bridge. In the years after the World War II, further streets supplemented the connection. The only channel in the north was closed during the further development of the residential area. The inner pedestrian connection consists of four parallel streets, which are interconnected by several smaller streets. While almost all inner open spaces have public access, the only private spaces are located at the areas's boundaries. Buildings are lined up on the longer main streets.

The streets even recall the image of older Venetian buildings that are located on former channels. There are numerous so-called *rii terà* (it. sing. *rio terà*) all over the city that have been closed either to improve the pedestrian network or to resolve hygienic problems. In 1931 Elio Zorzi (1892-1955) describes the streets of Santa Marta as clearly influenced by some of the most known examples of Venetian *rii terà* (cf. Zorzi 1931: 521).[12]

Figure 3: Calle Largha Rosa, locally inspired facade design of the third construction stage from 1933 to 1935

Photograph: Jannike Fichte, 2017

The development of the residential area can be divided into three stages. Regarding the continuity of the urban form, the first construction stage from 1922 to 1927 shows the highest ambition. The spatially complex buildings vary in their locally inspired facade design. The large-scale buildings that were built during the second constructing stage from 1929 to 1931 lack the complex cubatures of the first building period but some value was placed on the facade design. The buildings that were erected by the state railway cooperative to the west and south copy the simple cubatures of the first railway constructions that were already erected in 1914. They are more complex in their facade design in order to connect to the constructions

---

12 "Le case che si affaciano su queste arterie arieggaino a un certo tono di venezianità. [...] Anche gli edifici popolarissimi hanno un'impronta di architettura veneziana."

built by the IACP. The third construction stage takes place from 1933 to 1935. The facade design of the simple buildings is still inspired by the local architecture, but instead of a reproduction of existing features, it is more of a modern interpretation.

The military field to the north of the former Mendigola was built under Austrian rule in the first half of the 19th century. It filled in a blank spot in the fishlike *forma urbis* of the city. The massive triangular extension in the late 19th century aimed at the industrialization of the island. The urban structure of the residential area itself is limited by surrounding industry and has no connection to the lagoon, but is developed out of the former fishing village. This connection is still visible in the names of streets. This was possible due to the successive stages of construction, which initially used the newly created terrain north and south of the Mendigola island before replacing the old buildings. The original urban structure of the Mendigola was connected to the main part of the city in the east. It was cut off and isolated by the construction of the cotton factory at the end of the 19th century. The architecture is influenced by the Venetian residential buildings of the past, but the floor plans of all construction stages follow contemporary organization patterns.

Figure 4: Campiello Longhi, group of buildings built in 1930, schematic floor plan, first floor

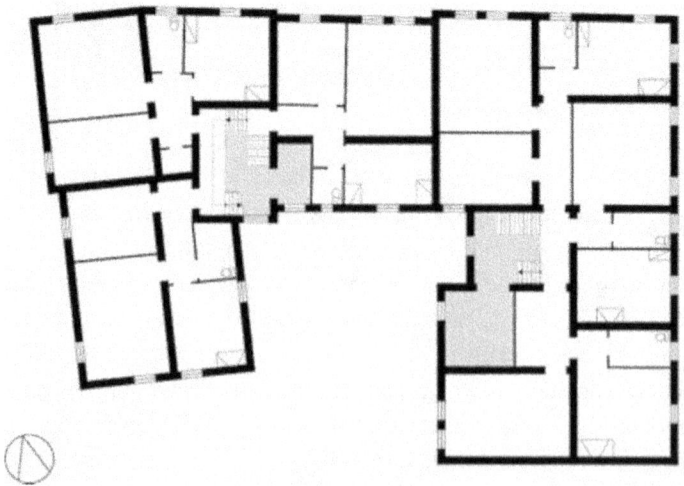

Drawing: Alexander Fichte 2019, after Paolo Bertanza
(Archivio municipale di Venezia 1926-1930 IX-2-6),
printed in Somma (1983: 114)

CONCLUSION

The breaking with the *forma urbis* has its roots in the connection of Venice to the continental railway system in 1846. This was followed by the construction of the island harbor and the attached industrial area. Being located in the middle of the industrial zone, Santa Marta has no connection to the *forma urbis* of Venice. Because there are no channels inside the residential area, there is no access to the lagoon. Nevertheless, the urban structure and the architecture correspond to the form of the existing city. That the *rio terà* has become a spatial reference shows a paradigm shift for building practice in Venice. The first channels were closed under Austrian rule in the first half of the 19th century. This practice was common, but rejected by large parts of the Venetian population until the beginning of the 20th century. With the closure of the waterways, it was feared that Venice would lose its peculiarity (cf. Molimenti 1884).[13] The building of new residential areas was bound by legal requirements that were no longer compatible with small narrow streets and channels that characterize many parts of Venice. Thus, the interpretation of Venetian urban form had to change. Even if the channels, which normally characterize the Venetian urban environment, are missing, a continuity in urban structure and architecture is produced by the residential buildings also because they are developed out of the fishing village. Santa Marta shows the necessity and ambition to create a continuous urban environment even in remote places of the city that are shaped by industrial production. The established continuity in urban structure and architecture remains isolated because of the surrounding industrial structures that are not compatible with the urban form of Venice.

REFERENCES

Bettini, Sergio (1960): La Forma di Venezia, Venice: Consorzio Venezia Nuova.
Bodenschatz, Harald (2009): „Diktatorischer Städtebau in der Zwischenkriegszeit: Besonderheiten Italiens mit Blick auf das nationalsozialistische Deutschland und die Sowjetunion." In: Mattioli, Aram/Steinacher, Gerald (eds.), Für den Faschismus bauen: Architektur und Städtebau im Italien Mussolinis, Zürich: Orell Füssli Verlag AG. pp. 46-62.

---

13 See the open letter of Pompeo Molimenti, Delendae Veneziae to the mayor written in 1887.

Calabi, Donatella (1993): "Un'itinerario di storia dell'architettura della città." In: Guido Zucconi, Venezia: Una guida all'architettura, Venice: Arsenale Editrice srl., pp. 8-21.

Concina, Ennio (1989): Venezia nell'età moderna: Struttura e funzioni, Venice: Marsilio Editori.

Concina, Ennio (1998): A history of Venetian architecture, Cambridge: Cambridge University Press.

Cosmai, Franca/Sorteni, Stefano (2007): "L'economia del fango: La 'sacca' come ridefinizione dei limiti urbani tra Sette e Ottocento." In: Quaderni: Documenti della manutenzione urbana di Venezia V/17, pp. 49-55.

Cristinelli, Giuseppe (1987): Cannareggio: Un sestiere di Venezia; La forma urbana, l'assetto edilizio, le architetture, Venice: Officina Edizioni.

Di Sivo, Michele (1981): Normativa e tipologia dell'abitazione popolare, Volume primo: L'origine e lo sviluppo nelle leggi della casa dal 1902 al 1980, Florence: Alinea Editrice.

Donatelli, Plinio (1928): La casa a Venezia nell'opera del suo istituto: Relazione del presidente dell istituto autonomo per le case popolari di Venezia, Rome: Stabilmento poligrafico per l'amministrazionie dello stato.

Favilla, Massimo (2002): "Delendae Veneziae, la città e le sue trasformazioni dal XIX al XX sec." In: Giuseppe Pavanello (ed.): L'enigma della modernità, Venezia nell'età di Pompeo Molmenti, Venice: Istituto Veneto di scienze, pp. 170-185.

Giovannoni, Gustavo (1931): Vecchie città ed edilizia nuova, Turin: Utet.

Howard, Deborah (2002): The Architectural History of Venice, New Haven/London: Yale University Press.

Miozzi, Eugenio (1957): Venezia nei secoli: La città; secondo Volume, Venice: Casa Editrice Libeccio.

"Per la più grande Venezia." In: Rivista mensile della città di Venezia V/6, June 1926, pp. 234-244.

Piacentini, Marcello (1922): "Nuovi orizzonti nell'edilizia cittadina." In: Nuova Antologia di lettere science ed arti, Sesta Serie, anno 57/fascicolo 1199, Rome. pp. 60-72.

Romanelli, Giandomenico (2005): La Forma del tempo, Sergio Bettini e l'idea di Venezia, Venice: Consorzio Venezia Nuova.

Ruskin, John (1845): "Letter to his Father 10th September 1845." In: Ruskin in Italy: Letters to his parents, Oxford: Harold I Shapiro Clarendon Press. pp. 198-199.

Somma, Paola (1983): Venezia Nuova: La politica della casa, 1893-1941, Venice: Marsilio Editori S.P.A.

Settis, Salvatore (2014): Se Venezia muore, Turin: Giulio Einaudi Editore.
Torres, Duilio (1924): "Urbanismo Veneziano." In: Rivista mensile del comune di Venezia III/8, Venice: Prem.Off.Graf.C.Ferrari. pp. 210-213.
Zorzi, Elio (1931): "Il nuovo Quartiere urbano di Santa Marta." In: Le tre Venezie: Rivista Mensile della città die Venezia IX, Venice. pp. 515-524.
Zucconi, Guido (2000): "Grande progetti per una più grande Venezia." In: Quaderni Documenti sulla manutenzione urbana di Venezia, Venezia '900, 2/44. pp. 61-67.

Innocenzo Sabbatini and the Construction of Modern Rome

Lorenzo Ciccarelli

Innocenzo Sabbatini (1891-1983) was one of the most talented architects employed in the Projects Office of the Istituto Case Popolari di Roma during the 1920s. With reference to some of his innovative buildings – the public baths, the cinema-theater and the suburban hostels at Garbatella, and the Casa del Sole – this paper analyses Sabbatini's attempt to build a modern Rome, using a vocabulary balanced between the ventures of the international avant-gardes and the still-persuasive expressions of ancient, Renaissance and Baroque Rome.

In the first thirty years of the 20th century, the buildings and housing projects completed by the *Istituto Case Popolari di Roma* (ICP) played a major role in Rome's growth. By 1930 some 60,000 of the city's 900,000 inhabitants were living in such buildings (cf. Cocchioni/De Grassi 1984:7; Bartolini 2001: 4-5). What is most interesting apart from the numbers is the fact that many of these developments were designed as parts of the city, in a dialectical relationship with the historical city of Rome (cf. Fraticelli 1982: 295; Vidotto 2006: 126-135; Conforti 2019). In addition to its intention to curb the excesses of building speculation and provide decent housing for the workers who came into the capital of the Kingdom of Italy, the ICP set itself the social and humanitarian goal of integrating the disadvantaged sections of the population into the dynamics of the city. Innocenzo Costantini (1881-1962), director of the ICP in Rome from 1917 to 1946, described workers' housing first and foremost as "a powerful means of social education" (Costantini 1922: 134; cf. Costantini 1930: 3-4; Toschi 1984).[1]

---

1   "[…] un possente mezzo di educazione sociale".

The Istituto Case Popolari di Roma was founded in 1903, in implementation of the first public housing law promulgated by the former treasury minister Luigi Luzzatti (1841-1927). Later, on the initiative of Rome's mayor Ernesto Nathan (1845-1913),[2] the first nuclei of San Saba (1906-1914, Quadrio Pirani) and Testaccio (1909-1917, Giulio Magni and Quadrio Pirani) were built. The tenants of the new projects were selected on the basis of income. The intention was to create social groups that were uniform with regard to class, but varied in terms of their occupations and the nature of their employment. This provision reveals a strategic and refined social sensibility, which sought to prevent the workers from becoming ghettoized (Cocchioni/De Grassi 1984: 27). Though restricted by small budgets, the housing built by the ICP was characterized by elegant layouts and was erected in locations separate from but adjacent to the historic city, integrated into the urban development plan (1909) drafted by Edmondo Sanjust di Teulada (1858-1936).

In the 1920s, under the direction of Innocenzo Costantini, the Institute reached its peak of production and quality, drawing on the work of outstanding professional architects. Among them, Innocenzo Sabbatini (1891-1983) was notable for his original and innovative solutions (cf. Accasto/Fraticelli/Nicolini 1971: 325-327; Regni/Sennato 1982: 35-40; Kallis 2017: 273-275). This paper analyzes Sabbatini's aims in designing new housing projects engrafted onto the older districts. The following examples of Sabbatini's design strategy are discussed here: the buildings for the public baths (1926-29), a cinema-theater (1927-30) and suburban hostels (1927-28) at Garbatella, and the Casa del Sole (1929-30) in Via della Lega Lombarda.

After spending his early life in Osimo and earning his diploma in Architectural Design at the Brera Academy in Milan, Sabbatini was hired in 1918 by the ICP's Planning Department in Rome, probably through the influence of Costantini, his maternal uncle. At that time, immediately after the World War I, the Institute's building activity was key to the provision of affordable housing. The ICP was in fact strengthened in 1919 with substantial allocations for a five-year plan, which allowed it to take out long-term loans with the Cassa Depositi e Prestiti (cf. Cocchioni/De Grassi 1984: 44-45). Likewise in 1919, it was granted the ability to build low-cost housing in addition to public housing; in 1927 this was further extended to individual rent-to-buy housing. The resulting typological multiplicity

---

2 A secularist and a republican, Ernesto Nathan was one of the most important mayors of Rome in the 20th century, and decisive also in the management of urban building projects in the early decades of the century (cf. Dizionario Biografico degli Italiani (2012), s.v. Ernesto Nathan; Toschi 1980: 189-200).

provided a formidable incentive to the creativity of young architects and engineers.

Sabbatini took full advantage of these opportunities and engaged in the composition of the facades of the great residential complexes at the "Trionfale II" (1919-22), as well as in projects for some of the buildings in the "Piazza d'Armi I" complex (1919-21), today the Piazza Mazzini (cf. Calza Bini 1924: 305-318). The opportunity to collaborate with Gustavo Giovannoni (1873-1947) in establishing the first nucleus of the working-class neighborhood of Garbatella (1920-22) and the Città Gardino Aniene (1921-23) at the end of the Via Nomentana, today Monte Sacro, was particularly incisive. In the ensuing years, Sabbatini designed numerous apartment blocks and some refined bourgeois housing in which he refined his unique ability to combine creative geometric formulations with heterogeneous decorative languages. In 1926, these achievements won him admission to the Professional Register of Engineers and Architects and an appointment as Head of the Institute's Projects Office (Ordinamento del Servizio Tecnico, 1926). From this time until 1931, when he left the ICP for personal reasons that remain obscure, Sabbatini built his most mature and convincing buildings, working to incorporate unusual typological variations and experimenting with a vocabulary balanced between the experiments of the Italian and international avant-gardes and the still-persuasive expressions of antique, Renaissance and Baroque architecture.

In the 1920s, Gustavo Giovannoni was among the most influential figures in the architectural and urban culture of Rome and Italy. From 1915 onward he presided over the commission for the reform of the Master Plan; in 1920 he was one of the most passionate promoters of the foundation in Rome of Italy's first advanced school of architecture (cf. Del Bufalo 1982; Zucconi 1996; Gustavo Giovannoni tra storia e progetto 2018; Benedetti/Dal Mas/Delsere/Di Marco 2018). It was Giovannoni who awakened in Sabbatini an aptitude for studying and designing new housing projects to be grafted onto older districts, all the while maintaining, not least in the architectural language itself, the cohesion between the "old cities" and the "new buildings" that Rome seemed to require (Giovannoni 1931; cf. Giovannoni 1918). Their close collaboration on the buildings of the Piazza Sempione at Montesacro (where Sabbatini designed the Palazzo Pubblico and Giovannoni the church of Santi Angeli Custodi), and on the design of some small villas in the first nucleus of Garbatella, was a profoundly educational experience for the younger architect, who was capable of drawing useful lessons from it without lapsing into the bland historicist formulas so elegantly practiced by his mentor. Giovannoni's close and careful study of ancient monuments, which entailed an attentive and meticulous redesign of details and ornaments, laid the foundations for the cultivated and audaciously abstract elaboration of the stylistic and constructive features of monuments which Sabbatini applied brilliantly in his works in the years that followed (cf. Giovannoni 1925 [speech 1920]: 18-24).

In 1926-27 Sabbatini's appointment to design the service buildings at Garbatella marked a turning point in his career. This working-class development in Rome was built for the workers of the Ostiense district and the manufacturing facilities at Testaccio. Designed as a garden city by Giovannoni and Massimo Piacentini (1898-1974), a little-known cousin of the more famous Marcello, Garbatella had absorbed part of the population expelled by the demolition of the historic center of Rome, and by the razing of clusters of proletarian huts at Ponte Milvio, Portonaccio and Ponte Lungo (cf. De Michelis 2009: 509-520; Stabile 2012: 107-190). As a result it had grown from its original core of 3,000 inhabitants to a population of some 23,000. Such a massive influx required expanded collective services of a hygienic-sanitary nature as well as leisure facilities. These buildings were designed by Sabbatini: they included public baths as a proletarian version of the ancient Roman baths; a cinema-theater for the people's leisure time (and the spread of official propaganda); and four hostels as temporary accommodation for people evicted from their homes and awaiting rehousing.

The substantial dimensions of these edifices, which appeared monumental when juxtaposed with the low-density, small-scale buildings of the first residential developments at Garbatella, are evidence of Sabbatini's innovative and experimental spirit; so too are the typological innovations that he introduced to convey original functional forms. He launched into vigorous and audacious interpretations, completely ignoring the Secessionist influences being pursued by other designers in Rome at the time, such as the *barocchetto* previously borrowed from his teacher Giovannoni.

The buildings housing the public baths and the cinema-theater became distinctive landmarks of the development. Set side by side on the Piazza Bartolomeo Romano, the two buildings faced the first nucleus of Garbatella around Piazza Benedetto Brin and Piazza Pantero Pantera; like eccentric monumental propylaea, they pointed the way into the streets of the new expansion, marked by the church of San Francesco Saverio, completed in 1933 by Alberto Calza Bini (1881-1957) (cf. Monzo 2017: 488-491). Placed opposite the building with the highest density of residents in all of Garbatella at that time, at the so-called "lotto 8" (1923-26) by Plinio Marconi (1893-1974), Sabbatini's two buildings stand out by their volumetric and expressive restraint and their lack of decorative elements, thus seeming to offer an historicist commentary on Marconi's building. Both the public baths (Fig. 1) and the cinema-theater (Fig. 2) construct an architectural and urban identity by the simple amalgamation of powerful, regular volumes; these are enhanced by smooth surfaces plastered with intense colors and underscored by the simple geometries of string courses and cornices. Synthetic, solemn works of architecture, they share the powerful elegance of the backdrops in the 20th century paintings of Achille Funi (1890-1972) or Mario Sironi (1885-1961).

Figure 1: Innocenzo Sabbatini, Public baths at Garbatella (1929)

Archivio Vanna Fraticelli

The five-story building containing the public baths originally included health clinics on the ground floor and basement level, while the upper floors had apartments and studios for artists; the semicircular, colonnaded shower block opened out in the middle of the central body, on the axis of the main entrance, while the great baths themselves were located on the top floor, under an attic inspired by the roofs of the baths of Diocletian. This attic, with its six large thermal windows, is just one of several instances in which Sabbatini drew on the constructional forms of ancient Roman architecture, as studied by the architect Italo Gismondi (1887-1974) in Ostia Antica and revealed in the monuments brought to light by demolition work (cf. Muntoni 1993: 74-82). Others include the undulating arches of the base, the lunetted vaults that are a feature of the mezzanine level, and the stylized, trabeated aedicule that frames the synthetic trilith of the entrance. Together with the gables of the lateral facades, these forms seem to pay homage to the common search for the "Latin origins of modern housing", as touted in the propaganda of those years and published in the review *Architettura e Arti Decorative* (cf. Calza 1923: 3-18, 49-63). The use of reinforced concrete is restricted to the interior, where there is no shortage of refined constructional virtuosity, such as the glass-brick floor in the ambulatory on the ground floor, which gives a view of the boiler room in the basement (Fig. 1).

In the cinema-theater, Sabbatini interpreted this same compositional logic in surprising terms, enriching it with curved geometries and very skillful concave-convex joints. The six-story building is shaped as a concave volume with curved porticoes at the base and marked by a regular pattern of square windows. The severity of the building's appearance is enhanced by its slightly overhung porticoes, simply plastered surfaces, and regular pattern of square windows. To this housing block Sabbatini welded the low, semicircular volume of the cinema-theater, which follows the fluid line of the two merging side streets and in this way models the urban space. Sabbatini contrasted the simplified functionality of the apartment block with the refined rhythmic cadence of this curvilinear cinema-theater, where a sequence of blind arches framed by projecting pillars is interrupted at the entrance by glazing and and a portico with four free-standing columns. The use of contemporary materials is again confined to the interiors, and specifically to the roof over the great auditorium, where imposing reinforced concrete beams are skillfully interlaced to generate triangular patterns, in an oblique allusion to Borromini (cf. Remiddi 1982: 12) In the same summer of 1927, while engaged in the design of the cinema-theater and the start of construction on the public baths, Sabbatini planned four impressive suburban hostels at Garbatella, which are particularly significant in his design work. The hostels were intended as temporary housing for families displaced by the demolition work in Rome's historic center and the dismantling of shanty-towns in various parts of the city, pending the provision of permanent new accommodations (cf. Costantini, 1928). Small apartments alternated with shared facilities located on the ground floor: police offices, storage spaces, kitchens, refectories, kindergartens, clinics etc. (cf. Cocchioni/De Grassi 1984: 193-194). Unfortunately, it is impossible to grasp the interior layout of these buildings today, since they were rapidly modified to adapt the small apartments into more generous and comfortable permanent accommodations (Fig. 2).

This planimetric system makes a complete view of the building impossible; rather, the visitor always perceives different and visually foreshortened segments of it. This undoubtedly represents a tribute to the architecture of 16th and 17th-century Rome, which Sabbatini studied passionately in those years (cf. Remiddi 1982: 12).

Figure 2: Innocenzo Sabbatini, Red Hostel at Garbatella (1928)

Archivio Vanna Fraticelli

Of the four sub-urban housing facilities, the so-called "red hostel" (*Albergo Rosso*) – immediately identifiable by the particular color of its plaster rendering, made by adding iron peroxide to the mix (Muratore 1990: 485) – is particularly important. Oriented toward the Ostiense ring road, this imposing building is the gateway to the district from the north. The planimetric system – a pentagonal body with an open central open courtyard, to which a further rectilinear arm is attached at the south vertex – is fragmented by the stepped profile of the cornice, blunted by the curvilinear contours of the fronts, and furrowed by loggias that mark the entrances or lighten its compact mass. The impressive housing complex could accommodate up to 1,212 people in 449 rooms on the upper floors (cf. Kallis 2017: 21). The "red hostel" imposed a leap of scale on the buildings of Garbatella and disrupted its planimetric structure, much as the runaway red horse causes an upheaval in the construction of the Futurist painting *The Rising City* (*La città che sale*, 1910-11) by Umberto Boccioni (1882-1916). If its stepped profile hints at the contemporary Parisian building blocks of Henri Sauvage (1873-1932), the convexity of the facades and the clock tower with its perforated metal dome are a clear homage to

Borromini's Oratorio dei Filippini; the semicircular loggia of the entrance, on the other hand, formally cites the design of the entrance to the Casina Valadier, as the architect himself made clear (cf. Remiddi 1982: 12; Muratore 2004: 97). This refined polysemic balance was fully apparent to contemporaries. Although Sabbatini asserted that his intention was "not to abandon the classical", the red hostel was included in the catalogue of the first exhibition of the *Movimento Italiano per l'Architettura Razionale* in 1928 (Remiddi 1982: 10).

Figure 3: Innocenzo Sabbatini, Casa del sole, Plan of the second floor (1928)

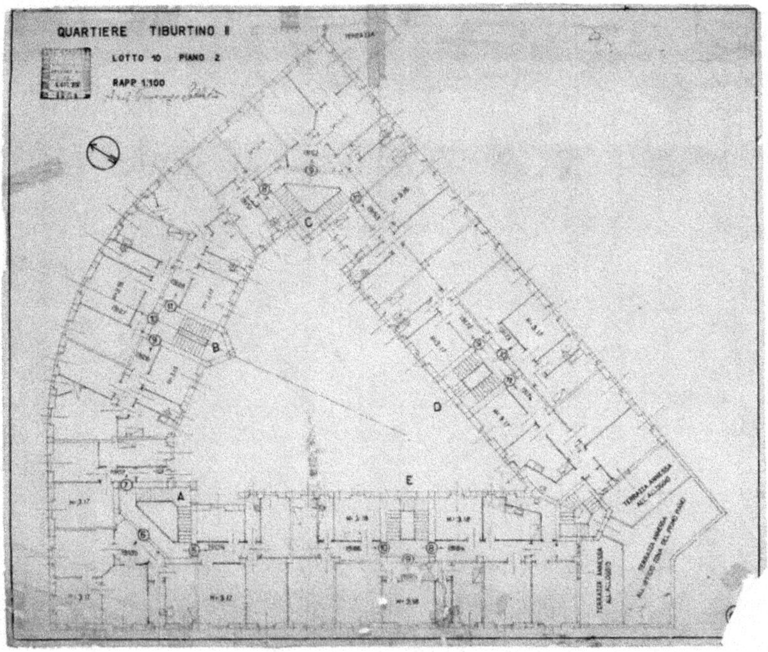

Archivio Storico Iconografico ATER, Tiburtino II, lotto 10, fabbricato unico

The celebrated Casa del Sole (Fig. 3, 4), designed a year after the hostels at Garbatella, was the final step in the course of architectural research that Sabbatini conducted as head of the Planning Department at the Instituto Case Popolari di Roma. Located immediately adjacent to the "Tiburtino II" housing project (1926-30) by Giorgio Guidi, with its buildings characterized by fragmented heights, irregular layouts and rich ornamentation, Sabbatini's structure is a regular prism which completely occupies its narrow triangular lot and is distinguished by the rationality and modularity of its stepped facades (cf. Regni/Sennato: 40; Cundari 2014; Conforti 2015: 28-30). Here the architect folded and adapted the type of the courtyard building to the hygienic and functional requirements of this particular location. The restricted size of the site would have made the small central courtyard very dark had the buildings around it been eight stories high, as required by the number of tenants to be housed. To avoid this, Sabbatini imposed a stepped pattern on the side wings, lowering them until they reached just two levels in the southwest corner, thus opening up both the courtyard and the terraces of the apartments on the upper floors. The facades were purified of all ornamentation; only the entrances, colonnades and tympana contrast with the stringently functional layout, which is based on repetition and the obsessive overlapping of a box-shaped module with a window at the center. Six stairwells placed in both the corners and in the center line served the 89 housing units, each with two or three rooms. Triangular in form, the stairwells make clear reference to those inside the walls on either side of the entrance to the Pantheon – which Sabbatini greatly admired – and to the Villa Madama. The facades are reminiscent of the megablock of rent-controlled dwellings that Henri Sauvage had built a few years earlier in the Rue des Amiraux (1913-30) in Paris; it is also possible that they contain suggestions of the master plan prepared for Allabanuel (1920) by Piero Portaluppi (1888-1967), whom Sabbatini may have met during his short stay as a student in Milan.

Figure 4: Innocenzo Sabbatini, Casa del sole (1930)

Archivio Vanna Fraticelli

Having completed the construction of the Casa del Sole, Sabbatini suddenly left the ICP in 1931. The political setting and the tasks being assigned to the Institute had changed greatly since the years of Ernesto Nathan. After a first phase of substantial continuity following his seizure of power in 1922, Benito Mussolini's famous 1928 article, "Sfollare le città" ("Evacuate the Cities"), published in *Il Popolo d'Italia*, had clarified the urban policy that the Fascist regime would pursue in the following decade (cf. Susmel 1957: 360-390; Nicoloso 2008). The forceful Fascist action following the kidnapping and murder of the socialist politician Giacomo Matteotti (1885-1924) in 1924, and the regime's consequent authoritarian clampdown, was complete by the late 1920s. The progressive restriction of local autonomies, the institution of the *podestà* and the fascistization of the prefects subordinated all urban initiative to the central power. In Rome, the extensive demolition work in the historic center, and the need to rehouse the masses of inhabitants, increasingly led the Governorate to limit the work of the ICP to the construction of villages, where the need for speed and economy trumped any concern for architectural quality and social cohesion (Ciucci 1998: 80).

In 1927 the structure and tasks of the Istituto Case Popolari di Roma were progressively altered, largely subordinating it to the contracting authority of the Governorate and depriving it of any freedom in either the choice of sites or the architectural design of buildings (cf. Fraticelli 1982; Ciucci 1998: 86-87). The regime's substantially anti-urban policy curbed the ambition to develop a common vocabulary in the construction of modern Rome that had united the architects and engineers working for the Institute. The intention to design outer-city areas – the *borgate* – that were organically connected with the established city as engines of social cohesion was forced to give way to the production of detached villages lacking even the most essential services and reserved for the sub-proletariat. This brought an end to the attempt to design parts of cities by public initiative and to model an architecture for modern Rome as a delicate balance between the needs of modernity and the profusion of history. These discourses would be resumed after the World War II, in the INA-Casa public housing projects (Istituto Nazionale delle Assicurazioni, 1949-1963), and in the competitions for the Mausoleum of the Fosse Ardeatine (1944) and the Termini station building (1947) (cf. Conforti 2015; Weststeijn/Whitling 2017).

REFERENCES

Accasto, Gianni/Fraticelli, Vanna/Nicolini, Renato (1971): L'architettura di Roma Capitale, 1870-1970, Rome: Golem.

Bartolini, Francesco (2001): Roma borghese: La casa e i ceti medi tra le due guerre, Rome-Bari: Laterza.

Benedetti, Simona/Dal Mas, Roberta Maria/Delsere, Ilaria/Di Marco, Fabrizio (2018): Gustavo Giovannoni: L'opera architettonica nella prima metà del Novecento, Rome: Campisano.

Calza, Guido (1923): "Le origini latine dell'abitazione moderna (part I and part II)." In: Architettura e Arti Decorative n. 3/January-February 1923, pp. 3-18 and 49-63.

Calza Bini, Alberto (1924): "Le nuove costruzioni dell'Istituto per le Case Popolari in Roma al quartiere Trionfale." In: Architettura e arti decorative n. 3, July 1924, pp. 305-318.

Ciucci, Giorgio (1998): Gli architetti e il fascismo: Architettura e città, 1922-1944, Turin: Einaudi.

Cocchioni, Cristina/De Grassi, Mario (1984): La casa popolare a Roma: Trent' anni di attività dell'I.C.P., Rome: Kappa.

Conforti, Claudia (2015): "Le Fosse Ardeatine: Un'architettura per non dimenticare." In: Casabella 79/846, pp. 5-16.

Conforti, Claudia (2015): "Costruire con i vuoti di Roma." In: Casabella 79/849, pp. 28-30.

Conforti, Claudia (2019): "Roma nei luoghi di capitale d'Italia (1852-2017)." In: Roma: Luoghi, persone, visioni, Rome: Istituto della Enciclopedia Italiana, pp. 2-51.

Costantini, Innocenzo (1922): "Le nuove costruzioni dell'Istituto per le Case Popolari in Roma: La borgata giardino Garbatella." In: Architettura e arti decorative n. 2, March 1922, pp. 119-137.

Costantini, Innocenzo (1928): Appunti sull'opera svolta dall'avvento del regime, Anno VII, 3, Allegati II/XVII. Historical Archives of the ICP, ATER/Aziende Territoriali per l'Edilizia Residenziale Pubblica del Comune di Roma.

Costantini, Innocenzo (1930): "Note sul controllo dei risultati economici per l'edilizia popolare." In: L'Ingegnere, n. 4, February 1930, pp. 3-4.

Cundari, Gian Carlo (2014): Elementi di analisi della casa popolare ICP Sant'Ippolito 2 di Innocenzo Sabbatini a Roma, Rome: Aracne.

De Michelis, Antonella (2009): "The Garden Suburb of the Garbatella, 1920-1929: Defining community and identity through planning in postwar Rome." In: Planning Perspectives, n. 24, April 2009, pp. 509-520.

Del Bufalo, Alessandro (1982): Gustavo Giovannoni, Rome: Kappa.

Fraticelli, Vanna (1982): Roma, 1914-1929: La città e gli architetti tra la guerra e il fascismo, Rome: Officina.

Giovannoni, Gustavo (1918): "Le questioni edilizie romane attinenti al Piano delle comunicazioni cittadine." In: Annali di Ingegneria e Architettura 33, pp. 15-16.

Giovannoni, Gustavo (1925): "L'architettura italiana nella storia e nella vita: Prolusione inaugurale della nuova Scuola superiore di Architettura di Roma, 18 dicembre 1920." In: Gustavo, Giovannoni, Questioni di architettura nella storia e nella vita: edilizia, estetica architettonica, restauri, ambiente dei monumenti, Rome: Società editrice d'arte illustrata, pp. 18-24.

Giovannoni, Gustavo (1931): Vecchie città ed edilizia nuova, Turin: Utet.

Gustavo Giovannoni tra storia e progetto (2018), Rome: Quasar.

Kallis, Aristotle (2017): "Rome's Singular Path to Modernism: Innocenzo Sabbatini and the 'rooted' architecture of the Istituto Case Popolari (ICP), 1925-1930." In: Papers of the British School at Rome 85, pp. 269-301.

Monzo, Luigi (2017): Croci e fasci: Der italienische Kirchenbau in der Zeit des Faschismus, 1919-1945. 2 vol. PhD diss., Karlsruhe Institute of Technology.

Muntoni, Alessandra (1993): "Italo Gismondi e la lezione di Ostia antica." In: Rassegna 15/55, pp. 74-82.

Muratore, Giorgio (1990): "Il cantiere romano del Novecento." In: Maristella Casciato/Stefania Mornati/Paola Scavizzi (eds.), Il modo di costruire, Rome: Edilstampa, pp. 475-487.

Muratore, Giorgio (2004): "Edilizia e architetti a Roma negli anni Venti." In: Giorgio Ciucci/Giorgio Muratore (eds.), Storia dell'architettura italiana: Il primo Novecento, Milan: Electa, pp. 74-99.

Nicoloso, Paolo (2008): Mussolini architetto: Propaganda e paesaggio urbano nell'Italia fascista, Turin: Einaudi.

Ordinamento del Servizio Tecnico (1926, January 29). Allegati, 1926/XIII. Historical Archives of the ICP, ATER/Aziende Territoriali per l'Edilizia Residenziale Pubblica del Comune di Roma.

Rappino, Sergio (2017): "Sabbatini a piazza Brin e al lotto 10." In: Garbatella, lo stabilimento dei Bagni pubblici: Innocenzo Sabbatini l'architetto visionario, Rome: Iacobelli, pp. 37-44.

Regni, Bruno/Sennato, Marina (1982): Innocenzo Sabbatini: Architetture tra tradizione e rinnovamento, Rome: A.A.M. – Kappa.

Remiddi, Gaia: "Incontro con Innocenzo Sabbatini del 26 aprile 1982." In: Facoltà di architettura dell'Università di Roma: Bollettino della biblioteca, 10/29, pp. 7-12.

Stabile, Francesca Romana (2012): La Garbatella a Roma: Architettura e regionalismo, Rome: Dedalo.
Susmel, Edoardo/Susmel, Duilio (1957): Opera Omnia di Benito Mussolini, Florence.
Toschi, Livio (1984): Costantino e Innocenzo Costantini: Progetti e realizzazioni, Falconara: Industrie grafiche Errebi.
Vidotto, Vittorio (2006): Roma contemporanea, Rome-Bari: Laterza.
Weststeijn, Arthur/Whitling, Frederick (2017): Termini: Cornerstone of Modern Rome, Rome: Quasar.
Zucconi, Guido (1996): Gustavo Giovannoni: Dal capitello alla città, Milan: Jaca Book.

Acknowledgements

The idea for this book was born in 2015 at the international conference on Gustavo Giovannoni held at the Accademia Nazionale di San Luca in Rome. There, given the sixty-six lectures hold by colleagues from seven countries and three continents, it seemed desirable to further deepen the exchange and bring the different interests and knowledge of scholars researching Italian architectural history from inside and from abroad closer together. This wish gave rise to the idea for a new cross-cultural conference initiative to start a broader discussion of the transformation of Italian town- and landscapes in the first half of the 20th century, especially between the two world wars. As a result, we linked our respective different research fields, urban design and architecture, for preparing two international conferences which took place in 2018. These meetings were held embedded in excellent, albeit distinct, institutions:

We are particularly grateful to the American Association for Italian Studies (AAIS) and the Bibliotheca Hertziana (Max Planck Institute for Art History in Rome) for their support to the "Townscapes in Transition" project. Without their encouragement, neither our double session at the 38th Annual Conference of the AAIS in Sorrento – adorned with grandiose views of the Gulf of Naples – nor the conference "Continuare la città" at the wonderful Villino Stroganoff of the Bibliotheca Hertziana in Rome would have been viable.

Particularly we would like to thank Dr. Elena Past and Dr. Emanuela Zanotti Carney, who signaled the specific interest of the AAIS in themes of architectural history. Both of them encouraged us to contribute and thereby to further expand the already broad horizon of the AAIS. We are also indebted to Marco Marino of the Sant'Anna Institute in Sorrento for his inexhaustible patience with all aspects of the organization.

For us, as scholars with a focus on Italy, Rome has almost become our second home. Over the years of our work, the Bibliotheca Hertziana has been a reliable place for us to come, to find valuable contacts and exchange fruitful ideas. Thanks to the support and hospitality of its director, Professor Dr. Tanja Michalsky, we were able to meet at this preeminent research institution in Rome – a city so famous for the history of Italian architecture and urban development. Thanks to the enthusiastic and informed support of our co-organizer Dr. Christiane Elster, this research encounter became a success. This result is not least due to Professor Paolo Nicoloso, who provided an ideal conclusion to the conference papers with his evening lecture. We would also like to thank especially Dr. Aban Tahmasebi for guiding us in a follow-up excursion through the Garbatella district.

Compiling the contributions from the conferences in a book became possible due to the funding of the Deutsche Forschungsgemeinschaft (research project "Geplantes Erbe: Gustavo Giovannonis und Theodor Fischers Stadtplanungen für historische Stadtbereiche der Jahre 1889 bis 1929" of Carmen M. Enss) and the additional generous financial support provided by the Center for Heritage Conservation and Technologies at the University of Bamberg (KDWT). In this regard, we would like to thank in particular Professor Dr. Gerhard Vinken, who holds the chair of Heritage Sciences in Bamberg, for his support in all phases of the project.

We are also grateful to our publisher *transcript* and in particular Annika Linnemann for guiding us through the production process. In Bamberg and Berlin, we could rely on the help of Farah M. Berger and Scott Budzynski. Without Johanna Blokker's generous and extremely competent linguistic editing of selected texts, the publication in English would probably have remained a dream. A warm thanks to all colleagues and friends who helped us in compiling this book.

Last but not least, we are most thankful to all the contributors, without whom neither the conferences nor these proceedings would have been possible.

'Terms and Conditions' of Interwar Architecture and Urbanism in Italy
A Tentative Glossary

Carmen M. Enss and Luigi Monzo

Ambientismo
Ambientismo refers to an approach of urban design developed by Gustavo Giovannoni in which the urban environment, or the context of structural interventions, are regarded as the criteria for design. By carefully thinning out and arranging interventions in the historical building substance (→*Diradamento*), a structural and creative modernization that harmonizes with the environment is to be initiated. The urban fabric should not be fragmentarily deformed by individual and independently conceived large-scale buildings, but should rather be understood as an ensemble to be considered as a whole, on which further work can only be carried out when appropriately taking into account the existing conditions. Architectural and urban heritage will not be negated, but recognized as a substrate of its own design activity. Giovannoni thus represents a standpoint that, in contrast to the international avant-garde's urban development trend, asserts the approach of a conservative renewal of the old town in Italian urban development. His influence continues to make itself felt in individual cases in which the effects of radically changing or contrasting urban planning are softened or even prevented; through the garden city projects in Rome that he shaped, his ideas also influence the development of an architectural language of site-related, reflective and historically informed urban planning. The idea of *Ambientismo* stands at the beginning of a modern Italian urban planning theory. As such, it also finds its way into the reform of architectural education strongly influenced by Giovannoni. The first Scuola Superiore di Architettura, founded by Giovannoni in Rome in 1919/20, taught a discipline of urban planning (*Edilizia cittadina*, later *Urbanistica*) for the first time in Italy.

Antichità e Belle Arti

Antichità e Belle Arti was the denomination which subsumed the Superintendence for Antiquities and Fine Arts related to the Ministry of Public Education before the establishment of the Ministry for Cultural and Environmental Heritage in 1975. The institution was responsible for the public surveillance and protection of the cultural heritage in all its forms of expression.

Architect (profession)

Before the legal protection of the professional titles of architect and engineer in 1923 in Italy, there was a typical confusion which can be resolved by looking at the educational curricula: previously, building professionals were organised according to their education in the *Federazione Architetti Italiani* (for graduates of art schools) and in the *Società degli Ingegneri e degli Architetti Italiani* (for graduates of engineering schools and polytechnics). The situation changed only through a process of educational reform and reorganization of the professions which saw for the first time in Europe the legal protection of the professional titles 'architect' and 'engineer' (24 June 1923). Furthermore, in 1925 the transition from studies to professional life was linked to a state examination, which is still required today, for the ability to exercise the profession.

Architetti dell'Urbe

→*La Burbera*.

Associazione Artistica fra i Cultori di Architettura

The *Associazione Artistica fra i Cultori di Architettura* (AACAr) was founded in 1890 and existed until 1935. It was an influential association of architects and artists with an overarching national organization and subordinate local sections that were founded and led by local cultural professionals depending on their own initiative. The most important section was the Roman one, led by important protagonists such as Gustavo Giovannoni, Marcello Piacentini and Arnaldo Foschini. The organization's multifaceted work focused primarily on an integral approach to architecture that went beyond structural issues and treated architecture as an object of social responsibility. The *Associazione's* main objective was to promote the development of architecture as an object of social responsibility. Therefore, its main mission focused on education and appreciation of architecture through the protection, preservation and communication of its built heritage, and to promote its further development through prizes, competitions, publications, conferences, etc.

Blackshirts
The Blackshirts (*Squadristi*) were originally the paramilitary wing of the National Fascist Party (PNF) and, after 1923, an all-volunteer militia of the Kingdom of Italy.

Conciliazione
→*Lateran Treaty.*

Corporatism
Fascist corporatism as authoritarian dictatorial (classical) corporatism is part of an economic model in which a limited number of associations with compulsory membership are separated from each other according to functional aspects and do not compete with each other in any way. The open structure of trade unions and employers is thus replaced by unitary associations that absorb both sides. Fascist Italy explicitly referred to itself as a corporate state.

Diradamento
Carefully thinning out and arranging interventions in the historical building fabric of towns and cities.

Duce
Duce is a word derived from Latin *dux* which translated means 'military leader' or 'guide'. *Duce* was the appellative assumed by Benito Mussolini as the leader of Fascism. The term was already in the Italian courtly language use to indicate the *condottiere*. Casts of it can be found in other languages in the appellative of various dictators, such as Adolf Hitler (*Führer*), Francisco Franco (*caudillo*), Nicolae Ceaușescu (*conducator*).

Engineer (profession)
→*Architect (profession).*

Federazione Architetti Italiani
The *Federazione Architetti Italiani* (Federation of Italian Architects) was founded in 1905 by Giovanni Rosadi as a corporate association that brought together the so-called professors of architectural design, graduates who had studied architectural drawing (*disegno architettonico*).

Genio civile
The *Genio civile* is an Italian statutory corporation with the task of controlling, monitoring and supervising public works at peripheral and local levels.

Gioventù Italiana del Littorio (GIL)
The *Gioventù italiana del littorio* (GIL) was created in 1937 and existed until 1944 as the consolidated youth movement of the National Fascist Party of Italy. In 1937 it replaced the *Opera Nazionale Balilla*.

Gruppo Urbanisti Romani (GUR)
The *Gruppo Urbanisti Romani* (GUR) was a group of Roman architects active between the 1920s and 1930s. The GUR, which included former students of Marcello Piacentini and now renowned architects like Luigi Piccinato, Gino Cancellotti, Giuseppe Nicolosi, Cesare Valle and to which was added as group leader Marcello Piacentini, proposed in 1929, on the occasion of the Congress of the International Federation for Housing and Town Planning, an important design for the urban plan of the city of Rome (*Piano Regolatore Generale di Roma*). The group's proposal picked up on Piacentini's work on the variant for substituting the still valid *Piano Regolatore* of 1909 and developed it into a clear functionalist plan. In Piacentini's logic, the core component of the city's reorganization is the relocation of the Termini railway station and the use of the space freed up for a new city center that relieves the historic city. In addition, the previously arbitrary expansion of the city is to be stopped and directed into a single-directional expansion towards the Alban Hills. Further members of the group were Luigi Lenzi, Roberto Lavagnino, Eugenio Fuselli, Mario Dabbeni, Eugenio Montuori and Alfredo Scalpelli.

International Federation for Housing and Town Planning (IFHTP)
The *International Federation for Housing and Town Planning,* a the network of professionals founded 1913 by Ebenezer Howard, held a conference in Rome in 1929.

Istituto Autonomo Case Popolari (IACP)
→*Istituto Case Popolari* (ICP).

Istituto Case Popolari (ICP)
The *Istituto Case Popolari* (ICP) or *Istituto Autonomo Case Popolari* (IACP), literally (Autonomous) Institute for Subsidized housing, was created in 1903 by the legislative initiative of Luigi Luzzatti and is a type of Italian statutory corporation,

with the aim of promoting, implementing and managing public buildings aimed at allocating housing to the less well-off, especially with low rents.

La Burbera
The grouping of the *Architetti dell'Urbe (La Burbera)* was an assembly of Roman architects active between the 1920s and 1930s. It competed especially with the *Gruppo Urbanisti Romani* (GUR) in proposing a more academic approach for solving the task for the new *Piano Regolatore Generale* of Rome. The plan propounded a clear cut that would have been radical for the baroque part of the historical centre, in order to implement a schematic Cardo-Decumanus system, which saw the Milvian Bridge connected in a straight axis with the Lateran Basilica and St. Peter's Church connected with the Termini station. *La Burbera*, which included renowned architects like Pietro Aschieri, Enrico Del Debbio and Vincenzo Fasolo, was lead by Gustavo Giovannoni and Arnaldo Foschini. Further members were Giuseppe Boni, Giacomo Giobbe, Alessandro Limongelli, Felice Nori and Ghino Venturi. Its ideas were inspired by earlier urban plans of Armando Brasini.

Lateran Treaty
The *Lateran Treaty* (*Patti Lateranensi*) is the name that was established for the mutual recognitions agreements between the Kingdom of Italy and the Holy See signed on February 11, 1929, with which for the first time since the Unification of Italy (1861) and the Capture of Rome (1871) regular bilateral relations were established between Italy and the Holy See. It consists of three parts: a treaty of recognition, a financial convention and a concordat. The Lateran Treaty was also subsumed under the Italian word for conciliation: *Conciliazione*. To commemorate the successful conclusion of the negotiations, Mussolini commissioned the Road of the Conciliation (Via della Conciliazione, 1936-50), which would symbolically link the Vatican City to the heart of Rome. Another important symbol of commemoration was the setting up of a new diocese in La Spezia, the first in unified Italy, and the corresponding project for a new cathedral which was initiated through a nationwide architectural competition in 1929 and whose subsequent realization was supported by Mussolini himself.

Littorio style
→ *Stile Littorio.*

Matteotti Murder
The socialist politician Giacomo Matteotti (1885-1924) gave a passionate speech in parliament on May 30, 1924, in which he contested the parliamentary elections

of April 6, 1924, blaming the fascists for the electoral forgeries and finally addressing Mussolini directly. On June 10, he was kidnapped and murdered by six *Squadristi* (Blackshirts). The "Matteotti crisis" was a turning point in Mussolini's politics. After having tried to cooperate to a certain extent with parliamentary institutions, he then relied on a consistent suppression of the opposition, restrictions on freedom of the press and the establishment of the secret police (OVRA).

Movimento Italiano per l'Architettura Razionale (MIAR)
The *Movimento Italiano per l'Architettura Razionale* (MIAR) was a group of mostly young Italian architects devoted to the fight for a clearly modern if not radical modern architecture. The founding nucleus was formed and inspired by the Gruppo 7, a group of avant-garde architects and art theoreticians from Como lead by Carlo Enrico Rava. The MIAR held two significant exhibitions of modern architecture in Italy (1930, 1931), which brought to light the Italian discourse on architecture and urbanism, before being dissolved on behest of the Fascist Architectural Corporation by the absorption of some of its leading members (Adalberto Libera, Sebastiano Larco, Carlo Enrico Rava) into the newly formed *Raggruppamento Architetti Moderni Italiani* (RAMI) controlled by Marcello Piacentini and Alberto Calza Bini.

Opera Nazionale Balilla (ONB)
The Opera Nazionale Balilla (ONB) from 1926 to 1937 was the Italian Fascist youth organization which provided youth from the age of six to seventeen with paramilitary, physical, cultural and professional education. In 1937 it was merged into the Gioventù italiana del littorio (GIL).The name Balilla derives from the nickname Giovan Battista Perassos (1735-81), a young Genoese who, according to tradition, started the revolt against the Austrian occupiers in 1746. Seen as an exemplary national hero, the young boy's nickname became the synonym for youngsters during the Fascist regime.

Opera Nazionale Combattenti (ONC)
The Opera Nazionale Combattenti (ONC) from 1917 to 1977 was an Italian charitable organization set up to provide assistance to veterans of the First World War.

Podestà
The institutional figure of the *podestà* was established by the regime in 1926 and was maintained until 1945. By suppressing the democratic principle through the mechanism of the state nomination, the *podestà* replaced the mayor at the head of the local administrations.

Piano Regolatore

The most important urban planning instrument in Italy is the *Piano Regolatore* (PR) or *Piano Regolatore Generale* (PRG), introduced by law in 1865. It is an urban development plan or regulatory plan, which approximately corresponds to a plan for the urban division (zoning) and use of land (land-use plan/urban development plan) and should not be confused with the much more detailed *Piano Particolareggiato*, which fulfils the function of a larger-scale development plan.

Raggruppamento Architetti Moderni Italiani (RAMI)

The *Raggruppamento Architetti Moderni Italiani* (RAMI) was the result of an initiative of the Fascist Architects' Corporation to direct the various Italian architectural currents into a dynamic complex of creative homogenization. By the absorption of some of the leading representatives of the avant-garde (MIAR), especially Adalberto Libera and Carlo Enrico Rava, into the newly formed *Raggruppamento Architetti Moderni Italiani*, the Corporation strove to dissolve the inhibiting contest between differing architectural tendencies by forcing an identifiable fascist architectural language. The appeasement was realized by formal mediation and by organizational subjugation to Mussolini's architectural stakeholders Marcello Piacentini and Alberto Calza Bini. The most prominent showcases of this appeasement policy were the Milanese Triennale exhibitions of 1933 and 1936 and the Florentine exhibition of modern architecture organized by Giovanni Michelucci in 1933, which originally should have been the third MIAR exhibition on rationalist architecture.

Scuola Romana

Scuola Romana (literally Roman school) refers to the loose aggregation of a Roman architectural class formed at the Scuola Superiore di Architettura di Roma or by previous institutions like the Istituto di Belle Arti di Roma. The architectural language of its protagonists' designs was inspired by historicist and eclectic references to the Italian and especially Roman art and architectural heritage (*romanità*).

Sindacato Nazionale Architetti Fascisti

The *Sindacato Nazionale Architetti Fascisti* (National Fascist Architects' Corporation), also written *Sindacato Nazionale Fascista Architetti*, was the fascist professional representation of architects founded in April 1923 by Alberto Calza Bini who will take over the leadership until its dissolution. The architects Ghino Venturi and Vincezo Fasolo were also members of the first directorate. At first, the *Sindacato* did not succeed in winning over the older architects' association

(*Federazione Architetti Italiani*, founded in 1905 by Giovanni Rosadi). It was only in the course of the authoritarian and corporative reorganization of the State (1926) that the *Sindacato* gained its primacy as a professional organization of Italian architects until the end of fascist rule in Italy.

Stile Littorio

The appearance of buildings and urban spaces designed and built in Fascist Italy which refer to a striped down Classical architecture in mostly simplified rhetorical and monumental forms, are subsumed by architectural historians under the expression *Littorio style*. This style or rather formal tendency was named after the Roman *fasci littori* (bundles of wooden sticks tied by leather straps, used as a symbol of Fascism) as one of the emblems of the Fascist Party. As an expression of creative homogenization and state architecture it merged monumentality and classicism to rationalism, searching for a unitary, nationally connoted and recognizable style in service of a new built image of the Fascist State. The first use of the term came with Saverio Palozzi's publication of the results of the first competition for the national headquarters of the Fascist Party of 1934 (Palazzo del Littorio).

Squadristi
→*Blackshirts*.

Sventramento

Urban redevelopment strategy based on a profit-oriented radical rearrangement of the roads and building masses in the city center and a very dense and rigid road network in the outer areas of the city, which does not provide for any zoning or qualitative structuring (urban development plans) and, in addition, gives free rein to land speculation over the resulting areas.

Ventennio

In Italian, *Ventennio* (literally twenty years) or *Ventennio fascista* generally refers to the rule of the fascist party that lasted more than two decades from 1922 to 1943 in the whole of Italy (Kingdom of Italy) and then from 1943 to 1945 in a northern fraction of the country (Italian Social Republic).

Authors

Micaela Antonucci (PhD) is an architect and assistant professor in History of Architecture at the University of Bologna, member of the PhD Research Board in Architecture and Design Cultures at the University of Bologna and Coordinator of the publishing series of the Department of Architecture in Bologna. She studied Italian Renaissance architecture, focusing particularly on Rome and on the work of Antonio da Sangallo the Younger; on topics and protagonists of contemporary architecture, particularly Otto Wagner and Pier Luigi Nervi.

Christine Beese (PhD) works as a research associate and lecturer at the Art History Department of the Free University of Berlin. As art historian she did her doctorate at the Technical University of Dortmund, Department of Architecture and held a scholarship at the Bibliotheca Hertziana in Rome where she organized the conference *L'Urbanistica a Roma durante il ventennio fascista* (proceedings published at Campisano Editore in 2019). In 2014 she received the Hans-Janssen Prize of the Göttingen Academy of Sciences and Humanities for her research about the urbanism of Marcello Piacentini published in *Marcello Piacentini. Moderner Städtebau in Italien*.

Scott Budzynski (PhD) is an art historian concentrating on modern and contemporary art and architecture. He studied and completed his doctorate in art history and criticism at Stony Brook University (New York) and has lived and worked in Berlin and taught at the Justus Liebig University in Gießen (Germany) where he worked as research assistant at the collaborative research centre for Memory Cultures. Since 2012 he has been professor of art history at the Savannah College of Art and Design. His current research is focused on the themes of memory, modernity, and representation in urban spaces in post-World War II Milan.

Lorenzo Ciccarelli is a research fellow in History of Architecture at the University of Florence. He is a member of the Scientific Committee of the Renzo Piano Foundation. His studies are dedicated to the ties between Italian and European and North American architecture of the nineteenth and twentieth century's.

Alberto Coppo (PhD) is a scholar in architectural history. He studied architecture and completed his doctorate at the Sapienza University of Rome in 2017 with a study that explores the architectonic activity of Pietro Aschieri (1889-1952) in Rome during the interwar period. Coppo collaborated with Éupolis Foundation (Milan) for the creation of a cultural itinerary composed by the churches of the last Century in Milan. At the moment he is a research fellow at the Accademia di San Luca in Rome and works on researches focused on twentieth century's architects' archives.

Cecilia De Carli is a professor of History of Contemporary Art at the Catholic University of Milan. She teaches History of Contemporary Art and is the Director of CREA (The Research Centre for Education Through Art and Cultural Heritage Mediation in the territory and museums). Her research focuses primarily on the relationships between art and architecture, art and faith and art and education. Her published works include the books *Le nuove chiese della diocesi di Milano 1945-1993* (1994) and *Brunate tra Eclettismo e Liberty: La villeggiatura progettata dal 1890 al 1940* (2009). She is also editor of numerous art history books like *I racconti dipinti degli ex voto: Il caso di Ossuccio tra storia, restauro e valorizzazione* (2015) and *Attraverso l'arte: Percorsi filosofici ed esperienze educative* (2013). She recently published in *Arte Cristiana* 'Il Refettorio Ambrosiano, opera d'arte totale e la sua committenza' (2018/11-12, pp. 124-147).

Carmen M. Enss (Dr.-Ing.) is a research assistant at the Centre for Heritage Conservation Studies and Technologies at the University of Bamberg. Her research links urban planning with heritage conservation. She studied architecture and received her doctoral degree in architectural history at the Technical University of Munich. Together with Gerhard Vinken, she published *Produkt Altstadt: Städtebau und Denkmalpflege für historische Stadtzentren* (2016). Her monograph *Münchens geplante Altstadt: Städteabau und Denkmalpflege ab 1944 für den Wiederaufbau* (2016) examines Munich's post-war city planning and monument preservations. Enss' research project "Produced heritage" investigates early heritage planning concepts of Gustavo Giovannoni and Theodor Fischer at the beginning of the twentieth century in Germany and Italy.

Giulia Favaretto is an architect and PhD-Student in architecture at the University of Bologna. Her research focus is on architectural restoration. Her particular research topics are the restoration of the twentieth-century heritage, conservation of the 'autarchic' materials and rationalist architecture in Forlì.

Alexander Fichte works as an urban planner in Cologne. In addition to his professional activity, he is doing a PhD-Research at the Technical University of Dortmund and the Ca' Foscari University of Venice. Thanks to a scholarship at the German Study Center in Venice (Centro Tedesco di Studi Veneziani) he was able to do the essential research for his project in 2017.

Cettina Lenza is a full professor of History of Architecture at the University of Campania Luigi Vanvitelli, where she teaches History of Contemporary Architecture and History and Principles of Architectural Design. Her research interests focus on the history of architecture from the eighteenth to the twentieth century and critical and methodological issues, published in numerous essays, articles, monographs and conference proceedings. She has edited collective volumes and the critical edition of the writings of Salvatore Vitale. Her published works include *La stazione centrale di Napoli storia e architettura di un palinsesto urbano* (2010) and *L'estetica dell'architettura e altri scritti di Salvatore Vitale* (2010). Together with Vincenzo Trombetta she recently edited the exhibition catalog *Baldassarre Orsini tra arte e scienza, 1732-1810* (2017).

Chiara Mariotti (PhD) is an architect, research fellow and adjunct professor at the Department of Architecture at the University of Bologna where she did also her doctorate in Architecture. Her research focus is on Architectural Restoration. Her particular research topics are the restoration of fortified architectures, preventive and planned conservation of historic buildings and sites as well as adaptive reuse of cultural heritage.

Luigi Monzo (Dr.-Ing.) works as an architect in Germany and teaches architectural history and architectural design in existing built contexts at the Department of Theory and History of Architecture at Leopold Franzens University in Innsbruck. He did his doctorate on church architecture in fascist Italy at the Karlsruhe Institute of Technology and was holding a scholarship of the Friedrich-Ebert-Stiftung. The related monograph on the modernizing of Italian church architecture, *Croci e fasci – Der italienische Kirchenbau in der Zeit des Faschismus* (2017) explores the multilayered impact of fascist architectural policies on various typological scales of architecture as well as on urban strategies. Monzo's research addresses the intersections between architectural culture, design process and political conditions in regimes of totalitarian aspiration, especially in fascist Italy. Among others, he published texts examining the various conditions of shaping an identifiable national architecture between the two world wars.

Sofia Nannini is a PhD-Student in History of Architecture at the Polytechnic University of Turin. She graduated at the University of Bologna with a Master's Thesis on Pier Luigi Nervi's Tobacco Factory in Bologna. Nannini is an editor of the journal *Histories of Postwar Architecture* and journal manager of *in_bo*. Her research interests focus on the history of concrete, from the work of Pier Luigi Nervi to her current doctoral studies on the use of concrete in Icelandic architecture.

Paolo Nicoloso is an associate professor in History of Architecture at the Department of Engineering and Architecture at the University of Trieste. He graduated in 1984 at the IUAV University of Venice with Giorgio Ciucci as examiner. He worked as a research fellow in architectural history at the University of Udine. His research focuses on the history of Italian architecture of the twentieth century with a particular interest in the work of Gustavo Giovannoni, Giuseppe Terragni, Marcello Piacentini and Giulio Carlo Argan. His published works include the books *Gli architetti di Mussolini: Scuole e sindacato, architetti e massoni, professori e politici negli anni del regime* (1999, 2004) and *Mussolini architetto: Propaganda e paesaggio urbano nell'Italia fascista* (2008). Recently he published a biographical study on Marcello Piacentini: *Marcello Piacentini – Architettura e potere: una biografia*.

Angela Pecorario Martucci is an architect. After the degree in Architecture with a thesis about historical disciplines for architecture with a monographic work on Ernesto Nathan Rogers and the architectural culture of the 1950s, she devoted herself to the professional business. She is currently a PhD student in Environment, Design and Innovation at the University of Campania Luigi Vanvitelli, with a research project focused on the Autarchy period and its experimentations.

Elena Pozzi (PhD) is an architect. She works as an architect at the Ministry of Cultural Heritage [MiBAC] and adjunct professor at the Department of Architecture at the University of Bologna. Pozzi did her doctorate in Architecture at the IUAV University of Venice. Her research focuses mainly on architectural restoration where she works on the topics revival phenomena, restoration of the twentieth-century heritage and theory of architectural restoration.

Marco Pretelli (PhD) is an architect and works since march 2016 as full professor at the Department of Architecture, University of Bologna. He did his doctorate in Architecture at the University of Naples Federico II. His research focus is on architectural restoration, and he works on the subject of preservation and restoration of historic buildings. His particular research topics are the adaptive reuse of cultural heritage, HIM-historic indoor microclimate and preservation of the twentieth-century heritage.

Sandro Scarrocchia (PhD) is an architect and art historian, he was a professor at the Academy of Fine Art of Brera until 2018 and is now teaching History of Art at the Polytechnic University of Milan. He did his doctorate in Architecture at the University of Bonn. His research focus is on architectural restoration with a particular interest in architectural design methodology and theory, and he works on the subject of preservation and restoration of historic buildings. Scarrocchia is the author of numerous essays, articles, monographs and contributions in conference proceedings including *Albert Speer e Marcello Piacentini: L'architettura del totalitarismo negli anni Trenta* (1999; 2013), *Oltre la storia dell'arte: Alois Riegl vita e opera di un protagonista della cultura viennese* (2006) and *Max Dvořák: Conservation and Modernity in Austria, 1905-1921* (2009; 2019). He also edited two proceedings on Alois Riegel's writings (1995; 2003) and recently edited the German edition of Max Dvořák's writings on conservation (2012) and a two-volume book on Camillo Boito (2018).

Leila Signorelli (PhD) is an architect. She works as an architect at the Min-istry of Cultural Heritage [MiBAC]. Until March 2018 she was researching fellow at the Department of Architecture at the University of Bologna where she also got her doctorate in 2011. Her research focuses on architectural restoration. Research topics are post-war reconstruction and creative cultural industry applied to cultural heritage and preservation of the twentieth-century heritage.

Anna G. Vyazemtseva (PhD) graduated in art history in 2007 in Moscow. She obtained scholarships from the Italian Ministry of Foreign Affairs for research works at the Sapienza University of Rome which were related to her doctoral thesis on the reconstruction of the city center of Rome in the 1920s-1930s (submitted in Moscow). In 2015 she discussed her second doctoral thesis *Art and Architecture, economics and politics between Italy and USSR, 1910-1940* at the University of Rome Tor Vergata. From 2016 to 2019 she has been a post-doc fellow at the University of Insubria (Varese) working on the project *Russian women in Italian art and architecture during the fascism*. In Russia, she published the monograph

Art of Totalitarian Italy (2018). Since 2010 she is in role at the Institute of History and Theory of Architecture and Urbanism in Moscow (since 2013 as a senior researcher). Since 2015 she works as an adjunct professor at University of Rome Tor Vergata, Polytechnic University of Milan and Roma Tre University.

GPSR Authorized Representative: Easy Access System Europe, Mustamäe tee 50, 10621 Tallinn, Estonia, gpsr.requests@easproject.com

www.ingramcontent.com/pod-product-compliance
Lightning Source LLC
Chambersburg PA
CBHW051532020426
42333CB00016B/1890